ECHOES *in the* WALLS

KATRINA MORGAN

Copyright © 2019 by Katrina Morgan.

ISBN Softcover   978-1-950580-63-7
      Hardcover   978-1-950580-64-4
      eBook   978-1-950580-65-1

All rights reserved. No part of this book may be reproduced or transmitted in any form or by any means, electronic or mechanical, including photocopying, recording, or by any information storage and retrieval system without express written permission from the author, except in the case of brief quotations embodied in critical reviews and certain other non-commercial uses permitted by copyright law.

Printed in the United States of America.

To order additional copies of this book, contact:
Bookwhip
1-855-339-3589
https://www.bookwhip.com

Acknowledgment

Whether tackling a ramshackle old house, writing a book, or following any heartfelt dream, we all need the support of friends and family. To take on major life changes without such support would leave us flailing and floundering in a sea of uncertainty. In saying such, I would be remiss if I did not take the time to acknowledge those who had lent sweat and muscle to our dream, encouraged when all hope seemed lost or cheered us to the finish line.

To my friends and neighbors, many of whom are named in this book, I thank you. We, as a family, thank you. Despite not understanding our dream, or even being able to visualize what we wanted to do, you lent us your unwavering support. You made us laugh when we wanted to cry. You lifted us up and came through in ways that still leave us humbled to the very soles of our well-worn boots. I am so blessed by each of you.

To my incredible parents and wonderful in-laws, know that your support, your unconditional love, and your faith have shaped who I have become. I've tried to chronicle your help throughout our journey, but words can never truly express my deep gratitude. You gave of your time and efforts, appearing when we most needed the steadfast love that only parents can give. It has always been so, regardless of where I found myself along life's twisting roads. You listened to a dream about an old house, and my dream of a book (Mom, you're a great editor!). You smiled and nodded and said, "We believe in you." I am so blessed by each of you.

To my best friend, Karen Haydon-Pemberton, who knew, before I did, that I needed to write, I thank you. You have been a steadfast companion since before we could even walk. And as we've learned to walk, run, soar or fail, our friendship has been a bedrock and foundation on which I knew I could always stand, to either shout my joy or voice my fears. You read early chapters which were awful; full of grammatical errors and deep flaws. You somehow saw past the mistakes and encouraged me to keep trying. I am so blessed by your friendship.

To my own amazing little family, know that I am prouder of each one of you than any other thing I've ever done or accomplished. My beautiful daughter, Deanna, you've grown into an amazing, intelligent woman, capable of attaining anything your heart desires. That you married a wonderful man, my favorite son-in-law, Chris, is evidence of your great wisdom. Your infectious smile and laughter are a balm to my soul. My son, Michael, you've grown into an incredible, smart young man. The world is laid out beneath your feet, only waiting for you to decide your direction. Your mix of charm and clever sarcasm always make me smile and shake my head in wonder. Spencer, my youngest, you're still evolving and changing each day. I know you too will be a bright and remarkable man, able to tackle any challenge that comes your way. Your antics still make me laugh, and your generous spirit leaves me in awe. My husband, John, you've always lifted me high to reach my goals, and chase my dreams. For all the years you've worked to turn a vandal's delight into a warm family home, for all the nights you sat and listened (glazed and glossy-eyed) to edits, for the decades you have loved me, know that I am eternally thankful. I am so very blessed.

Contents

Chapter 1. The Dreamer and the Fixer... 1
Chapter 2. Awakenings.. 7
Chapter 3. Love Is Blind...13
Chapter 4. Pom-poms and Tool Belts 21
Chapter 5. Can You See What I See? 30
Chapter 6. Parental Discretion Advised....................................... 40
Chapter 7. Move Dem Bones...50
Chapter 8. Strangers in Our Life 61
Chapter 9. What Lies Beneath 71
Chapter 10. How Much Wood Can a Wood Duck Chuck?............ 80
Chapter 11. Scotch on the Rocks..89
Chapter 12. Bat Wars Episode I: The Discovery............................99
Chapter 13. Fiddling on the Roof..107
Chapter 14. Miscommunication..115
Chapter 15. Calling Up the Reserves... 124
Chapter 16. This Aint Gonna Work! 133
Chapter 17. Enlightening 143
Chapter 18. We Are Not Alone...152
Chapter 19. Stop the Ride, I Want Off...160
Chapter 20. Crow Pie...169
Chapter 21. Who Else Has a Problem Today?............................177
Chapter 22. Ready, Set, ~~Move~~ Stop 186
Chapter 23. Bat Wars Episode II: "They're Back" 195
Chapter 24. The Exorcism...205
Chapter 25. Bat Wars Episode III: Incoming...............................214

Chapter 26. Bat Wars Episode IV: B Day 223
Chapter 27. Silk Purses and Sow Ears 230
Chapter 28. Mired in Mud 243
Chapter 29. A Little Warning, Please 252
Chapter 30. With a Cherry on the Bottom 260
Chapter 31. I'm Stuck 270
Chapter 32. Good Things Come to Those That Wait 279
Chapter 33. I am So Blessed 288

Chapter 1

The Dreamer and the Fixer

The wind tugged at loose shutters, and cold wind slithered through a cracked window somewhere upstairs. The snow had finally melted, and the ground was saturated from trying to absorb it all. The Old Woman looked at the two trees in the front yard, comforted that they, at least, were still there and relatively unchanged. Tiny shoots were timidly pushing through the soggy, brown-green grass, anxious to bloom, but still afraid. The lady shivered as spring rain wept down her windows. The weather had triggered memories, swirling in time with the few leftover leaves from fall. She couldn't help but think back to the day her last, beloved family had moved away.

What a sad time that had been, and, although several years had slipped by, she felt as if she'd never truly recovered. The beautiful antiques and the oriental rugs had been carefully wrapped and placed into the back of the moving van. Lamps were removed, and dishes sat in neat boxes in the kitchen, which had seen many boisterous dinners and holidays. Even the fireplace sat cold from days spent packing instead of relaxing.

She'd spent almost eighteen years with them, watching the children grow, reveling in happiness and being lovingly restored. She'd laughed at the growing list of animals they'd brought home and ensconced in the barns. Silently following behind her family, she listened to the husband and wife as they'd walked through her gracious rooms, remembering Christmases and birthdays. They'd laughed about the day they'd finally finished the stairs and how the children had eagerly slid down each step. They'd looked out windows at the flowerbeds and smart white fences. Tears slipped by unnoticed. They'd held hands, shut off lights and slowly driven away, looking out the car window and waving until they could see her no longer.

She'd been heartsick and anxious over their leaving—wondering who the new residents would be and how they would treat her. "I'm getting too old for this," she sighed, thinking back over more than a century and suddenly feeling tired.

A few lonely and excruciatingly silent days passed before another moving truck pulled into her driveway. She watched with trepidation as it backed haphazardly across her lawn, crushing the flowers and having little regard for her carefully groomed appearance.

They'd rushed to get their belongings inside, not even stopping to say hello. The rooms, although filled again, did not ring with laughter. As the weeks slid into months, and months into years, she never grew accustomed to the constant bickering between the children, or the vicious arguments flowing out of the master bedroom. The floors were scarred due to furniture being carelessly pushed and shoved into place. Weeds grew where flowers should have been. The children, whom she'd looked forward to, had ruined her walls with scribbling and hideous paint. No one seemed to notice, let alone care.

The years of abuse had seen many of her beautiful accessories destroyed: light fixtures and hickory planks pulled away and sold for profit, new and inferior replacements installed. She wondered if she would ever be the same again. Slowly, she felt herself shift with neglect and crumble with loneliness. She wasn't ready to give in though, and silently asked, "Is there some chance I'll stand tall again? Is there someone out there that will love me once more?"

Little could she know that five hundred miles away, the fates were already hard at work, tumbling the gears that would bring a dreamer and a fixer together to make wishes come true. She would need to endure more and wait patiently, but help was definitely on the way.

Katrina

Tamping down the rest of the dirt, she looked over to watch her skinny girl copying every move. "That should about do it," Mom said, satisfied with the row of flowers they'd just planted.

"Let's do more," Katrina suggested. She'd never planted anything before and had loved the whole process: warm dirt in her hands, new life in the soil.

Mom shook her head. "Can't, there aren't any more seeds, silly girl." They'd been out in the heat for well over an hour, but in her normal fashion, Katrina was eager for more. She was at that odd age, a mix of child and teenager rolled into one. Mom looked at her daughter's long, lanky legs that Katrina had just learned to shave and smiled at the scraped knee. Beginner's mascara was clumped on long eyelashes, yet she'd smeared dirt across her nose. Looking at her own dirty nails, Mom smiled, acknowledging that maybe the girl came by such anomalies naturally.

The girl quickly scrubbed and ran up the street, eager to find her friends. Disappointed to find no one home, she headed for her room and her pet project, disappearing for hours.

"Katrina? Katrina! Do you hear me?" She was getting annoyed. "Where is that girl?" she muttered to herself as she strode down the hall and opened the bedroom door. There, amidst a pile of old catalogs, scissors and paper, she found her answer. She hadn't been ignored, just unheard.

Her gaze softened. Katrina was sitting cross-legged in the middle of the room, strawberry blond hair shoved behind her ears and lines of concentration drawn on her forehead. She was paging through hundreds of clippings, dreaming, lost in her own world. She hadn't even noticed that her door had been opened.

Mom, taking in the mess, realized another house plan was in process. Katrina spent hours creating meticulous floor plans, always to scale using graph paper and rulers. Some of the houses were bungalows; others were multi-storied mansions with *Gone with the Wind* columns and wide porches. Regardless of style, each plan was sure to include a large family room, a fireplace, tall, sweeping windows and areas connected to nature, probably a result of the hours spent wandering the woods behind their small home.

Once the plan was done, the real fun began. She paged through countless catalogs and cut out pictures of furniture and accessories for the house she'd drawn, blending colors and textures like an artist with his palette.

Looking over Katrina's shoulder, Mom smiled at the flower garden her daughter had just drawn, remembering their morning. *Where will these dreams and gifts take you?* Her heart lurched at the thought of her best friend growing up and away. Rolling out of her thoughts and away from the doorframe, she forced a smile. "So, this is where my JCPenney catalog went?"

Sheepishly, the girl looked up. Surprised at having been caught, she grinned. "Sorry, Mom. It's an old one, I think."

Mom craned her neck to see more detail. "So, when do I get to see the completed masterpiece?"

"Hey! No peeking." Katrina slid the drawings away. "I want it to be perfect first."

"Alright, alright, I'll wait. Set the table, please. Your dad will be home soon."

"I'll be right there," the girl answered as she replaced the catalog and carefully slid her clippings and drawings into a drawer to be indulged in another day.

John

The man opened the door allowing the light to enter first. "Wake up, John! Come on now, wake up!"

Sprawled across his bed, the teenager opened one eye to peer incredulously at the alarm. Eight a.m. *He's got to be kidding. It's Saturday, man.* He thought these things belligerently but never said them aloud. It was not his nature to argue. Shoving thick, black hair out of his eyes, he struggled with blankets and sheets in an effort to sit up. Stretching, he felt his muscles twinge and smiled smugly, remembering the game-winning double he'd hit the night before.

"Come on now. Daylight's wastin'. We got things to take care of, son." The man pushed his head further through the doorway to make sure his words had the desired effect. Sensing movement, he continued, "Heard you had a good game last night. We're gonna have to buy you a bigger hat to go with that head." He laughed at his own joke even as his own chest puffed with pleasure. He'd pulled an overtime shift the night before and had missed the game again. He'd listened intently though as Mom gave the play-by-play over coffee that morning. "Sorry I keep missing things you kids are doin'. Them bills gotta be paid though."

"Don't worry about it, Dad. We know how it is."

He looked toward the bed, nodding at his son. *You make me proud, boy.* John looked so much like him already, this almost man of his. They were so similar, although it would be years before the son would admit to it. The hair, the mannerisms, even the birth date were the same. He was determined that John be able to stand on his own two feet and never want for anything.

"I want so much for you and your sisters," the father whispered on a sigh. He'd come from a place poor in cash but rich in values, and he'd used the hard lessons he'd learned to build a good life. It hadn't been easy, but, as he looked around at his house and little family, he knew it had been worth it. He stepped away from the door and his reflections, and headed toward the yard, knowing John would join him shortly.

So began another day of raking, clearing and painstaking instructions on not only how to use the tools, but how to take care of them or fix them if they broke. One of the hard lessons learned growing up poor on a tiny, tobacco farm in Kentucky was that money wasn't always easy. You fixed, and never threw away. This lesson he drilled into his children whenever the opportunity arose.

"Lookit here, see how this handle's loose?" He held the offending equipment under John's nose. "We gotta tighten that up right now 'fore the thing falls apart."

"Yes, sir," John answered, already heading toward the open toolbox on the patio.

Although the young man grumbled a bit and may have even rolled his eyes when Dad wasn't looking, he worked hard, his hands instinctively understanding what to do. Perhaps it was a genetic trait, taking after his father. Maybe it was a personality trait, trying to be perfect and pleasing to those around him. Regardless, the job was always done well, and his dad would always smile.

As the last of the tools were put away, John called out, "I'm heading over to Wayne's to play some ball." Glove and bat slung over his shoulder, dark hair glinting in the sun, he took off at a run, forgetting he was supposed to be tired.

He played when his work was done. Lessons, all of them, that would follow him forward to another day.

CHAPTER 2

Awakenings

I leaned closer to the mirror, not really believing how deep and dark the circles were. I smeared makeup under my eyes, attempting to disguise the discoloration. With my hands up to my face, I couldn't help but notice the details. My nails were jagged and dirty. The chorus of calluses running across my palms had nearly grown together, forming large, leathery appendages. Mottled bruises ran up and down my forearm, mixed generously with cuts, scrapes, and Band-Aids. "Jesus, girl," I said to my reflection. What the hell had happened to me, and how did it get so bad?

I'd lost at least ten pounds and so had John—weight we could ill afford to give. We hardly recognized ourselves anymore. John looked worse than I did, since he wasn't comfortable applying makeup. We both avoided mirrors and calendars as much as possible. I shook my head trying to remember the last four months and how the insanity had begun.

Perhaps it had been the bitter cold blowing malcontent through chinks in our walls. Or, maybe it was moving into a new century and the self-examination such a milestone brings. Whichever, the year or the cold, January had found us edgy, unhappy and myopic in our view of each other. We felt closed in by the prolixity of our neighbors and our own incessant restlessness. Something needed to change.

We were living in our sixth house and still hadn't found a place we wanted to call home. The first few houses had been purchased with the idea of remodeling and turning ordinary homes into places that would make us proud. We'd sold them, and our dreams, for profit, forgetting why we'd started such adventures. We'd bought bigger and better, following society's map for success. We'd always upgraded but kept them carefully neutral in case something better came along. The current address, despite having been recently built, was no exception.

Cautiously, carefully, we unfolded an old dream. We'd meant to protect it, had folded it away for safekeeping, but like an old newspaper, its edges were yellowed, brittle with eighteen years of lying dormant.

Homes for Sale booklets were stacked on the kitchen counter. The newest one was splayed open on the table while John sat with elbows propped, holding onto his forehead. It was nearly impossible to concentrate with the noise and confusion.

We had seven children at the house—our own three and four additional neighbor children we were watching for a sick friend. I was wild-eyed and frazzled with trying to get kids, aged two to seventeen, fed, showered and settled in for the evening.

"I can't find my pillow," someone complained. Was it Michael or my friend's son? Being nearly joined at the hip, their eight-year-old voices and mannerisms were barely discernible.

"Who spilled Kool-Aid on my homework?" The girl, Aimee, glared suspiciously at her brother and Michael.

Pulling at my sleeve, my chunky two-year-old Spencer demanded attention, "I need a 'nack."

The other two neighbor children, also toddlers, came running at the prospect of food. Spencer wedged himself between them, and me establishing his territory.

"Deanna! I could use some help down here!" I yelled up the staircase, desperate to find my daughter. As one of the older teenagers in the neighborhood, she pulled down a fortune in babysitting fees. She watched these particular kids all the time. Surely, she'd know what to do, or at the very least, could come downstairs and help.

She bounded down the steps, long minky hair swinging around her shoulders. She laughed at my expression. "Having some trouble there, Mom?"

"Yeah. You could say that," I answered while disengaging Spencer and my friend's baby from my legs.

Usually patient with his own children, John had less tolerance for anyone else's. The additional four and the constant noise were making him crazy. "God, we have got to get out of this neighborhood. I swear it's something all the damn time!"

The phone rang. Once. Twice. Three times.

"Get the phone, John!" I called from the bathroom where I was supervising teeth brushings. "Jeez! What's your problem?"

"Hey, Rick!" I heard John's greeting and knew he'd be involved in yet another long conversation with our realtor. We'd spent almost two months crisscrossing the county, looking for our dream house, something old with acreage, something being sold "As Is" and needing renovations. Rick, however, was losing patience with our picky requirements and inability to commit.

"This one sounds pretty good, more like what you two have been looking for. I haven't seen it though," Rick warned, erecting a quick caution sign, as he listed dimensions and features.

"How old?" John asked, obviously surprised. He paused, listening.

"Free? Cool. That sounds more like it!"

I popped my head out of the bathroom, straining to hear the one-sided conversation better. He sounded excited, and my pulse quickened.

Because it was nearby, and, I suspect because he was fed up with the whole bedtime torture process, John announced, "I'm gonna drive out and see this one. It's not far from here, and it sounds pretty good. I'll be back in a bit." He aimed a kiss in my general direction, "You've got the kids squared away, right?"

I just nodded and rolled my eyes. It's not as if he'd been involved. It was 9:30 p.m., everyone was late for bed, and I was too harried to argue. An hour later, with the house finally, blessedly quiet, John rushed inside.

"Oh my God, hon. This is it. It's awesome!" He gushed before the kitchen door clicked close. "You've got to go see it now! These things disappear fast, you know?"

"Hello?" my voice dripped sarcasm, "we have seven kids here. I *just* got them to sleep. I can't leave. What if their mom calls?"

"I'll stay here and watch them. Just go!"

I knew the house had to be quite something if he was willing to supervise all those kids, even if they were sleeping. His excitement was contagious though, and I was hurriedly looking through a mountain of coats trying to find mine. John was attempting to draw me a map but having difficulty. He kept jumping up from the table and running hands nervously through his blue-black hair. He was describing things about the house in between bursts of energy. "It's got two little sheds out back."

Having found my coat, I was head-first in the closet, searching for matching gloves.

"There's a porch too. You'll love that, I bet."

"What?" I backed out, trying to hear his muffled speech, and caught my hair on someone's Velcro strap.

"Why don't we wake up Deanna? She can watch the kids, and I can go with you."

"Ha!" I spun around and pointed playfully at him, "I knew you wouldn't watch the kids." I was still stuck to the Velcro and trying to remove my long, blond hair a strand at a time.

He came up behind me, trying to help. "No, seriously, I just want to see what you think when you see it."

Deanna was summoned grumpily from her warm bed. "I just fell asleep," she complained on a yawn. We set her up on the couch, tossed the remote in her general direction and ran out the door before she could ask too many questions.

John pulled into the driveway, picking out sections of the house with the beams of the headlights. My breath caught, and I knew that house was the one I'd always been searching for, dreaming of, drawing.

Trying to be statuesque, despite leaning slightly toward the back yard, it seemed solid, dependable, and just large enough to be comfortable. Sitting in the middle of the property, it emanated a sense of pride; sure of its place in the world, even if everyone else had forgotten. Not understanding the nuances, I mentally connected with the house, and, for the first time in all our married life, saw myself at home. I looked at John to gauge his reaction.

Catching my glance, he asked, "It's great, isn't it?" His eyes were big, and he looked like a little boy, eager and ready to play. I nodded, strained against the seatbelt, and squeezed him into a hug. The gesture was awkward and rusty, and I wondered at how we'd grown apart, not talking, not touching. Maybe this house, this venture would infuse new life into our marriage.

In the dark and frozen mix, John and I held hands as we crept up to the house and peered through her windows. With noses pressed against the grime, we saw past the large piles of junk in the foyer and began to toss around our dreams enthusiastically. "Oh my God, there's a curved staircase! The boys will love it!" I envisioned them sliding down the rail. I squinted against the darkness, trying to see beyond the foyer to the rooms on either side.

John grinned beside me. "We could have this cleaned up in no time." He nudged me aside so he could see the staircase better.

We gave each other high-fives, and our pact was sealed. The house came with just enough acreage to make it interesting, boasted a pond and "free gas." It was too good to be true and, hugging each other, we turned circles of excitement on the old porch.

In doing so, we woke The Old Woman that the house had become. Sleep had become a welcome companion. There, she could dream of happier times. Opening tired eyes, she grunted in surprise to find strangers glorifying her. Catching pieces of our enthusiasm, she tried on a slow and creaky smile. As she watched, she caught strains from a long-ago waltz and remembered being dressed beautifully and twirling to music and laughter. She sighed at the memory, afraid to give in to such longings. She'd waited so long, dismayed to feel herself drooping and decaying. Over the years, she'd opened her doors to many strangers, only to have them walk away, unwilling to bring her back to life. She had never had anyone dance on her porch though. *I think I might like to dance once more.* She listened more intently.

"I want to see more!" I shoved against the door, noticing it wasn't quite closed.

John stopped me. "It's too dark. Someone might see us and call the cops. We'll come back and see it tomorrow." He was already pulling me toward the car.

I followed him reluctantly; my head turned back trying to see every detail. We drove like idiots back to the neighborhood, talking excitedly and interrupting one another. Not noticing the late hour, we called Rick and made an appointment to see the old house first thing in the morning. We knew we had to act quickly, or our treasure would disappear.

Hearing our enthusiasm, Rick cleared sleep from his voice and readily agreed.

Unable to close our eyes, John and I tangled into one another, laughing and unencumbered by the mundane any longer.

Chapter 3

Love Is Blind

Eager to see the old house again, we poured cereal, sloshed milk, and hustled all seven kids off to school and babysitters. Arriving before Rick, John and I sat in the driveway, looking things over through the pale February mist. It wasn't nearly as captivating in the daylight.

Without a doubt, the old girl needed some serious, cosmetic surgery. Her skin was blistered, and long ribbons of paint curled up along the edges. Most of her windowpanes were broken, allowing winter to drift in and out at a whim. The occasional upstairs shutter was missing, giving her the appearance of having applied make-up haphazardly. We jumped out of the car, eager to greet her despite her rumbled appearance. Hands jammed in pockets, we stomped our feet and blew cold smoke.

She'd been sleeping again and was startled to see us. *Oh, it's you two again. I thought maybe I dreamed about you last night.* She tried to stand a little straighter, embarrassed to be caught in such a state.

Rick pulled in behind us. His eyes, behind thick lenses, widened as he took in the house. Getting out of his truck, he tugged at the corners of his jacket to get it zipped against the cold. "Hey, I'm sorry. I had no idea it was this bad. I should've looked at it before calling you guys."

"What are you talking about? It's great!" Like puppies with a new toy, John and I were sidestepping and practically shaking with anticipation.

Rick scowled at us, absently stroking his salt-and-pepper beard, trying to determine if we were being sarcastic. Deciding that we really wanted to see the thing, he fished in his pocket for the keys.

We followed him to the back of the house where the realtor lock was attached to an ancient door. I gaped at the crooked, falling-apart stoop we were to balance upon to get inside and announced, "A house like this requires proper entrance through the front door." I turned on my heel and headed once again for the porch where we'd danced. We hadn't wanted to take chances the night before, but daylight and an official Realtor presence, had me shoving against the door again.

John followed my lead, and together we shoved our way inside, surprised to find that it had been a broken toilet blocking the door. In fact, it looked like the pieces of an entire bathroom had been dumped there. Chunks of tile, porcelain, rusted plumbing pieces, and a partial shower stall littered the entire entryway. A thin coat of plaster dust had settled on everything, and for a moment, I thought of Pompeii. Rick squeezed in behind us, shooting furtive glances at the road.

The guys stood in the middle of that mess, gawking in silence. Unable to wait, I picked my way through the foyer and headed toward the curved staircase. "Look at these! They're absolutely beautiful." I craned my head back to see the whole set, not noticing they were scarred and worn. Hearing snickering behind me, I turned.

John was pointing at my shoe, and Rick was trying not to laugh. "Uh…Darlin', you've managed to step into the old seal from the toilet." He shook his head at the messes I seemed to always get myself into. "So much for your grand entrance."

"Ooooh. Gross." I wiped gluttonous, yellow slime off my shoe and onto the broken shower stall leaning against the wall. No use messing up those wonderful stairs.

I assumed the foyer was the worst and all could be redeemed. I'm not sure, but I'm fairly certain that I've never been more wrong in my life. To the right of the entry, we walked into the dark and dreary kitchen. Homemade cabinets hung limply from spent hinges. Mouse droppings decorated every surface and spiders scurried out of our way. The walls were lined with dark, knotty pine and blackened beams ran across the low ceiling. The windows were crusted in grime and soot, most of which had probably come from the wood-burning stove squatting dejectedly in the middle of a wilting floor.

"This room is really cool. Look at the beams in the ceiling here." John seemed oblivious to what he'd just walked into. He was impressed, and I had no idea why.

"My God! This is filthy." I ran the toe of my shoe across a room-length crack in the vinyl flooring. "How could anyone have cooked and eaten in here?" I wondered. Rick nodded, agreeing with my assessment.

The Old Woman peeked around the wall into the kitchen and sighed. *This used to be cozy and clean.* She turned away sure the condition of the kitchen would make us change our minds. It certainly had for everyone else that had come to look.

John continued to expound on the construction and age of the beams. "Do you know how old the trees had to be to be cut this thick? Look how they're notched."

I frowned, wondering what was wrong with him. Backing out of the kitchen, I worked my way through the chaotic and cluttered foyer to see the other front room. "Oh man. Look at these doors!" I opened and closed the mammoth, curved doors guarding the entrance to the living room. "Amazing…these really date the house, ya know?"

The Old Woman beamed.

"What are you talking about? They're all beat up." John had followed behind and was now wondering about *my* mental faculties.

"Look though," I pointed, "all the original hinges are here. See the scroll work?"

John stepped forward, not to see the hinges, but to run his hands across the holes and dents in the woodwork.

Standing in the middle of the living room, we took in a pile of broken furniture and noticed the wallpaper had started to mold in the corners and was creeping down the walls. Dust armies swirled, and spider webs swayed, ready to do battle at the unaccustomed disturbance of air. Gray winter's light, struggling to break through years of dirt, cast a smoky haze over everything as it gingerly stroked each surface. Graffiti artists had dropped by to leave their signatures haphazardly on walls. Future marksmen had sneaked inside, blasting BB pellets in every direction.

John and I wandered the first level, confused and overwhelmed by the decay and abuse. There were a dozen doors, boxing everything into unusable compartments. Shelving had been nailed haphazardly to most walls, and old canning jars—some still containing mysterious liquids, lined each space. We shrugged not understanding.

"Check this out," I called to John. I'd opened a door in the hallway and was leaning into a hole where stairs should have been.

John peeked over my shoulder, confused. "Whoa. This just drops into the basement!"

I laughed, "We'll just direct any undesirable guests here."

"Good idea. We'll tell them it's the bathroom." John laughed along with me.

We were unaware that we'd just claimed ownership. The Old Woman and Rick, who had been following our progress, both smiled. She heard the excitement. He heard a possible sale.

Giving up on the first level, we charged up the curved staircase, skipping past several steps in our haste. At the top, we were greeted by two saloon doors. We sauntered through, like Old West gunslingers and immediately grew quiet. The low-ceilinged sitting room and bedroom were dark and heavily vandalized. Blood red handprints had been painted on the ceilings and walls. The paint had been allowed to drip down from each print, giving the appearance of a grisly crime scene.

"Jeez! This is creepy!" My body did a full, involuntary shake. "Remember Amityville?"

John was seemingly unaware of his surroundings. "This room's pretty big. With a little work, it could be a bedroom." John was circling the room, unfazed by the handprints, the names carved into the plaster, or even a bird's nest tucked into the corner of one of the broken windows.

"You're joking, right?"

"What? You don't think one of the kids would like this? I think it's cool."

"No way—look at what they're used to." I turned slowly, trying to see it finished: a closet in the corner, fresh paint, carpet on the scarred planks. "Maybe. I've got to give it more thought. It's possible." I fumbled for John's hand. Dragging him behind me, I was anxious to leave that ominous space and see what other surprises the house might hold.

The Old Woman followed more slowly, trying to decide if we were truly interested in her. *You've got children? Wonderful! I just hope they're nicer than the last bunch that was here.* She looked thoughtfully at the scarred walls.

We found three more bedrooms. The first, the master bedroom required walking through a closet to get inside. There was no lighting, and dark water circles stained the ceiling. We ran toward them, hand outstretched, and were relieved to find them dry.

Moving on, we stuck our heads inside a tiny bedroom and declared in unison, "It's snowing in here!" Both windows were missing, allowing the elements to pile inside.

"Are those animal tracks?" John asked in alarm. He visually tracked muddy paw prints from a window ledge to a pile of furniture in the middle of the room. He was my anomaly—a tough guy who hated all creepy, crawly things.

"Yep, looks like a raccoon. Isn't country living going to be great?" I laughed at his face, screwed up in concern.

The last bedroom was so dark we could only guess at its color. The windows were intact though, and we nodded and gave each other a thumbs up sign, as though we were somehow responsible for that small miracle. "This room is nice. The kids will be fighting over it, I bet." I said to the empty air. I'd thought John was behind me, but he'd moved on already.

"Hey, I found the missing bathroom!" John called out to me, excited and pleased with himself. His head popped back out through the doorframe. "Or at least what's left of it!"

I stepped into a room completely stripped down to lathe boards and plaster. Someone had evidently decided to gut the thing, tossed the pieces over the railing into the foyer, and then changed their mind. I couldn't say I blamed them as I stood there staring at exposed plumbing and wiring. The flooring had rotted, revealing holes open to the first floor.

Rick, still overwhelmed and less enthusiastic than we were, had lost track of us somewhere along the way. "Where are you two?" We heard him call out from downstairs.

Grinning, John leaned down to call through one of the holes in the bathroom floor. "Hello? We're up here. You've got to see this!"

I smiled at John. It had been a long time since I'd seen him play. Following the sound of John's voice, Rick was more than surprised to look up through the hole and see John waving.

"What are you two doing? This house is gone. I mean really gone." He shook his head.

"No, it's not! You're not seeing it done. It could be beautiful!" I called over John's shoulder. I wiggled in beside him and waved down at Rick too.

The Old Woman was in the hall, grinning too. *I like these two. They're going to be fun, and Lord knows we could use some fun around here again.*

Rick shook his head. "I'll just wait down here."

Squinting in the dim hallway, I noticed a small attic access. "Hey, John, come here and hold me up so I can look at this thing."

The Old Woman started praying. "Please, please do not open that attic."

"We can't get in there right now. Are you kidding? It's gotta be ten feet up there. I can't hold you up that high."

Spying back stairs, we quickly forgot the attic and changed direction.

Thank goodness. The Old Woman let out a sigh of relief. The attic was not for the faint of heart, and she knew we needed more time before venturing there.

"Back stairs! Can you believe it?" John shook his head at our descent. "These steps are crooked as hell."

We were both tilted against what seemed a funhouse wall, trying to make our way down the dark and narrow stairs.

"So?" I shrugged nonchalantly.

"Well, there's got to be a reason for that. They weren't made this way."

"Well, we'll just fix 'em!"

"You're clueless, you know that?" He smiled though, as I hopped and skipped down the stairs like a child on Christmas morning.

"Nah, I'm an optimist. That's why you love me!" I grinned up at him.

We raced through the house and exploded out the back door, anxious to see the yard. "This is crazy out here," I yelled, leaping over trees and branches thrown around the yard like forgotten toys.

"No kidding. Nobody's touched this in years!" John called over his shoulder, shoving his way through tall grasses.

Reaching the edge of the pond, I was met by a solid wall of thorns. I was trying to step on them and work my way forward when one whipped back and caught the back of my hand.

"Back out of there! You're going to tear yourself to pieces!" John admonished. He'd already given up the fight and was halfway back across the yard.

"Too late," I muttered quietly, not wanting him to know I'd already done damage. Sucking on the back of my hand, I jogged toward him and the house.

His head was thrown back, staring up at the chimney. "Jeez, look at the vines crawling up this thing. They're as big around as my arm!"

Pressing against him, I quietly asked, "What do you think?"

"About the vines?"

"No, you idiot, the house. What do you think about the house?"

"I like it. It's what we've been looking for. How 'bout you?"

"Me?" I threw my arms around him, "I…love…this… house!"

The Old Woman leaned on her cane hardly believing her ears. "Please…" she whispered, afraid to hope, but unable to help herself.

John and I grinned at each other. "We can do this!" We were suddenly deeply in love, with the house and with each other. Eager to begin something so big that we'd never be bored again, we brushed easily past the overly obvious obstacles. We'd done extensive remodeling in our previous homes and felt sure that we were up to the task. The graffiti, the lack of plumbing and lighting didn't matter. She was gorgeous, and we shared the same vision. Holding hands, we ran to find Rick. He was standing in the foyer, keys out and ready to go.

"Can you believe this house?" John and I asked in unison.

He shook his head, misinterpreting our question, and headed toward the door.

"Man, the things we could do here."

"It's awesome." John and I were tripping over each other's sentences.

Rick, confused by our enthusiasm, stopped mid-stride. "What are you saying?"

John grinned. "We want to put a contract on it right away!" I nodded happily.

Rick's eyebrows shot sky high, but who was he to argue a sale? He readily agreed to meet us at our current house and set about locking things up. Rick bounced behind us in his truck, gas pedal floored, trying to keep up with our break-neck speed.

"We're gonna start in the kitchen first, right?" To my way of thinking, it was the room furthest gone, and I hated it with a passion. The rest of the house was great or would be.

John had a very different agenda as to where we should begin. We playfully argued the merits of his plan vs. mine the entire way home. Never, not for a minute, did we consider the possibility of not owning that home. It was ours, and we were anxious to begin.

Entering the newer, cleaner house, which now seemed dull and contrived in comparison, we wrote a contract toward that living, breathing opportunity. Rick left, contract clutched in his hand and shaking his head—sure that we'd lost our minds.

John went to work making out mental lists of supplies. I rummaged around for a ruler and paper and began to sketch The Old Woman's nooks and crannies to scale.

Huddled alone and cold again, The Old Woman wondered, "Are they the ones?"

Chapter 4

Pom-poms and Tool Belts

John and I waited all day for a response to our offer. We filled the void by calling each other repeatedly, talking and refreshing our memories on the layout and still arguing about where to begin. As the day wore on, John grew more and more nervous. I attributed his mood to the endless waiting and nothing more. I should have been more astute. I knew he hated change and that things left undone made him unhappy and stressed. I'd witnessed it over the years, with every "project" we'd ever tacked. I just never imagined an anxiety attack.

He woke up at eleven-thirty that night, sweating and swearing. "What the hell are we thinking?" He sat up and clicked on the bedside lamp. "How can we sell a new house to work on that thing?" The light was glaring.

I was glaring too. I'd been dreaming all kinds of wonderful things about the old house. He was intense, waiting for a reply to a question I couldn't quite comprehend.

"What are you saying?" I asked cautiously.

"We are out of our friggin' minds. There is no way in hell we can take on a project like that. It's too far gone and needs to be bulldozed!" He was nearly shouting.

I blinked sleep from my eyes. "Why are you yelling at me? You were the one all excited—'This is it! You have to see it!'" I repeated his earlier self in a singsong voice.

"It was dark."

"Whatever."

"I am not buying that house!"

I sat staring at him, waiting for a punch line that never came. Understanding that he was serious, I pounded home my point, "*We* have a contract we signed and sent off today."

"Cancel the son-of-a-bitch!"

"You're kidding, right? It's almost midnight. The office is closed."

"Then call Rick at home."

Silence.

"Hello? Did you hear me? You call Rick at home and tell him we cancel," John insisted and pounded his pillow for emphasis. It was strange behavior indeed and surely something I had never witnessed before. Normally, he was an easygoing guy—laid back and non-combative. I had, however, heard his co-workers describe a very different man who was intense and temperamental. I'd never believed them before.

"What's wrong with you all of a sudden?" I sat up, untangling myself from blankets.

Trying to calm down, he rubbed his hands up and down the sides of his face, "I'm lying here thinking about all of the things that need to happen at that house and wondering why we're doing it. What's wrong with where we live? It's done, for God's sake."

"And we're bored out of our minds. I thought we wanted an old house to restore, something to keep us busy. We've talked about having land for years. Why are you changing your mind?"

"Work is crazy right now. I'm going to be traveling all the time. I can't fix that house too. You have to call Rick and tell him we've changed our minds. I mean it."

"*We* haven't changed our minds. *You* have. Sleep on it. It will be better in the morning." I pulled the covers back up, signifying an end to the conversation.

Tapping me on the shoulder, John pulled back the comforter, leaned in until we were nose to nose, and enunciated each word with measured care. "I saw it *this* morning. Tomorrow ain't gonna matter. Call!"

Thrashing around and fighting for space, I shoved him off me. "Why the hell am I supposed to call? I like the house. You're the one who's chicken all of a sudden. You call."

"Damn straight I'm chicken. I hate heights. Have you seen those rooflines? I hate spiders and snakes. Did you see that dark basement? The description says crawl spaces, for God's Sake! We don't know about the electric, the water, nothing. All we know is that it has free gas. It's a hell of a lot of work for free gas!"

"I'm still not calling. It's late." I yanked the covers back into place.

"We called him the same time last night, and he was fine."

I sat up, my spine ramrod straight. "That's because we might have been buying, not canceling!" It was my turn to yell. I was also seriously considering pounding a pillow.

"If I make the call, I'll say things I don't mean. You're better at smoothing things over. Please, Katrina," he softened his tone and made a puppy-dog face. "Please."

Had he stayed pissy, I would never have made that call. I decided, given John's mood, that I'd better play along and keep my marriage on an even keel. If I forced him to buy the house, we'd all end up miserable. He'd do it too; take on something he hated, to make me happy. He would then mope and fall into a depression over being talked into doing something he didn't agree with, in the first place. I'd feel bad because I'd somehow manipulated the situation. I'd been down that road before. Living with a martyr, or as a martyr didn't appeal to me.

As I dialed, I was sick to my stomach with the thought of losing that house. I explained things as best I could to a sleepy Rick. I was right, he wasn't glad to hear from us. He mumbled some things about a binding contract and hung up with the promise of talking to us about it in the morning.

I pouted and sat plotting. John leaned in for a kiss, which I ignored. I wasn't willing to give up on the old house, or the way it had briefly rekindled our relationship.

Over coffee and the newspaper the next morning, I tried reverse psychology. Laughing about what a mess the old house was, I wondered aloud if there were other ones on the market, in better shape. "Maybe we should just keep looking. We'll find the right one, Babe," I assured him with a smile as I poured him more coffee and waited on him hand and foot. Those actions were unusual, but he didn't seem suspicious at first.

"Those staircases sure were great though, weren't they?" Sly and subtle, I continued such tactics.

He grinned. "I know what you're up to. You're not fooling me at all. I know you love that house. And, you're right. It's not as bad this morning."

I waited with my lips pursed, hoping he had truly changed his mind.

"I'll make you a deal," he offered. "You do the attic and the crawl spaces, and I'll handle the rest." He smiled.

I would have given my right arm, and he knew it. "No problem! You've got yourself a deal." I leaned across the table and actually shook his hand.

"I guess you'd better call Rick and cancel the cancellation."

I danced around the kitchen, kissing John as I twirled by, and checked the clock to see if I could make the call yet.

Michael came downstairs looking for breakfast and stopped mid-stride, taking in his mom's strange behavior. "What's going on?"

I picked him up and kissed him too. "Nothing, Honey. Mommy is just happy."

We hung in the balance for a week, waiting for the owner to respond to our offer. During that time, John would panic, and I would cheerlead. We were going to follow the dream by God, and nothing was going to stop me—it wasn't a group project anymore.

Everyone seemed to be balking, even the kids. Deanna and Michael were less than thrilled when they took the tour. They stood in their prospective bedrooms and gaped. Deanna, always wanting to please, tried to smile but didn't pull it off very well. Michael's eyebrows seemed permanently stuck to the top of his forehead. He was our literal child, and gray areas made no sense to him. Only Spencer seemed excited. He'd never moved before, and, at two and a half, seemed to think the old house was a plaything. He yelled just to hear his voice echo through the cavernous rooms.

I could not seem to get them to see how things would look once we'd fixed it up. John tried to convince them too, but his words rang hollow, with his own doubts dangerously close to the surface. He continued to ask ridiculous questions of his own. "When am I supposed to put in bathrooms? Do you know how long it will take to replace flooring? I have a job, you know."

Unbelievable. I rolled my eyes and painted the rosy picture over and over. I whispered about the rooms, the charm and the vision we shared. I reminded him of the land and space. "Think about all that privacy. We could run naked! Wink. Wink." I gave a lot of exuberant hugs and wore clothing I knew he liked. I even started wearing lipstick, something I'd given up along with my career, six years prior. Whatever it took to get that house, I was game.

I was crazed with the idea of starting over. I'd felt like we were heading down the wrong path for a long time but had had no idea as to how to get us turned around. We'd fallen into the trap of buying bigger and better, and I hated the image and lesson we were sending our children. The competition, the obligations, and the fast track had blinded us to what was important. Taking on that old house was the way for us to get back on track.

On the home front, things were smoothing out, when Rick finally called. "The seller has agreed. Go ahead and get financing."

He hung up, and John started talking right away, "We can't sell this house yet. There's no way we can move into the other one for six months or so."

This was not good news to me. "Where are we going to get the money? We can't afford two houses. And, we'd still have to come up with the cash to start fixing the other one too!" I'd been concentrating on owning with little thought to the more mundane topic of paying.

"I've been working on that, and I made some calls during lunch. The best we can do is a bridge loan. It's kinda like a re-finance and will give us some cash."

I frowned, not really understanding.

It turned out not to matter. Every bank we approached had serious issues with the fact that there was no working bathroom. "It's against the law to finance a home in which the inhabitants cannot get themselves clean and remain sanitary," one such financial manager intoned. He frowned over the description of the old house a home inspector had faxed to his attention.

John smiled. I knew him and what he was thinking. There was light at the end of his tunnel. If we couldn't get a loan, it would all fall through. He could then walk away, and none of it would be his fault. I couldn't get mad, and life would continue as normal.

I secretly plotted and coerced the owner into allowing us into the house for two weeks to finish the upstairs bathroom, the one missing all plumbing fixtures and sporting holes in the floor.

It was undoubtedly a risk, and one of those times when I knew, without question, that my husband loved me. He should have throttled me for that whole plan but didn't. I was so excited and happy he couldn't help himself. It wasn't roses or champagne, but a gentle giving-in to please. What better form of devotion can there be than to bend? I thought we were on the same page and eagerly moved forward.

Securing a few hours of babysitting for Spencer, I went to the old house to take inventory of what we would need to finish the old bathroom. It was my first time there on my own, and I called out, "Hello, house! It's me! Ready to get cleaned up?" I peeked in all the rooms again, stopping to think about which pieces of our furniture would fit where. I'd brought a notepad and pulled a pencil from my back pocket to make notes. Because it was too quiet and a little scary, I talked to myself the whole time, just to hear a voice. "I think the couch will need to go on this wall." I decided while standing in the living room. "I wonder if Spencer's furniture will even fit in that little bedroom." I jogged up the curved staircase to check out the dimensions, scribbling as I went.

I stood in what was going to be a bathroom and sketched basic dimensions into my pad. I needed to think about tubs and sinks and commodes. I'd never bought such things before and was looking forward to getting it just right.

Putting away the notes, I surveyed the mess of a room. John had given in to my wishes. The least I could do, in return, was to empty the room and get it ready for the work we were to begin that weekend. "Okay, time to get moving."

An hour later, the room was completely cleared. It had been pretty easy since I'd basically just thrown everything out the window. Still talking to myself, I promised, "I'll pick that up, I swear. It's just easier than going up and down the stairs." Hacking, I backed out of the room, laughing at the dust I'd stirred up. "I am woman hear me roar!"

The Old Woman had thumped her way up the stairs, following the sounds of my voice. She wanted to see what the ruckus was about. "Who you talkin' to, girl?" She shook her head, puzzled, trying to decide what I was doing.

I stopped on the landing upstairs, whipped my head around, sure I'd heard something. My hair stood on end. "Hello?" I called out, walking slowly down the stairs. Looking around, I decided it had been my overactive imagination, located my purse and headed home.

Meanwhile, The Old Woman had stopped mid-stride too. "Did she hear me?" She was intrigued. "That's never happened before." She, too, headed back downstairs and watched me drive away, thinking about what had happened upstairs.

I rescued Spencer from the babysitter's house, read him a story and settled him in for a nap. He never complained about such things, generally wearing himself out all morning with his constant motion. His round, little face peeked out from under his blanky, and I couldn't help but smile.

I tiptoed to the kitchen and sat down to work out my plan for the bathroom. I dug through my notes and began to sketch the room to scale, marking the placement of the window and existing drains. I looked up, surprised to hear Spencer coming down the stairs. An hour had flown past.

I put the drawing on top of the fridge, away from little hands. It was one of my better drawings if I did say so myself. A beautiful cabinet and large mirror were in place on one wall. I'd had a little trouble drawing the claw feet on the tub, but the overall image was fairly convincing. I'd even labeled the walls with "deep maroon" and the vanity as "cherry." I couldn't wait to show John. As he sat down at the kitchen table, I remembered my other experience. "I had the weirdest thing happen today."

"What do you mean?" He turned the paper sideways to read my notes.

"I don't know really. I was at the old house, and I swear there was someone else there."

Alarmed, he looked up. "Did you see anything?"

"No, it was more a feeling. It wasn't bad though."

"If it's haunted, we ain't moving!"

"I wasn't like that. Probably just creaks and groans I'm not used to." I shrugged, to signify it was no big deal. John frowned, and I changed the topic by pulling my drawing off the fridge and handing it to him with much fanfare. "What do you think?"

He cocked his head to study the sketch. "This stuff is expensive. We can't afford this."

Later at the local hardware store, I had to agree. Who knew that a bathtub could cost over a thousand dollars? Sadly, I chose lesser cabinetry and boring fixtures.

The weekend arrived, and we worked like crazy, tearing out walls, running new pipes, installing lights, a commode, and sink. We were exhausted before we even knew if we would own the place. We'd also uttered more cuss words than I would have thought possible. "Sorry," I would whisper.

The Old Woman pretended to be offended. "You two need your mouths washed out!" She grinned though, knowing our efforts could only be to her advantage.

On day fourteen, nearing the end of February, the bank arranged to have an appraiser come out to the house to review the upgrades before they would secure a loan. Unbelievably, he was early. We weren't quite done, but at least the toilet flushed, and the shower sprayed. He looked at our hard-won bathroom for all of three seconds, nodded his head, wrote on his paper and announced he was going to go look around outside. We didn't care. "Knock yourself out."

The room was dusty as hell due to our drywall sanding, so we opened the window, despite the forty-degree temperatures, and started our clean-up operation. Not sure what the scribbling meant, we figured every improvement would be to our benefit.

Through the open window, we suddenly heard a splash, a screech, and a "Shit!" John and I stuck our heads out the window to see what had happened. Mr. Appraiser had inadvertently stepped on the rotted lid to an old cistern and lost his footing. His leg had gone down into the hole he'd made, and he hung in the balance, clutching what remained of the lid and sides. He glanced up at us, and more than a little embarrassed, admitted, "I think I need some help here."

John went to straighten out the latest mess. I followed closely behind, worried the cistern episode would turn the tide against us. We pulled the appraiser free, and John lay on his stomach to fish out his shoe that had been lost along the way. The appraiser stood in the soggy yard, holding his wet shoe away from his body and crinkling his nose at the musty smell of old water.

I approached cautiously. "Does this mean we won't be approved?"

He half-laughed. "No, my humiliating moment has nothing to do with your approval. This sort of thing has never happened to me before." He reluctantly replaced his shoe and marked on the paper again. "I guess that's about it," he said, holding out his hand to shake on the deal, signifying that we'd passed.

The Old Woman cheered. Having more energy than she'd had in years, she limped quickly through her rooms. She knew she was going to dance.

Chapter 5

Can You See What I See?

As the inspector shook our hands, realization sank in for me. I did an impromptu cha-cha across the backyard, chanting, "We're gonna get this house, we're gonna get this house."

I tried to get John to join me, but he wanted no part of my childish behavior. Embarrassed by the presence of another man, he rolled his eyes, conveying that *he* never broke into spontaneous dance, apparently forgetting our first night on the porch.

The Old Woman had followed us outside and snickered at the appraiser, who was still unwilling to put his weight down on that soggy foot. Watching me dance, her heart soared. We seemed to be kindred spirits, and the weight of loneliness was lifting. She absorbed my excitement, feeling it ebb and flow.

John, still trying to control me, reeled me toward him, silently appealing to me to be quiet. He jerked his head slightly to the side as a reminder that we still had company. *You're acting like an idiot,* his eyes said. I didn't care and started singing again. It turned into a game, with John trying to cover my mouth.

The inspector watched us play, shook his head and made a quick exit. Noticing the band on his left hand, I imagined he suddenly felt the urge to play with his wife too.

John and I rushed inside to put away the last of our tools and locked *our* house. I was eager to get back to the neighborhood and start spreading the news. To date, we hadn't told anyone that we were trying to buy the old house. It had been a precautionary measure in case things went south.

As we pulled into our street, friends and neighbors happened to be milling around. "Hey, we're in luck. Everybody's out!"

John grunted, "Great," and slumped down in his seat.

Parents had shoved their children into coats and hats and pushed them outside to enjoy pale sunlight and unseasonably high temperatures. Given the number of families outside, I realized we hadn't been the only ones feeling trapped.

We ran inside to relieve Deanna of her babysitting duties. John doled out money, and I hurried Michael and Spencer into their own coats, anxious to get outside before our friends got cold and headed back indoors.

"Come on!" I called out to John. "Everyone's still out."

"I'll be out in a little bit," he answered. He sat in his favorite chair, pretending to watch college basketball, which I knew he hated.

Checking on the boys through the front window, I saw they were busy kicking slush at one another. I went back to the family room and slid my hand along John's shoulder. "Hey, what's wrong? We got the house! Don't you want to go tell everyone?"

"No, not really. They're gonna think we're crazy or something worse."

"Worse? What do you mean—worse?" It made no sense to me.

"You know…worse. Like we're in over our heads and can't afford this house."

"They will *not*. They'll be happy for us. Come outside with me. Please." I tugged at him to pull him away from the chair and T.V. He unfolded himself and reluctantly slid back into his coat. I grabbed his hand and laughed at his pout.

Kids seemed to have exploded from houses. The noise was shocking. Small groups of adults were gathered on both sides of the street near the mouth of our cul-de-sac. It was cleverly disguised as a safeguard to keep the children from running out into the busier road that connected to ours, but I knew a social gathering when I saw one and hurried us toward our friends.

They saw us coming and began to call out greetings. The newest to the neighborhood, Mike and Karen, were fast becoming two of our favorites. Mike stepped forward, hand out toward John. "Whazzup, man?" He drew the words out and grinned.

Karen, long hair pony-tailed into a ball cap, stepped around her towering husband to give me a hug. "Hey, girlfriend! Good to see ya." Her eyes sparkled, and I knew she meant what she said.

Another friend, Jennifer, rapped on her kitchen window and waved. Having five children, she hadn't made it out the door yet. Her husband, Doug, was strolling down their driveway. "John…. Katrina…where you guys been? Haven't seen you much lately."

It was all the encouragement I needed. I ran over to give Doug a quick hug and launched into a narrative. "Well, funny you should ask. We bought a house!" I smiled so big, my cheeks stretched.

"Do what?" Doug stopped walking.

"What are you talking about?" Mike spun around.

"You're moving?!" Questions seemed to come from all around us.

John looked pitiful. "Yeah, we bought an old house to fix up. It's not far though."

"Where? What's it look like?" Karen managed to talk over everyone else.

"It's an old farmhouse about eight miles from here. It needs some work though," John said, with little inflection and downcast eyes.

The sidewalk was getting crowded, and Karen and I scooted our skinny butts closer together. Doug and Mike were looking at John, waiting for some sort of explanation. They knew my dramatics and needed the more logical Morgan to explain things.

"What kind of fixing up?" Doug asked. He was pretty handy himself and seemed intrigued.

"How bad is it?" Mike asked, already reading into John's body language that this was no stroll in the park.

John shook his head sadly. "It's bad, I mean really bad. She's trying to kill me, man." He appealed to his male friends, distancing himself from the project, somehow making it my fault.

"I am not!" I defended my honor. "He's the one who found the place! He just doesn't want you to know he likes it. It's awesome! It's got all these nooks and crannies, and there's even a curved staircase." I was gesturing wildly, as was my norm.

"She lies. The basement has a dirt floor, and one of the bathrooms is falling off the back of the house." He was starting to enjoy himself now that he had sympathetic men listening.

"The rooms are big, and they have these tall windows. There's even a back staircase. Oh! And a fireplace in the kitchen! It's incredible." I talked loudly to drown out John's negatives.

Karen was grinning and trying to fill in the blanks for Jennifer, who had finally made it outside. She'd been drawn to the animated conversation and was trying to make sense of what John and I were saying.

John reached over to give Jen a hug. "She's trying to kill me, Jennifer. There are red handprints all over one room and somebody shot up all the plaster."

"No way," Doug laughed, sure we were just kidding now.

"What the hell are you doing?" Mike demanded.

"I have no idea."

"Did you two go look at the same house?" Jennifer laughed.

"You guys wanna see a picture?" Not waiting for answers, I ran for my sketches.

John turned to the group, "It's going to be a lot of work, but she loves it. What can I do?"

"You're getting whipped, boy. You need to watch that!" Mike wiggled his eyebrows.

Cindy and Jim, another favorite couple, came around the corner with their two kids. They lived behind us, but often walked to our street where there were more kids—twenty-seven to be exact. They were quickly brought up to speed.

"TLC project, huh?" Jim asked, walking up to shake John's hand.

"More like BST—blood, sweat, tears," John answered.

"What? Like you haven't found enough to do around here? You two never stop," Cindy shook her head in exasperation.

She had a point. In the three years we'd lived there, we'd put in extensive landscaping, finished the basement into a second family room and bar, and wallpapered all the other rooms twice. We weren't known for relaxing.

More people exited houses, and before John and I knew what had happened, the news spread like wildfire, jumped our street and made its way two roads over.

Two days later, I called Cindy and Karen. "Okay girls, time to be spontaneous. Let's get an hour of babysitting for our little ones, and I'll run you out to see the house."

Always up for an adventure, phones buzzed, children were quickly re-aligned, and we three lady musketeers headed out to the country. The radio was blaring, and jokes were bandied about. Karen kept sticking her head between the front seats to hear the conversation. The car got strangely quiet when we pulled in the old driveway. Both women stared wide-eyed. We trudged up to the porch, and I shoved my way inside.

"Should we be doing this?" Cindy asked, surprised I didn't have a key.

Karen's took in the mess and pulled her coat tighter.

Ten minutes later, we walked down the curved stairs to the foyer. We'd made a complete circle, with me doing most of the talking. I was trying to judge their reaction, and they were trying to find something nice to say. "So, what do you think?" I had to ask.

"You're nuts you know that? You couldn't pay me to live here. I mean, look at it, girl! It's creepy." Cindy's blond hair was bobbing.

"Yeah, and are you sure that's rust in the toilet?" Karen pointed toward a tiny worthless bathroom off the foyer. Years of well water and rusted pipes had tinted the sink and commode dark brown.

"Who cares?" I asked. "Nothing works in there anyway. Come on, work with me here." I launched into the new bathrooms we'd be installing, the flooring we had planned. I waxed poetic about colors and where our furniture would sit. "She's gonna be great. I know she'll look better immediately, once we clear out the junk."

They both scrunched up their foreheads and tried to visualize what I was describing.

"Why do you keep saying she?" Karen wanted to know. "Is it haunted or something?"

"Do I? Hmm, weird." I tilted my head, thinking. "Well, to tell ya the truth, there does seem to be something here sometimes." I let the statement float and watched my friends.

Cindy's eyes grew huge, and she moved toward the door.

I grabbed at her arm. "No, no, it's nothing bad—more like I'm just being watched. I guess it feels like a woman. I don't know. I'm sure it's just my imagination." I laughed and changed the subject. I didn't need anyone thinking we were any crazier.

Seconds ticked by, punctuating the silence. Karen finally responded, "I can see you love it, and I know it will be great." She was trying to smooth and be supportive.

Cindy laughed again. "It's not for me! But if it's what you want...."

The Old Woman smiled. *Get your friends behind your dream, girl, and it will be all right.*

Cindy and Karen reached in, wrapping me in a circle of hugs. I breathed in warm friendship and knew I had their unwavering support.

It lasted less than an hour. Those two traitors must have talked to everyone as soon as they go back home. My phone never stopped ringing for the rest of the day. The conversations all started with, "Is it true about...?" and they would launch into some unbelievable detail they'd heard about the house. They wanted to see it for themselves and appease their curiosity.

As a result, John and I filled up the rest of the week with tourist duty, handing out maps and explaining our renovation plans in detail. I took women over during the day. He met some of the guys there after work. We learned that not everyone is a visionary. Most of our friends could not get past the superficial. The dirt and decay offended the women. "It's so gross! How are you going to move your kids there?" The sheer volume of work overwhelmed the men. "This is a bad excuse to get new tools, John. Where do you even begin?"

"See? I told you they'd think we were crazy." John reminded me Thursday evening.

"They won't, once it's cleaned up," I reassured.

Friday finally came, and John and I were greatly relieved. It had been an emotionally flagging week as we kept opening the door to hope, only to greet disappointment instead. Trying to convince our friends had been hard work.

As we often did on weekends, the neighborhood began to gather around a bonfire area we'd all made at the end of our cul-de-sac. The adults pulled out chairs and coolers. The kids pulled out toys. We parents formed a semi-circle around the fire, talking and laughing. The kids would bike, skate, squeal and yell as they circled us.

That night, John and I had to endure being the butt of many jokes as our friends picked on our lovely old house and us. "The thing is crooked as hell!" Tony, our immediate next-door neighbor, started in, pointing in general with his beer.

"You two aren't quite right either." Kerry, his wife agreed, brushing thick hair away from her face, all the while checking the location of their three small kids.

"The men in white suits are coming any day now," Karen piped in and began chanting, "They're coming to take you away, ha-ha. They're coming to take you away."

We accepted their ribbing as part of the game. Our neighbors were having a wonderful time talking about our demented state. They made up headlines chronicling our demise, each one jumping in for a turn.

"Couple Falls to Death Through Rotted Flooring," Jennifer started, using a deep, announcer's voice.

"No. No. No. It'll say, Man and Wife Mysteriously Disappear in Dungeon," Mike said, stretching long legs toward the fire.

"Electrical Failure Blamed in Strange House Fire," Doug said, standing behind me. He never did seem to sit, and I suspected it was a result of all their kids.

It was kind of funny, and we sat back to enjoy the show. John and I briefly made eye contact and just shook our heads. We obviously weren't going to get the "hell yeah" response we'd been hoping for. More comments and questions were thrown our way, and the tone began to change subtly.

"This just isn't right!" Mike said, angrily snagging a beer and heading home.

What's wrong with him? Is he mad at us? It was getting more serious. We needed an evasive maneuver before things got out of hand.

John and I looked at our watches, feigned surprise at the time, and began to move Michael and Spencer toward home and bed. Other parents, following our lead, began to gather toys and shuffle the younger versions of themselves towards pillows too.

That was also part of the weekend custom. We let the kids play and then tucked them into bed. Once that was done, the adults would re-group around the fire for a quieter time. It was a fair and reasonable system, and one we hoped would sidetrack our friends.

Two by two, parents straggled back to the fire, harried from fetching last-minute drinks of water and convincing children that, "Yes, you really do have to go to sleep."

Chairs were shuffled as people got more comfortable, positioning themselves closer to the fire to ward off the chill. We each opened another beer, mellowing a bit as we did so. Another can burst open behind us as yet another harassed mom or dad worked their way back to the circle.

Doug, the calmer of our friends, leaned into the circle and asked the questions everyone had been dying to ask. They'd been too nice up until then. The beer had leveled the playing field.

"What are you two doing? Are you nuts? Look at what you're leaving." His arms opened wide to encompass the people, the beautiful homes, and manicured yards. The neighbors followed the arc he'd drawn. His questions seemed to sum up everyone's feelings, and they all began to nod.

Mike joined in next. "Everybody has dreams of a house in the country, but we don't walk away from everything else to do it." He flicked a cigarette into the fire for emphasis.

"Dreams are good. They keep us sane. Actually moving—giving up everything you've worked for—it doesn't make sense," One of the ladies stated, surprising me. I had at least expected the women to see the romance of our project.

Chairs were re-arranged so that everyone could see and hear better. They sat sipping, waiting for enlightenment. John and I were silent too, hoping for divine intervention. The fire popped and settled back down as if to listen too.

So much for the sidetracking technique. How am I going to explain our need to move away and not offend?

I stared into the flames trying to get my thoughts together. John wasn't making eye contact with me anymore, so I had to assume it was up to me to try to appease their uncertainty. Firelight flickered in time to old movies playing in my head; me drawing pictures; the two of us, newly married with no money, searching for old houses to fix; our years of restless activity.

Taking a deep breath, I started, "Look, we're not moving away from *you*, you're wonderful, the neighborhood's wonderful. It's what we're moving *to* that's important."

The group turned toward me, sensing, perhaps, that I would make sense of things.

"Ever since I was a little girl, I've dreamed of an old house to fix and restore." My voice wavered, and I shook myself to get my nerves in place.

They leaned in, trying to hear me better.

"There's something magical about an old house, you know? I mean...they've stood the test of time. They've helped families celebrate. They've...I don't know...held them when things went wrong. I know it sounds crazy, but there's something about that...image. Something strong and solid that pulls at me. Can you understand that?" I stopped to ask the hushed circle.

There was no response. Since I hadn't really expected one anyway, I rushed on. "Bigger houses, better cars... They just don't fill us up anymore. We've spent years looking for an old house to restore, a place to...start over, get back to basics."

"She's right about that. We have always looked." John finally entered the conversation. Relieved, I blew bangs off my forehead. He went on, "You know how we are. We're always looking for something to do. We're bored. Maybe that old house will do it for us. Who knows?"

John tilted his head at me and smiled. I matched his grin, and continued, "It's not just about the work, and staying busy. John's doing this as much for me as for our family." I looked directly at John. He needed to know that I knew why he had signed on the dotted line. "He's lifting me up to reach for a dream." I leaned toward him in his chair, and he reached for my hand.

"I don't know where the dream came from. Maybe I was born with it. I only know that I need to take on something awful and make it beautiful. I need my kids to learn that nothing is too big to try. They think everything's easy, that all the toys and gadgets will just fall in their laps." I gestured toward the neighborhood, again. "Grow up, get a job, and buy a house, end of story. They don't understand it takes hard work."

"And you know what else?" It was John's turn again and, like a tennis match, heads turned for his volley. "No matter how hard we work, how much money we make, it still never feels like it's enough. Personally, I'm tired of it."

Eyebrows went up at that statement. I guess John had hit a sore spot or at least found common ground. I pulled myself closer to the fire. Fear of failure had made me cold. If we couldn't convince our neighbors, how in the world were our parents going to react? It was worrisome, to say the least.

I took one last stab at conquering the doubt that curled in the air, playing tag with smoke from the fire. "We really want to do this, but it would be easier if we had your support. My family is far away. Most of you are in the same boat, and we've learned to rely on each other, ya know?" I turned to look at each person. "We could really use your support here."

The half circle of faces looked away from us and toward the fire. The flames had grown smaller, having gone unattended, and the coals pulsed against each other trying to stay warm. What could they say, those friends of ours? They'd listened to my fervent speech. They'd heard John be more honest than they expected. How could they argue against such passion?

Heads turned to the side, eyebrows raised and lowered on thoughts. Slowly mouths began to smile—softly. "Man, you guys are still nuts, but if anyone can do it, you two can," Mike said, stretching out of his chair and heading for home. He slapped John on the back as he went past.

"Go for it," Doug agreed, leaning against Jennifer and reaching for her hand.

"We'll do what we can to help," Karen chimed in, nodding and encouraging the other women to nod too. Cindy came over and squeezed between John and me, and Jim reached out to shake John's hand. I knew it would be all right. I settled in, to finish my beer and enjoy the rest of the evening. All we had to do now was tell our parents.

Chapter 6

Parental Discretion Advised

Thinking we had the neighbors quieted down, we were looking forward to telling our parents. Initially, we were so excited with our exuberant, "Guess what?" that, in my parents' case anyway, they thought we were going to have another baby.

Throwing me off track with their assumption, I paused to regain my momentum and mentally wiped away pictures of diapers and bottles. I corrected their assumption, "No, three is enough!" and went on to explain my excitement. "We have found *the* house! *The* one. It's the greatest, and you've just got to come to see it!"

Both sets of parents were way ahead of our neighbors in appreciating our need to have an old house to play with. They knew who we were and where we'd been, having spent time in our previous homes and witnessed all the work we'd done in each. They knew, although they may not have understood, that John and I were restless, and had been searching for "something" over the entire course of our marriage.

My parents, probably more than John's, knew of our burning desire to fix up a tumbling home. We'd lived near them during the early years of our marriage, and they'd watched us go through our first four houses in eight years. They weren't surprised that we were finally moving to a fixer-upper. They were simply astounded at the age of the house we'd chosen.

"It was built when?" they asked, incredulous.

"1840! Pre-Lincoln, pre-Civil War," we answered with chests puffed importantly.

"The Pony Express was still running back then," I added, just in case they didn't quite have the concept.

I painted a virtual masterpiece over the phone, glossed over the faults and highlighted only the charm and potential. It was easy to do as they had not seen the thing and had to take my accounting at face value. They were pleased and happy for us but had some very real concerns.

"What about lead paint?" my dad asked.

"You mentioned a cistern? And someone fell into it?" my mother questioned.

"There's a pond? Are our grandchildren going to be safe out there?"

"There's probably asbestos, Katrina. You know that, right?"

I was a little disgusted with all of their questions, some of which I had not thought about, and now, in good conscience, would have to consider.

"Just say you'll come. You'll see. It's gonna be great," I soothed, and elaborated the details of the old house, trying to move away from the issues they'd raised.

"What's the attic look like?" my dad threw out as a final question. There was a dreamy quality to the question, and I knew he was picturing the kind of attics portrayed in movies, mysterious rooms, soaring ceiling, trunks full of treasure.

I hadn't actually seen the attic in its entirety. Earlier in the week, a home inspector had stuck his head up through the access hole in the upper hallway. He'd been looking for old, outdated wiring or gaping holes in the roof. I'd been searching for antiques or romance and had squeezed next to him on the ladder. I was saddened to find it small, with pitched roofs and nothing to offer but insulation. The inspector nudged me down the ladder and closed the trapdoor. I wrinkled my nose at the stale smell and looked at him curiously.

"There's not one thing up there, Mrs. Morgan."

My dad's question made me remember just how quickly the inspector had looked over the attic. I should probably have been more curious about that and insisted on scrutinizing it for myself. Neither John nor I had wanted to ask many questions though. We needed him to approve the house so we could move forward with the loan.

I mulled those things over quickly, and a tiny red flag began to unfurl. I ignored the image and continued. "Sorry, Dad, but it isn't pretty. I looked. The access is narrow. There's nothing up there at all. In fact, I don't think anyone's been there in years."

My dad was disappointed by my reply, but my mom quickly quipped, "Just as well—you and John already have bats in your belfries."

We three laughed and made plans for them to drive in from St. Louis. They decided they could come in two weeks, taking us to mid-March. I could wait that long. Besides, we had plenty to keep us occupied.

Our realtor Rick, although happy about selling the old house to us, was periodically calling. He wanted to put the newer, more expensive home on the market.

"There's too much work to be done. We're not ready. We've already told you that." John was getting tired of explaining himself. He was plotting though, that realtor of ours.

In the interim, already filled with phone calls, paperwork and waiting for my parents to arrive, we invited John's mom and dad to take the tour. They lived nearby, so we set a time. They were excited for us and, like everyone else, pictured something wonderful. How could they not? We were practically gushing. They pulled in and experienced a moment or two of uncertainty.

"Are you sure this is it?" They looked at each other with surprise.

We knew they were having trouble since they stayed in the car, despite our standing right beside them and bouncing from foot to foot. *Why are they just sitting there?*

Normally, Gene and Nancy had lots to say. They would ask questions and generously affirm ideas and dreams. Both were positive people, particularly Gene, who could spin anything into gold. At least they had been until that day. They gawked at the house in silence.

We gently helped them from the car and led them inside. Hopefully, they'd feel better once they saw it from that perspective. Their silent condition did not change. They looked around and said nothing. Zilch. Zero. Nada. I pouted.

Gene kept taking off his ball cap to slick back his mostly gray hair. Nancy still had her car coat carefully buttoned and didn't look like she had any intention of staying. Gene rested his arm across her much shorter shoulders, and they stood armed against our insanity.

Not to be deterred, John and I jogged from room to room, calling out our ideas on how we would fix up each space and what it would look like when finished. "Ignore these old planks and picture the room carpeted." We tried to sell the 'after' picture. We pointed. We gestured. We put an exclamation point at the end of every sentence. Nancy and Gene weren't buying.

Gene finally spoke up, shaking his head. "Morgan, I don't know, son. All I can say is that it's a good thing you're young, cuz this baby… whooee. It's gonna take it outta ya."

He was Southern-born and, despite living in Ohio for almost fifty years, the drawl was still there. "This thing is months, I mean months, from fallin' in around your head, boy." He shook his own, wiser head and ran his hands once around his belly. "The land seems fine. The barns are good, but this house?" He left the question hanging there.

Nancy, searching for something to say since the silence had been broken, came up with, "I'm just not good at picturing things." Her curly hair bobbed in rhythm with the nodding.

The Old Woman harrumphed over their statements, a bit put out they'd not had anything nice to say. She'd been excited to see them, understanding that we were widening the circle, introducing her to people of import.

Meanwhile, John and I stood pondering their statements. *Hmm. Did we have their blessing or not?* We kept trying to nail them down on what they thought, but they carefully refused to commit. They truly thought we had lost our minds or that maybe we were in dire financial straits. "You two doing alright?" they asked with eyebrows arched.

They just could not come up with a logical explanation for our moving out of a beautiful new home and relocating to that crumbled house. They hugged us anyway. "We know you can do it." They left immediately, heading for the safety of their own four walls.

"They are out of their minds!" Nancy likely started the conversation on the way home.

Gene, prone to folksy sayings probably said, "I wouldn't take a three-legged mule for that thing!"

John and I didn't know what to think. We nervously waited for my parents' arrival. Surely, their reaction would be better, and they would be able to visualize. We needed *someone* to affirm our decision. All the silence and open-mouthed gaping we'd run into had caused our own little niggles of doubt to surface.

Our neighbors, seeing the out-of-state license plates, gave a collected sigh. To their way of thinking, the parents would straighten out the mess John and I were in neck-deep. I'm sure my mom and dad must have wondered at all of the enthusiastic "hellos" and "good to see yous" that were thrown their way as they got out of the car, but they just waved and smiled.

We Morgans all ran out to the driveway, eager to see them, touch them. My dad stepped out, grinning and stretching his legs. I ran up to get a kiss, his mustache tickling me as it had for years. I grabbed my mom in a long hug, still homesick for their company, despite having moved away more than seven years prior.

We all casually visited that evening, catching up and letting them recover from the eight-hour drive. The kids were hustling each other for time with Nana and Grandpa. John and I relaxed and showed no stress concerning our purchase. We talked easily, setting the tone.

The next morning, I got hung up at with cooking, kids and generally playing hostess. John and my dad decided they would drive over to see the old house and that the rest of us could meet them there. I was consumed by jealousy as I watched them drive away. I'd wanted to be there to show it to my parents at the same time and see their reactions. I raced through my chores, stuffed the kids and Nana into the car and drove like a maniac to the house. I took the curves on the back roads as fast as I dared and rolled through stop signs as though there was an emergency.

I pulled into the gravel drive and threw the car in park. Grinning all over myself, I turned to look at my mom; sure she'd fall in love with the house immediately. She looked at the house, the overgrown yard, the missing windows and turned to me with a laugh. "You're joking, right? This isn't it! Come on, let's go." She sat there with her seat belt fastened.

I was crushed. I'd been sure my mom would recognize the potential, having spent years looking at my rough drawings. My dream was right there in front of her. *Couldn't she tell?* Guess not, as she was still smiling at my supposed prank. The children, oblivious to the happenings in the front seat, undid their belts and jumped out eager to go find grandpa.

My mother's mouth dropped open at that.

"No joke, Mom. Isn't it great?" I was trying to recover for both of us.

She slowly creaked open the car door, unfolding her long legs apprehensively. Her eyes were huge as realization sank deep. She tried on a smile; worried that she'd hurt my feelings.

I reached for her hand and tugged her toward the house. "Wait 'til you see inside!"

I hoped, once I got her in the door, she would feel better. That didn't happen. The kids were running from room to room, calling to her or my dad. "Nana, look at the swinging doors. Grandpa, come see my room."

She couldn't seem to take it all in and even refused to go in the basement to see the old furnace, crawlspaces or outside cellar doors.

My dad, who had already been through once, trailed behind us listening to my narrative, hoping if he heard my inflection, saw my slant on things, that the rooms would miraculously change. His shirt was still carefully tucked into his size thirty-two jeans, and both hands were in pockets, as though he was afraid to touch anything.

They were as appalled and shocked as Gene and Nancy had been. They also wondered if we had lost our marbles and money. "You guys doing okay?" they asked, eyebrows raised.

The Old Woman had been listening and waiting for their reaction too. She was no more pleased by their visit than she had been by Gene and Nancy's. Always happy to see the kids, she turned her attention to them, reveling in their youth and energy. "I guess you wouldn't keep bringing people to meet me if we weren't going to go through with the dance." She would wait some more and decide later what she thought of the grandparents.

Not again, I thought. *Why can't anyone see this finished?* I shook my head, sad that my parents hadn't been able to visualize. I thought I'd raised them better than that. Taking a page from The Old Woman's book, I went off in search of the kids. I needed a refill of their laughter to keep me from crying in frustration.

My mom watched me trudge away and caught my dad's eye. They began to change their tune. "We love you, guys. You know that."

"You obviously have psychological problems, but if anyone can turn this wreck into a home, you two can."

They believed in us and never fully voiced their overall objections. They didn't place any roadblocks in our path either, probably because there were so many already.

We drove back to the other house a little more quietly. As we neared the neighborhood, my mom tilted herself toward me, even reached out her hand. "I'm sorry I didn't respond better baby. I know you love it but damned if I can understand why. What is it about that place?"

I smiled back at her. "I don't know, Mom. It's like I don't even see the mess when I'm there. I see it done, with us living there, happy. I swear it feels like I've already been there or something. I can feel it, waiting, wishing."

Her eyebrows went up at that. "I've never had your vision for such things. Maybe now that I've seen it, you could draw me a picture of how you think it will look?" She patted my hand and settled back to think.

We four adults congregated in the kitchen, grabbed coffee and settled around the table. We were hashing things out, throwing around ideas and enjoying the jibes and jokes, most of which were at John's and my expense.

My mom tilted her head at John, her red hair falling easily into place. He'd been listing what we would do first, second and third. She interrupted, "How long do you think it will take you to finish that house?"

He never skipped a beat, "A year."

"Are you serious? You don't think maybe three or four years will be more like it?" She was more than skeptical of his reply. "Did you hear that, Bob? A year?"

"No, a year. Seriously, Dee," John defended himself.

As we sat around the table, letting John's declaration sink in, the phone rang. John reached to snag it off the cradle. He mouthed to me, "It's Rick again."

I quietly explained to my mom and dad that Rick was the realtor. We eavesdropped on John's end of the conversation.

"Rick, I'm telling you, we aren't ready to list yet. We've talked about it before."

I rolled my eyes, conveying to my parents that it wasn't a new conversation. I was starting to get nervous as John's side of the conversation had grown quiet, and I scrunched my forehead at him. He held up a finger toward me, asking me to wait.

"I guess I hadn't added all of that up. Go ahead, then."

John hung up the phone, and I stretched across the table, grabbing at his shirt. "What?" I demanded, practically shaking an answer out of him.

"Rick was talking about how long it takes to sell a house here."

I waited, eyebrows still on alert.

"He thinks we should list soon because people will be out looking since Spring is here."

"Well, are we listing?"

"Yeah, we are. We'll need the money from this one pretty soon anyway."

Wow. I needed that to settle in my mind and sank back into the chair. I hadn't been thinking about selling yet.

Rick, knowing the listing was coming, had already printed out fliers, taken pictures and gathered all the necessary paperwork. He must have called from the corner because within seconds of John relaying the conversation to me, the front doorbell rang. Rick stood there with a "For Sale" sign tucked under his arm.

I ushered him toward the kitchen, making introductions. He shook hands all around, had John and I sign some papers and exited. He pounded the sign into the front yard and pulled away before we could change our minds.

An hour later, he called back sheepishly. "I know this is short notice, but there's a couple that wants to see your house tomorrow afternoon at 2:00."

There was total silence on our end. It was our turn to be shocked and appalled. All of our energies had been going to the other house and the repairs needed. We weren't ready to display perfection and cleanliness and neatly organized closets. Hell, I hadn't done laundry in three days.

We all absolutely panicked. My parents, who had driven in to catch up with all of us, were caught up in total chaos instead. The leaky kitchen faucet needed to be replaced, the brass footplate on the front door polished, the floors scrubbed and the yard mowed. We took off in four different directions, trying to do everything at once.

John was pissed. He had a few choice words for Ol' Rick as he wrestled with the faucet. He was conducting one of those conversations that we all hold in our heads, the ones in which we verbally trounce our opponent, the kind we always win.

My dad was picking up the yard and getting ready to mow. I assigned clean up of the garage to Deanna and Michael. I figured she'd keep her brother in line and busy.

I carried Spencer and an armload of toys to the deck. I locked the gates, denying him access to the yard. It was the worlds' largest playpen and might buy me some time. I figured I had maybe an hour while he tried different means of escape. Throwing another load of clothes in the washer, I joined my mom, who was on her hands and knees scrubbing the front door plate.

I'm sure our neighbors were extremely disappointed in my parents and their negotiating skills. They were supposed to have come in and talked some sense into us. Instead, there stood a damned "For Sale" sign in the front yard.

My mom and dad, exhausted from the whole experience, headed home that Sunday morning. They used the looming appointment as an excuse to escape. They practically peeled out of the driveway and hardly looked back. There were no neighbors out to wave good-bye either.

It was probably the fastest trip home they ever made. I imagine that the conversation ate up the five-hundred miles as they headed west.

"They've lost their damn minds."

"You think John may be in trouble at work?"

As it turned out, we had had every reason to panic. That first showing turned into a second showing, and our house was sold by Thursday night. Five days, not eight weeks, as Rick had suggested. The buyers, accommodating as could be, graciously allowed us ninety days to move out, instead of the normal sixty. Anyone else would have considered that scenario a huge success. We did not. It spelled disaster with a capital D.

Things were going to get crazy-ugly, to say the least. The only advantage I could see was that we were locked in and there was no turning back. The list of projects was so long and overwhelming that John didn't have time to talk me out of things anymore. My cheerleading days temporarily over, I put away the pom-poms and strapped on a tool belt instead. It would become a terrifying roller coaster ride.

"Keep your arms and legs inside the ride at all times. This ride is not recommended for persons with anxiety problems, heart problems, fear of heights, or tight spaces."

From the time the sale was completed late one evening in March, we had exactly ninety days to turn a vandal's delight into a family home.

Chapter 7

Move Dem Bones

With the other house sold, it was time to roll up our sleeves and start working. The stress and crunch of a deadline hadn't overrun our excitement yet. We were still enjoying ourselves and did the ridiculous first: removing all the old wallpaper. Standing in the living room, I announced, "This stuff is so faded and molded, it has to go!" Everyone was given tools.

Deanna had followed us over too. "I've got to go to work later, but I'll help for a while." She sat on the living room floor eagerly reading the directions on the heat lamp box. Although we'd never owned such a tool, she was soon bossing us around, telling us how to use the thing. "You can't aim it straight at the paper—you'll melt it! Here, let me do it."

Michael claimed the back hallway as the place he would fix and attacked the walls with a putty knife, gouging them as he went. His gusto surprised us. To date, he'd shown zero interest in tools. I corrected his death-grip hold. "Slow down! No use causing more damage."

On the flip side, Spencer, who loved all tools, was picking up everything he wasn't supposed to touch. "I'll help," he announced, holding up a hammer. His green eyes flashed with anticipation.

"No! Not with that," we yelled and then laughed at his eagerness. We finally persuaded him to shoot hoops in the kitchen with his junior-sized basketball net. He wasn't convinced it was more fun and kept leaving the kitchen to see what everyone else was doing.

John, having a history of doing such work, gave the kids frequent breaks. He even joined Spencer in the kitchen to do a lay-up or two. Overall, though, things were going as planned. Our children were involved in turning something awful into something great. I mentally punched the sky in triumph.

The Old Woman was laughing and generally enjoying the chaos. "You got your hands full with this crew. Strong minded, the lot of them."

We scraped, peeled, cut, sprayed and steamed for hours. All our effort resulted in the occasional narrow strip being pulled from the walls. Melted paint curled along doorframes. It looked much worse than when we had begun.

The Old Woman was beginning to frown. "You do know what you're doing, right?"

John stood in the living room, taking in the mess. "Everyone just stop what you're doing. This isn't working." Tools were laid aside, and we stopped to listen. "There's no way we've got time for this crap. The wallpaper isn't budging; the walls are dented and covered in holes." He blew out a breath and announced, "We're going to have to drywall the place instead."

I was the only one who really understood what that statement meant. I stood up to protest immediately. "No way! We're not going to undo all the beautiful work inside just to save a few days. The house is old. We should preserve it, not turn it into some modern monstrosity."

The Old Woman's eyebrows lifted at that. She'd had no idea what John was talking about but glared at him as a potential threat.

"We've got eighty-eight days left. Period. We can't spend them peeling wallpaper! We've gotta fix this shit, and I mean right now." He slammed a cigarette in his mouth and lit it fast.

"Can't I put up sizing and fill the holes? Come on! We don't have time to do every room in drywall either." I couldn't imagine the house looking so new and looked around wildly.

"It won't cover the waviness. It'll look bad. I'm telling you, this is the only way." With that final statement, he reached down and jerked the heat lamp cord free of the outlet.

Michael had been holding his putty knife in mid-air, watching John. His arm fell, his chin dropped, and his attitude slid in to the toilet. He'd been feeling quite grown up and was disgusted by the turn of events. "I could have been playing basketball with Spencer. Unbelievable." He shook his head sadly like a tired old man and muttered, "I lost a whole day for nothing."

I frowned at John but didn't argue. I needed time to think. He didn't usually come across so strong, and I needed a strategy to break through this new veneer of his. After a long night, I was ready for him the next morning. It was Sunday, usually a lazy time of newspapers and coffee, and, I hoped, strategic realignment. I was more than surprised to find John awake, dressed and heading out the door. "Where are you going?"

"Home Depot to get the drywall." He looked like a guilty teenager caught sneaking out of the house.

"What? We haven't agreed on that!"

"There's nothing to talk about. It's the only solution we have."

"But…" I stammered, but it was too late. He was already in the car.

He came home to an empty house. I'd gone over to visit The Old Woman, trying to salvage the situation. I was gently sanding the dents and dings and trying to come up with a smooth surface to prove my point.

"I ordered two hundred sheets of drywall, buckets of joint compound and boxes of screws," John said as his hello. He'd followed a hunch and driven to the old house to find me.

I shrugged, not bothering to turn around. "Big deal. Thanks a lot, by the way. I've been dreaming of this house all my life. In one fell swoop, you change everything. No discussion. No options. Nothing."

He tried to be soothing. "Hon, there really is no other way. I know more about this than you do. Trust me. It takes longer to fix than to start over."

"Why the whole house? Some rooms aren't that bad."

"It needs to look the same. The walls have to be the same or doorframes won't work. Besides, you can't mix textures and finishes—that would look stupid."

I spun around to face him. "That's twice in two days you've finished your argument by saying it will look bad or stupid. Are you still worried about what everyone will think? Afraid you won't have the model home anymore? Well, good. That's what this is all about, you know? Walking away from that."

"You're the one who wanted to walk away. I was fine."

"Right, sure you were. You're the one who was looking at real-estate ads, talking about being bored."

"That didn't mean I wanted to change my whole life or everything I've worked for." He sighed. "It doesn't even matter. It's done."

I shook my head, trying to remember when I'd lost so much control.

Taking my silence as agreement, he continued, "I guess this is as good a time as any to tell you I have to go out of town this week. I won't be here for the delivery, so, uh, you'll need to handle that, okay?"

I narrowed my eyes. "No, it's not okay. You ramrod through here, turn into a tyrant, go buy stuff I absolutely hate and then tell me I have to be here to handle it? Amazing." *Jerk.* I stopped to fume, and he wisely left me alone.

I didn't speak to him for the rest of the day, which made him crazy. He kept flirting and trying on puppy-dog faces. "Come on. How can you be mad at this face?" he would ask, leaning in close and pouting. For the first time in our marriage, those tactics left me unfazed.

He dragged out a suitcase and packed slowly, watching me for a reaction. "Have you seen my electric razor?" I said nothing, and he tried again. Shaking a nearly empty bottle, he asked, "Do we have more aspirin? You wouldn't want me to get sick while I'm gone, right?" Another silly face appeared.

I hid a tiny grin. "You're a big boy, used to traveling. I'm sure you'll find everything just fine. Me? I just wanna be mad for a while."

I shared a mostly silent cup of coffee with him the next morning and broke down to give him a hug before he left. "I do still love you."

He smiled, triumphantly, and leaned in for more than a hug. "I love you too. Want me to show you?" His eyebrows went up and down, Groucho Marx style.

"Oh no you don't!" I flounced away. "I may love you, but you're still in trouble."

On Tuesday, I went to the old house to wait for the damn delivery. Never able to stay mad for very long, my resentment had mellowed.

If we had to drywall, then so be it. I could handle a slight detour and figured I could decorate and paint to bring back the graciousness of her era.

"I thought you were mad," the Old Woman offered as a greeting. She watched me, head tilted. "You know what your problem is, don't you? You make everything easy for everyone else but you. Trust me. I know what I'm saying."

The drivers finally pulled in with a flatbed truck weighted down with John's requirements and an honest-to-God forklift to lift it down. My jaw dropped. The men hopped down from the truck, wanting to know where to stack things.

"Well, we'd like half downstairs in the living room for now, and the rest in the biggest bedroom upstairs."

They looked back and forth at one another. "Uh, ma'am, it doesn't work that way."

The two men, one tall and one short, were dressed identically in coveralls and red hats. They resembled Abbott and Costello, and I had trouble concentrating on what they said. "We can't carry this stuff into the house. There's a liability clause."

I waited for a punch line that never came. "Really. You don't say?" I finally muttered. I was temporarily at a loss for words and decided I was mad again.

John was really going to be in trouble when he got home. A person didn't rise to his level of management without learning to delegate and, in this case, disappear. I thought about him working and being unavailable during our last two moves. I got indignant knowing I was the one who seemed to hold everything together despite his long hours and constant travel. In my constant quest to prove myself, I'd never complained, but as he had said, handled it. *We'll just see about this buddy boy. You think you've got me all figured out, don't you? Well, it may not be so easy anymore.*

The men were backing the forklift off the back of the truck. Once down, they lined up the claws, grabbed huge piles of drywall and rocked and staggered the machine across the uneven yard. They made piles near the porch while I stood nearby trying to figure out what to do. It was March in northeastern Ohio, which said it all.

The drivers and I stood there in the yard, discussing the best way for me to keep the piles dry. "You need a tarp or some immediate help," they graciously suggested. The main driver, or Abbot as I was calling him in my head, was fascinated by the house. "I grew up in a place like this. Great for kids." I could almost see his memories swirling.

"How about a quick tour?" he asked, with an embarrassed laugh, and twisted his hat nervously in his hands.

"You're kidding, right? You leave me out here with all this stuff and want a tour? I don't think so." Sarcasm had always been my middle name. I smiled deviously.

He laughed and looked at his co-pilot. They seemed to reach a silent agreement. Men do that: size up a situation and communicate a solution to other men without saying a word. Women, on the other hand, must discuss, question and agree upon a plan. Being one such female, I wasn't sure what had transpired. They were smiling, and it was my turn to be nervous.

They each picked up two buckets of the joint compound, or mud, as we called it, and headed to the front door. "Where to ma'am?"

"I thought you couldn't put anything in the house."

"The clause specifically states *drywall*, due to size and weight." They grinned at each other and headed toward the door.

It sounded good to me. We'd had twenty of those buckets delivered and at sixty-two pounds apiece, I wasn't going to argue. I tried to get them to take a specified number of buckets to designated rooms. In my normal, ultra-organized and anal way, I'd made a master list while waiting for them. I knew I was pushing my luck with the drivers, but I had to try. We compromised. They carried half of the buckets upstairs. The rest were stacked in the foyer.

Always happy to share my dream, my mood improved dramatically. The delivery guys got the tour, I got a partial shipment hauled inside, and we were chatting like old friends. "This place is gonna be great!" Costello said.

Abbott nodded and looked around one more time. "It's a little hard to look at now, but it seems solid. That's the important thing." He held out his hand, and I shook it gladly.

I watched them drive away and felt my smile disappear. I slumped on the Old Woman's porch wondering what to do. She settled down too, wondering what this whole drywall business meant and whether she was going to like it or not. Based on my reaction, she wasn't looking forward to it at all.

I shook myself, suddenly determined. "Time to get moving, girl."

To be fair, I was no slouch when it came to delegating either. Or, if not delegating, then rallying the troops. Standing on top of one of the four-foot piles, I started making phone calls. I arranged for three of my nephews to be there by four that afternoon. I made up an emergency situation so the school office would page Deanna and let me talk to her. She was usually my fallback plan when I found myself in a jam. Being popular, I knew she'd find some guys that could help. On a whim, I offered up an incentive: "I promise pizza, pop and twenty bucks to you and any of your guy friends that can be here tonight from four to seven."

She giggled. "Dad's going to love the twenty-dollar bill part! He should know not to leave you in a snit!"

I laughed with her but didn't bother to dispute her words or defend myself.

"We're moving drywall doubles, so no wimps!" I ordered.

She'd done enough remodeling with us over the years to know what that meant. We'd finished off two basements in other houses, and she'd carried her share. A drywall double consisted of two pieces of four-by-eight-foot sheetrock bound together, weighing in at approximately ninety-two pounds. I did some quick math and squared my shoulders.

The cavalry arrived promptly at four, hoping for pizza immediately. I was no fool—work first, pizza later. All in all, we had the three nephews, Deanna, her tall, skinny, track star boyfriend Dan and two stockier guys from the football squad, Mike and Brian. Not bad. I walked over to Deanna and gave her a huge hug. She flashed one of her infectious smiles. She'd come to the rescue, no doubt about it.

Out came the master list, and I was once again in my glory, directing traffic and piles to the correct rooms. There was initially some posturing from the nephews and local jocks. Coming from different schools, there was a certain competition in the air. My nephews were wrestlers or baseball junkies and not about to be intimidated or out-maneuvered by track stars or football necks. Deciding to use the competitive spirit to my advantage, I paired them off.

"Dan and Deanna, you're obviously a pair. Grab some drywall and start us off. Take yours to the second story, the last bedroom on the left. Mike, Brian, you know each other, so you follow Deanna. I pointed at two of my nephews, "Chris and Nick, you're group number three."

I looked my remaining nephew in the eye, "Lou, you're stuck with me, but I promise you we can show 'em all up in no time flat!"

The groups began to shift around accordingly. "When you drop off the drywall, come down the back stairs, so you're not in the way!" I grabbed a pair of gloves, lifted my end and waited for everyone to file into a line. "Come on now. We've got a hundred trips to make!"

"Move it out...move it on...Rawhide..." Deanna sang, and the guys rolled their eyes, finally finding common ground against Deanna and me. They started acting macho, joking and egging one another on. By the time we got to the second pile, the staircases, narrow hallways and sheer weight of the stuff had taken its toll. The group was growing quieter, and I wondered if I'd ordered enough pizza.

John, ever the master of timing, pulled into the driveway as the last two trips of drywall headed through the door. He stepped out of his car, spiffy in his clean dress clothes and shiny black shoes. Smiling, the rat.

The entire group was dirty, sweaty and smelly. I, in particular, did not appreciate his timing. My arms felt three or four inches longer. I defiantly explained the situation, what I'd done to rectify the problem, and dared him with my tone to find fault with my plan.

The Old Woman stood right behind me, nodding in all the right places. "You tell him! What he did was not nice. Not nice at all."

"We're paying each of these people twenty bucks? Plus pizza?" He frowned.

"You weren't here. What was I supposed to do? Drag it all inside by myself?" I was spoiling for a fight, and he knew it. Smart man that he was, he grinned at my disheveled appearance and rubbed his hands through my hair. "How long are they here?"

"We're done." I slapped at his hands just in case there was even the slightest chance he didn't know I was disgusted with him.

"No, I mean how long did you tell them they'd be working?" He winked at me.

"Oh." I saw where John was going with his train of thought. "Three hours. They've been here for two." I winked back.

He looked at his watch, looked at me. We smiled at one another ever so smugly.

The Old Woman watched us completely confused. "What's going on? I thought you were mad. How come you're giving in again?" She followed us, trying to figure out our relationship.

John called the teenagers together and lavishly praised the work they had done, careful to explain that he'd just come in from out of town, and what a relief it was to know we had such great people to rely upon. I suspected he had actually driven by earlier and killed some time waiting for us to finish, but I said nothing.

"I know you're all a little tired, but," he looked at his watch for emphasis, "it looks to me like there's an hour left on the clock." With that, he marched importantly toward the back of the house. They followed him unquestionably. *The pied piper?*

He reached down and proudly flung open the cellar doors. "Welcome to the dungeon."

Taking that as my cue, I scrambled down the decaying steps, unlocked the doors and switched on the one hanging light bulb. The basement, if you could call it that, was not a happy place. The center area housed a furnace and piles of debris that had been haphazardly tossed down the stairs for years. There was even a large, old tree trunk, used to hold up the house.

"How about all of you strong young people dragging out all of the junk down here, before we stop for pizza?" John stated more than asked. "Unless you're too tired, of course."

They took turns leaning down and peering into that black hole. They seemed transfixed by the tree and stood staring at it for a long time. John had stroked their egos and then challenged them. What could they do but agree? Smart man, that husband of mine. Smarter still because he stood at the top of the stairs in his nice clothes and directed all of us, me included.

Slowly, the broken bits of furniture, twisted pieces of metal, rusted cabinets, rotted beams, and trash disappeared up the broken stairs, to be piled outside until a Dumpster could be delivered.

The kids joked about how scary the house was, giving Deanna a hard time because she was going to have to live there. "Man, this is nuts! You've got the coolest basement at the other house," Brian piped in.

"Yeah," Mike agreed, "we could play pool, darts, whatever down there."

"There's NO way I would stay here," Lou, normally reserved, announced loudly.

"You can stay at our house, Deanna," Nick, one of her baseball cousins, offered.

"Yeah, if Mom saw this, she'd let you move in permanently," his brother, Chris, agreed.

The conversation changed to haunted houses. "There's so much junk down here a person could hide a body for years," Brian, the jokester, began. He looked around the basement for emphasis, hoping for a laugh. So began speculation and spooky tales.

I'd worked myself over to the corner housing the last pile of crap. It looked to be rolls of the same crappy wallpaper we'd tried to peel off the living room walls. It was covered in slimy mildew and stuck together in a gummy mess. I disgustedly pawed through the wet stuff.

I was half-listening to the ghost stories when I discovered a complete skeleton underneath all the paper. It was a badger. I knew that but didn't enlighten those teenagers. Not able to resist, I held the skull up in the dim light of the dungeon and yelled, "We've got bones here!"

The kids turned, assuming I was kidding. Seeing the head and sharp teeth, they all screamed and scrambled their way up and out of the basement, fighting for purchase on the crumbling stairs. They pushed and pulled each other out of the way, trying to be the first to safety, and even rammed into John who'd stepped down to see what all the fuss was about.

I ambled up the stairs, laughing my fool head off. "It's just some little animal, ya'll."

They were not amused and were more than a bit embarrassed by their behavior. "Your mom is really weird, Deanna," Dan said, puzzled over his girlfriend's family.

"I know, I live with her," she answered, but she was still laughing at the memory of them shrieking and running. I'd given her leverage against six jocks, and she knew she was queen.

The pizza arrived, and most of them opted to grab a few pieces and eat it on the way home. We doled out twenty-dollar bills as they raced out of the driveway.

John tipped my chin towards him. "Still mad at me?"

"I can't stay mad for long, but I still can't believe you left me with all this, today."

"We got the basement cleared though, didn't we?" He was trying to sweet-talk me again.

"I don't know about the *we* part, but, yeah, the basement's cleared and with pizza and payroll, you're only out one hundred sixty-seven dollars and twenty cents!"

The Old Woman stood chuckling over my earlier prank. "You're gonna be alright after all, aren't ya? Lord that was funny. I'll tell ya, not everyone handles the skeletons in their closets like that, no siree!" *I think I'm gonna like you a lot.*

Chapter 8

Strangers in Our Life

Naturally, right after the drywall was hauled inside, the weather turned warmer and sunnier. I might have resented the irony except, with the change in weather, our entire front yard, from the porches to the road, bloomed with crocus and made me temporarily forget any other problems I might have had.

Thousands of miniature flowers cheerily waved their purple bonnets at cars and their passengers as they cruised slowly past. It was certainly not something a person would find in a subdivision, and I loved the wildness that came from having land and experiencing the seasons with a fresh outlook.

That first spring also brought us an influx of new people. Our first official visitors were two elderly ladies who opted to pull into our driveway rather than past. Eager to greet them, John and I laid down our tools and went outside.

They approached us with beautiful, dentured smiles. Their lined faces were carefully powdered and made up for visiting. The shorter of the two filled her dark pink suit quite snugly, and I noticed, due to the overly large cuff, that she'd hemmed the pants several inches. Her jacket was the exact color of the pants and her shirt carefully chosen for its matching, pink-flower print. I doubted whether the blouse was ever worn with anything else.

The other lady, several inches taller, wore dark, slimming slacks. Her jacket was a careful shade lighter, and the shirt, like her friend's, selected to match. Even the collar was ironed.

I couldn't help but compare how they'd carefully dressed and primped for a simple afternoon drive to how John and I had groomed for the day. I'd brushed my teeth and hair and slid into worn jeans and an old sweatshirt. John had rummaged around and found an equally used shirt and lawn-stained tennis shoes.

The two ladies crooked elbows and picked their way through the front yard, trying not to step on the flowers. They waved a greeting with their free hands, and I was charmed.

"I'm Alice," the tall one said.

I knew she'd be the leader. I smiled at John, wondering if he'd arrived at the same conclusion.

"We drive out every year to see these flowers."

"Oh yes," the more matronly lady answered enthusiastically, holding out her hand. "I'm Felicia. We came out here years ago with a local artist group to paint around your pond." She grinned and nodded her head, sure we would know what she was talking about.

John and I struggled with that mental picture, knowing our pond to be choked with thorns and covered with algae. Being optimists, we chose to believe them and garnered hope from their statements, shaking hands and smiling. The women captivated us with their tales and flattered us by asking if they could take our picture. "Stand in front of your house and flowers."

We were still new to our project, energetic, happy and full of plans. John and I put our arms around one another, stood by our front porch and mugged for their camera. The ladies left, and we went back to work.

Days slid by and a second visitor, who was far from charming, set the tiny hairs at the nape of my neck on alert. He pulled his rusted, dented van into the driveway and sat there unmoving. We stepped out onto the porch, expecting him to get out or, at least, speak.

His arm, totally covered with tattoos, rested casually along his open window. He stayed inside the van, smoking and looking at us between drags. He slowly exited, flicked his butt toward the yard and called out, "Are you all gonna rent?"

"No, we bought the house. We're planning on living here."

During another long silence, while we watched him walk toward us, I felt the first stirrings of unease. Although there was no sun that day, his eyes were squinted and glassy. They moved back and forth, assessing, missing no details. I looked at John, and his eyebrows were lifted as high as mine were.

"How about renting though?" the stranger asked again, standing too close to us. His skin had a gray pallor, as though he'd stepped through a cloud. I shivered once and took a step back to stand behind John.

"Nooo," we answered more slowly, not sure if he was daft or if we were just not speaking clearly.

At our puzzled tone, he elaborated, "No, I mean are you going to rent out the other half?"

Understanding dawned. The man thought the house was a duplex due to the double porches and two front doors. We could see how someone might think that and nodded at the notion. We set him straight, but he stood in place, silent once again. He ran a hand through slightly greasy, too long hair and turned his head slowly side to side and up and down, getting the full picture of the house. He took in our work clothes, old shoes and seemed to reach a decision.

"You interested in hiring some extra help around here?" he questioned. "I'm kinda outta work right now and my wife's expecting a baby soon. I could sure use some extra money." I took in his thin t-shirt, old jeans, and missing wedding ring.

John and I half-laughed, shuffled our feet and told him we needed to do the work ourselves or we'd be out of money too. We exchanged names and talked a little more. "Sorry," we said, feeling slightly unsure of ourselves and wondering how to get him to leave.

He reluctantly drove away, cruising slowly past, staring at us again. I let out a relieved breath I'd not even realized I'd been holding.

John shook his head. "That was just weird. I'm glad the kids weren't here. I'd just as soon he not see them." John reached for my hand, still watching the road.

We quickly forgot about him and the incident due to newer, more interesting guests. The frenzied and continuous commotion acted like a magnet, drawing people to us. The couple living way back and behind us brought pizza and a smile. We four exchanged mail as the rural carrier had gotten things mixed around. I tried to get them to keep our bills, but they declined. Although the Old Woman was not dressed for company, she enjoyed the attention. "It's been a long time since I had visitors stop in just to say hello."

Exploring the house and getting to know the project and us seemed to be a source of conversation and a door opener for a twenty-mile radius. "You the ones fixing up that old farmhouse?" It didn't matter if we were pumping gas, buying stamps, or getting more supplies.

What is it about this house? Everyone's got a story or knows someone who lived here.

It was fun to be the center of so much attention, and I loved the history, the stories, the feeling of being connected somehow. On days when I was there alone, I turned up the radio, sang off-key, tackled my jobs eagerly and forgot that not everyone who pulled in was nice.

Although we'd dismissed him, the handyman had not simply evaporated. Much to our surprise, he returned a week later. Spencer and Michael were with us that day, just messing around in the house, while we worked furiously to hang John's two-hundred sheets of drywall and generally make the old house habitable.

The boys ran through the empty house and exploded through the saloon doors at the top of the stairs. Spencer's chubby legs were pumping furiously to keep up with Michael's longer ones. An occasional argument would break out when Spencer got fed up with losing.

"They'll work it out," I assured John, who had stopped working and was listening to the yelling.

Problem solved, the boys slid down the staircases and screeched in delight. John and I smiled at their far-off laughter and tuned them out, until there came a knock at the door—one we didn't hear right away, being upstairs and in the back bedrooms.

The guy with the van had pulled in and come up to the front door. At his knock, Michael opened the solid front door and talked through the screen. "Can I help you?"

The guy looked Michael right in the eye and lied. "I'm a friend of John's. Are you his son?"

The familiar use of a name convinced an eight-year-old. "Yeah. You want me to go get him for you?" Michael was our charmer.

Spencer peeked around Michael's leg, "Who's that?"

The man ignored Spence and addressed Michael again. "That'd be great. He wanted me to stop by and maybe help him with some stuff. Can I come in?" the snake asked, rubbing his hands across sinewy arms, acting as if he was cold.

The Old Woman had been in the foyer watching the boys when the knock had come. She, too, had leaned around Michael to see who was there and decided immediately she didn't care for this particular visitor. "Don't open that door, son. Do not open that door!" Michael was, unfortunately, unaware of her.

"Oh, sure. I'm sorry," Michael replied as he unlocked the screen and pushed it forward. He left the stranger downstairs and jogged upstairs to find us. I'd already put down my sander and was headed down the hall, sensing something wasn't right. Mother's intuition? Sudden silence? A tug from the Old Woman? It didn't matter; I simply knew something was wrong. At Michael's announcement of a guest, John passed Michael and me in his haste to get downstairs.

He descended hurriedly and forcefully on the old steps, with me in hot pursuit. We were not pleased to see that particular man standing in our house. John could be imposing when he wanted to be. His eyes were glinting, and his muscles bunched. "We won't be hiring any help, okay? You need to go and don't stop by anymore. You got that?" He narrowed his eyes, and I noticed one of his hands was curled into a fist. He marched over to the front door, wrenched it open and stood there until the man left.

I was sure he'd finally gotten the point. We were nervous though. He'd seen all of our tools lying around, and they represented a lot of money. The old house was not what I would have called secure. It would be easy for someone to break in and walk away with all that we had, or worse.

John and I stood on the porch and made sure the jerk drove away. Doors were firmly closed, and feeble locks turned. Michael, taking it all in, was mortified. His thin shoulders sagged with failure. "I'm sorry Daddy. He said he knew you."

John knelt down to face level. "It's alright, but out here we just don't know everyone like at the other house. I'm not mad at you—just come get me first next time. Deal?" He got up, looked at me and said, "I want you to go to the store tomorrow and buy deadbolt locks for every single door." He went to explain things to Spencer.

"No problem." I nodded in understated agreement. I reached for Michael and pulled him in for a hug, brushing at his messy, brown hair. He remained silent, his eyes huge.

I began to think about the amount of time I spent at the old house alone. For the first time, I realized I was vulnerable and maybe not such a superwoman after all. There were a few houses near ours, close enough to see one another anyway. I decided, then and there, that it was time to meet the rest of our neighbors.

The people across the road never appeared to be home, so I tried the house catty-corner to ours. I walked up in torn jeans and a t-shirt, introducing myself and apologizing for the way I was dressed. The couple and their older daughter, in for a visit, stepped outside and stood with me in the driveway. They'd been watching all the activity and commented on how much was going on. "It sure isn't boring over there."

I told them we would probably be able to provide them with hours and hours of entertainment as we were always doing something. We talked awhile, and they told me what a showplace the old house had been in the eighties. "Those people really kept it up nice."

"It will be again, I promise."

Dave, the man of that house, leaned back against a car, arms folded, listening. He looked tough, despite a mostly gray head and mustache, and I hoped I'd chosen correctly. I started to relate our problems with the wannabe worker. "There's this guy who keeps stopping by, drives a kinda rusty red van. He's pretty skinny, dark hair. Anyway, we wondered if you could maybe keep an eye on things when we're not there."

"I know which van," the neighbor said, a faint New York accent coming through. He stepped away from the car and nodded at me as if he and I were in on a secret. "I've seen it there a couple of times. I kinda keep a watch on the road here."

His wife, Helen, rolled her eyes. "You can say that again." She turned toward me. "Man doesn't know what to do with himself now that he's retired."

Her daughter, Karen, nodded vigorously, "That's the understatement of the year."

"If that van shows up, it won't be okay." I clarified, looking directly at Dave.

Dave, thrilled at the prospect of finally having something to do, announced, "We don't put up with that kind of shit out here. I got a shotgun ready for just such things."

I didn't know quite what to think of the shotgun statement but accepted that we had a neighbor in our corner. I scribbled our number on a scrap of paper and ambled back to the old house.

More days passed, but the van never returned. I hoped John had scared him off and smiled at my fierce protector. A car turned in, and I ran quickly to the window, pulse racing. It wasn't the van. Surprised and pleased, I watched our flower ladies, Alice and Felicia, get out of their car and head toward the house.

Weeks had flown one into another. I'd forgotten about those charming women. Smiling, they presented me with a copy of the photo they'd taken. I was touched they would take the time and effort to do such a thing, and stood with them in the yard, talking and laughing at John and myself in that modern rendition of *An American Gothic*.

As I watched them drive away, I gave into my love of the outdoors and headed to the little potting shed out back. I'd been planning on clearing it of all the junk, and it seemed as good a day as any to tackle that. I looked inside. "This all has to go. I need room for our stuff." *At least until I can talk John into building a garage,* I plotted silently.

Spencer was with me that day and completely overjoyed to be playing around outside the shed. He was digging in the dirt and generally filthy from head to toe. I had just swept up a pile of glass and didn't want him in the shed until I was sure it was safe. Through one of the broken windows, I heard Spencer start talking to someone I could not see.

"Hi!" his little toddler voice rang out.

"Hey there, little boy. Is your mom around?"

Goosebumps chased each other up and down my arms. He was back. "Damn him all to hell!" I picked up the largest piece of glass from the pile and stepped outside. A tigress protecting her young, I wielded the glass in one gloved hand as I reached for Spencer with the other.

"She sure as hell is and I think you'd better go. Now!" I was shouting and may have even bared my teeth.

"Whoa," the guy laughed, put his hands up in mock surrender and took a step forward instead of back. "I'm just trying to be friendly."

"Leave." I stood my ground, pushing Spencer further behind me. I was trying to formulate a plan in case things got out of control. My legs trembled, and I willed them to stop. *Show no fear.* We were in the backyard and invisible to anyone passing by. Could I defend Spencer and myself?

I looked past my threat to see my gruff neighbor, and new best friend, Dave, cross the road. He was carrying his shotgun, as promised. His eyes were narrowed, and he was hunched over as if stalking prey. The handyman didn't see him coming since he was still watching my lethal weapon and me.

"This the son-of-a-bitch you told me about?" Dave called out, raising the gun.

I nodded, and my persistent pest turned at the addition of a new voice. Seeing the gun, the stranger's eyes grew large. Without saying a word, he moved quickly toward his van, finally dropping into a jog to shorten the distance. Fumbling for the handle, he managed to get inside, slam the door and throw it into reverse in one fluid movement. He was never seen in those parts again.

I'd given Dave my trust, and he had not taken the gift lightly. "Thank you, thank you, thank you. I'm not sure how that would have gone if you hadn't shown up." In one of my normal spontaneous actions, I hugged him. He pulled back and seemed embarrassed.

I thought he'd head home, but he plopped himself on a stump. Pulling up a blade of glass he chewed it thoughtfully and looked at me, the yard, the piece of glass I'd dropped.

"What?" I asked self-consciously.

Pointing what was left of the grass at me, he started in, "You got to be more careful around here. You're doing stuff normal women don't. I see ya over her, hanging off ladders, hauling broken windows when there ain't anybody around."

My mouth dropped open. I was being lectured. I stood there trying to be respectful but couldn't help grinning.

Dave saw the smirk and grew sterner, "I mean it," he waved the soggy grass for emphasis. "It ain't funny. I may not always be here to check on you, ya know? What if I hadn't been around today?"

Wiping the smile off my face, I had to admit he had a valid point. I walked toward him looking at him more closely. His grizzled hair was sticking out of a well-worn baseball hat. His old jeans hung loosely around his legs, and on closer inspection, I noticed his skin had taken on similar attributes—gray and worn.

Scootching onto the stump next to him I asked, "You okay?"

"Yeah…no…not been feeling too good lately, that's all." He brushed me away like a bothersome fly, shoving up from the stump. He gave a half salute as he headed toward home. I noticed a little swagger as he slung his shotgun up onto his shoulder. I chuckled to myself. *Helen's going to be hearing about this one for days.*

The Old Woman had been watching, in shock, from the back window, unsure what was going to happen or what, if anything, she could do to help me. "Well, I'll be. You're a pretty tough little cookie, aren't you? And David came all the way over here to help." He'd been her neighbor for years, yet they'd hardly met.

After dinner, I told John about Dave and the handyman incident. He was mad as hell. "We need to buy a gun," he declared, jumping up to pace.

No way was I agreeing to a gun. "He probably didn't mean to be so intimidating. And while we're sitting here judging him, I can't help but wonder how *we* come across to strangers. We don't always put the best foot forward either. Walking around with a gun isn't the answer."

I softened his mood by showing him the picture the ladies had left. John turned the picture to see it more clearly and grinned. I smiled in memory of our flower ladies. "You just never know who's going to show up, do you? I guess we take the good with the bad, huh?"

I shook my head, overwhelmed by the difference in visitors. The Old Woman beckoned though, and I imagine we did too. Work of that magnitude seemed noble and grand. People, even strangers, wanted to touch our dream.

We learned, soon after that, that Dave had cancer. He put away his shotgun and began a more urgent battle. I was haunted by his words of caution and tried to be more careful. It is appropriate that my gun-toting, sage-toothed neighbor was named Dave *Angell*.

CHAPTER 9

What Lies Beneath

The funny and charming things about our project occurred with less regularity. We were left with grimy, grueling stuff that wore us to a nub. The basement and foundations were like that. Back in February, when we'd first found the house, we'd named the area, "The Dungeon." I was about to find out just how apropos the name choice had been.

Early on yet another Saturday morning, we all pulled into the old driveway. Turning off the car, John laid out the day's plan. "I'm really going to try to get the rest of the drywall up on the first floor today. Well, except for the kitchen anyway."

"Sounds good," I replied, eager to move us further down that To-do list. It had been a long week, with John traveling again, and he'd been unable to work at the old house. We were feeling the weight of keeping up with two houses, moving two yards (sometimes in the dark), three kids, a job and tedious day to day activities that make up a family. I was determined to keep a decent attitude. It was laugh or cry. "What about me? What should I work on today?"

John shot me an arched look and laughed. "Crawlspaces. Today you get crawlspaces. You did promise, remember? It's time to get things ready to jack up the kitchen." He leaned over and gave a quick kiss.

I wasn't fooled by the show of affection. It seemed eons ago that I'd so stupidly agreed to "do" crawlspaces and attics. I'd hoped John would renege or eventually feel sorry for me. He would be a knight and save his damsel in distress. To date, he'd not been suave in that department. He was too busy slaying other dragons named drywall and plumbing.

I scowled and bit my tongue. I would not balk, complain or admit that I couldn't do what he was asking. Instead, I nodded as though it was a fine plan.

I had no clue as to what I was really supposed to accomplish in the dungeon and puttered around the house straightening, dragging out toys for the boys, and reminding them to be careful.

"You better get moving," John admonished from his ladder.

"I know. I'm getting there." Descending into what surely must be hell, I took in the basement in its entirety. Despite having removed the majority of the debris, it remained a dark and ominous place. A lone, naked forty-watt bulb hung sadly from the ceiling, inadequately trying to push back the gloom. Pieces of the old water system tilted against each other like fallen dominoes, casting murky shadows across the floor and my mind. Never having had to deal with well water, we weren't sure what their purpose was and needed to study them in more detail. The pump chugged to life, bringing in icy water from somewhere yet to be determined, and the overhead pipes dripped condensation, keeping the dirt floor damp and dank.

Resigned to my task, I rolled my eyes at the entrance to the crawlspace. A small window had been cut into the stone foundation and dragged various pieces of junk and constructed a wobbly step of sorts, under the entrance so I could get inside. I yanked and pulled myself up into the hole in a less than graceful fashion. Fishing out my flashlight, I sat cross-legged in the dark, cramped area, just taking it all in for a moment.

I looked at the sandstone boulders used as a foundation for the old house, some three foot across. They'd shifted and settled over the last century, and smaller rocks had been fit into their crevices. The result resembled a complicated jigsaw puzzle. One of my assignments was to make sure everything was packed tight and sealed. Seeing feeble rays of daylight filtering through, I knew I was in for quite a job.

I couldn't help but speculate on the sheer size of the rocks. *How did these get here? Who fit them together like this?* I envisioned draft horses straining under ropes as the builders coaxed and prodded them to keep moving, to pull and to stop. Sweat dripped, and hands blistered as pieces were moved into their final position. The sheer determination was humbling.

Even the thick oak rafters hanging quietly overhead were impressive; hand-hewn, their unhealed scars still showed the slices of ax and hammer. That was another thing I was somehow responsible for. "Make sure you check the rafters. They could be cracked, rotted or full of termites," John had lectured earlier. I'd listened as if he was speaking a foreign language but nodded my agreement, so he'd be quiet.

I hit one of the rafters with my hammer, surprised to feel it bounce back at me. "Jeez, these aren't going anywhere. It's like petrified wood down here." I thought about the trees that had been sacrificed for our house. The width of the beams surely meant they'd stood sentry on the property long before crashing to the ground. In my mind, that made them true Giving Trees. What was I really seeing down there in that dark hole? Two hundred years? More? It was embarrassing to think about the complaining we'd been doing.

Awed, all I could come do was start working. My tasks were paltry in comparison to what others had accomplished. Trying to clear a path, I pushed old boards and rocks out of the way. Crawling and yanking, I backed myself to the window over and over again, tossing and dumping debris into the basement. I poked at piles, mindful of slithery creatures or varmints. In such jabbing, I uncovered a few skeletal remains, a cat and possibly a rabbit. "We've got bones here!" I called out, remembering and laughing at the teenagers scrambling for safety a month before.

I stumbled, literally, over a much larger femur bone. Definitely not a cat. It looked like it had come from a large animal, or worse. I frowned at the thing, holding it close to my flashlight beam and turning it over and over. I thought about the Chippewa Indians that had lived nearby, hundreds of years prior. My mind then jack-rabbited to 1982, the movie _Poltergeist_, and the bones buried in *their* backyard. "No way! Not gonna happen!"

I exited the basement using the crumbled, old cellar steps instead of the main stairs into the house. John did not need to know what I was going to do. I snagged a garden trowel from the old shed, out back, and snuck back inside. Carefully, I wrapped the bone in newspaper and towels and buried it exactly where I'd found it. I sent up a quick prayer, a body shiver, and hoped John would never find out we had a femur in the dungeon.

With each passing day, he seemed to speak less, sleep less and eat less. His ears and neck had taken on the permanent flush of high blood pressure. I hadn't seen him smile in weeks. His mood had all of us tiptoeing around and whispering. He was a delicate balance and one I did not want to disrupt, especially since he kept threatening to sell my old house.

Two hours had gone with me re-packing the foundation, spraying expandable foam, and clearing out the area. I'd finally reached the area under the sagging kitchen floor. It needed to be leveled before we could do cabinets and flooring. I'd never set jacks before, but I wasn't worried. If I could do foundation work, putting in a few jacks would be easy. I was tired though and wondered if I'd get it all done that day. My thighs were shaking from the constant squatting position, my neck ached from leaning over, and my eyes seemed stuck in a permanent squint. The earlier emotions of awe and pride were slipping away, replaced by martyrdom.

"How come I get all the nasty jobs?" I scrunched my face up, thinking about everything I'd been asked to do. "Crawlspace, duty, darling. Go under the porch, honey." The attic was still looming out there too. Something was very wrong with our job distribution.

I heard the boys playing in the house and could just make out the noises of John's ladder sliding around. Bits of conversation filtered down through the planks and boards to reach me in the pit. I heard John's dad, Gene, laughing from time to time too. He'd shown up unexpectedly that morning, afraid like everyone else we weren't going to make the deadline. He'd put on coveralls and started mudding, a job that was usually mine. There I was, in the dungeon, a prisoner, incarcerated and alone.

The light from my flashlight caught and held heavily charred beams under the kitchen. I flipped to my back to see the flooring better and noticed the base of the fireplace, also in the kitchen, had been re-set with new concrete blocks. "Damn. This whole kitchen's been on fire!" Feeling out of my element, I went to find John.

He didn't care one whit that the house had been on fire. "Is it fixed now?" he demanded, a putty knife dangling from one hand, a palette full of drywall mud in the other.

"I guess so. I don't know. That's why I came to find you."

"I can't stop what I'm doing. You fix it. I'm busy. You know how to run a hammer. Make some cross braces with two by fours and move on."

"Yeah, sure. Why didn't I think of that?" I spit out a sarcastic reply, tiredly rolling my neck back onto my shoulders. "Oh, and by the way, thanks for checking on me. We have no idea what's down there, and you left me there for hours. Thanks."

He had the good sense to look contrite, but the crawlspaces were still mine.

Spencer and Michael had followed the sound of my voice to announce they were hungry. I looked at my grimy hands and sighed. "Damn, John. The least you could do is take care of the boys."

"They never said anything like that to me," he defended himself against my tone.

"It's not like you're approachable right now. They're just kids," I spit back at him.

"What's that supposed to mean?"

"Nothing. Forget it." I rummaged in the cooler for drinks.

Because my own stomach was making noises, I cleaned up and made sandwiches for everyone but John. "He can make his own sandwich," I muttered, slapping pieces of bread together. Once the kids and Gene were watered and fed, I headed back to prison.

Armed with boards, nails, and a temper, I set to work. I hammered and propped as loudly as I could in an attempt to either drown out the other sounds or garner sympathy. "Tell me to make cross braces, will ya?" Smash. The hammer hit home. "Is it fixed?" I asked in a false John voice. Smash. Another nail slammed home. All I had left to do were the jacks, and since we hadn't purchased them yet, I backed out of the area.

Walking across the basement, I stared at the remaining crawlspace. It represented another fourth of the house, and I knew it needed serious repair. The back staircase and landing located in that section were extremely crooked. That could only mean I needed to jack up that area too. Looking at the boarded-over access hole, I knew it wasn't going to be easy. *Imagine that.*

I bent under the ridiculous maze of vent work, plumbing and gas lines to get a better look. Prying off the boards, I jumped back as piles of dried grass, walnut shells, rocks and dirt spilled down on my head. "Great. A nest. Just what I wanted to see."

Not caring anymore, I dragged the mess out of the way and peered inside. It was much smaller, and I was getting nervous. I tended to suffer from bouts of claustrophobia and barely tolerated elevators. I could feel myself starting to sweat, and my hands were growing clammy. Pulling my measuring tape off my waistband, I held it up to the opening and held my breath. "Eighteen inches. Shit." It would mean belly crawling in there, and I panicked. "No way! I cannot go in there," I told the dreary basement. Letting the measuring tape collapse with a hiss, I ran up the cellar steps again, needing fresh air and a plan.

I took a lap around the house just in case I'd missed a better entrance to the crawlspace, hoping a door would magically appear. I peered briefly under the porches but quickly gave up on that possibility. The only other prospect I could see was the back of the house. I stood in the backyard looking at the room and frowning. The entire room was balanced precariously on rocks, bricks and whatever else had been available during construction. The ingenious builders had literally cut big holes through the sandstone foundation to push through plumbing, electrical and heat to the bathroom, leaving everything, including the underside of the main house, exposed to the elements. "No wonder the damn thing's caving in."

I kneeled in the dirt to look at the holes. The plumbing and electrical no longer worked in that bathroom. I was pretty sure they could be pulled free. I ran my hands across rot and moss. *Maybe we can make this bigger. Work from the outside in.* I had terrible visions, though, of being in there when the tired, sagging structure collapsed. I'd agreed to do the crawlspaces but didn't want to be entombed there. I'd really hate someone to find *my* femur in the crawlspace. I needed some advice.

Hoping for strength in numbers and a stay of execution, I approached John while his dad was nearby. "I need some help with this whole crawlspace thing. I did the one side, but the other one..." I let the sentence hang until I had their attention. "The way into that side is really small. I can't get in there."

"Hmm," they wondered simultaneously, still spreading mud across drywall seams and not really listening.

"I'm serious. I need you to come downstairs and look at this."

The two dusty men reluctantly laid down their tools and made eye contact with each other. "Women," the look said.

I coaxed them down to the dungeon, pointing at second crawlspace hole, explaining as I went. John absently kicked at pieces of the nest. Gene eyed the opening with me. "How about the ol' porch?" Gene asked, heading out of the basement and toward the front of the house.

"Can't. A groundhog lives there." I answered quickly, calling him back. There was no way I was crawling under a porch with a grumpy groundhog as a probable companion.

"She's right, Dad," John chimed in. "The damn thing comes out from under the steps every day and eats the front yard."

I thwarted their every suggestion and finally led them up the cellar stairs to the backyard, the old bathroom, and the open, rotting holes. Having effectively set the stage, I asked, "Can we make one of these holes larger? Cut through the beam and get under there?" I gestured, Vanna White style. *Will it be hole number one or hole number two?*

There was much talk and measuring and arguing over whether such a thing would be feasible. Like gunfighters, we'd all three pulled our measuring tapes from belt loops and were flashing them around in the sun. Finally, it was concluded, "Yes, we can cut out a three-foot section, work ourselves under the house, and add supports."

"Sounds like a big job," I called toward John, who seemed to have other plans and was heading back inside for more drywall work. "I can't do this!" I threw my hands toward the hole.

He turned around, irritated. "You'll be fine. Just add supports as you go."

I could feel my temper rising to the surface. Gene, also feeling a storm brewing, offered his assistance. "There ain't no way she can do all that by herself, John. I'll help."

John turned around to offer a rare smile and say thank you.

"Hell, son, I knew this area had to get fixed. I just didn't think I'd be the one doin' it." Gene wasn't happy either and sent a scowl at the hole and John's retreating back.

He and I worked in silence, removing boards, crumbling rock, rusted plumbing, and old insulation. We could clearly see the sagging floor joists. "Have ya'll got any hydraulic jacks over here?" Gene asked, eyeing the enlarged opening.

"Sure do." I ran to the potting shed and pulled out our car jack. Lugging it proudly across the yard, I smiled. Days earlier, I'd moved some of our tools from the other house to the shed. I was immensely proud of my forethought.

Gene took one look at that jack and plopped himself down in the dirt. "Whooee. Is that it?" He took off his ball cap and ran his hands through dusty, gray hair.

"Uh-huh," I replied. I wasn't sure what I'd done wrong but knew when a man took off his hat to rub his head, that something wasn't right. I waited to find out what I'd done.

"We need three-ton jacks, not car jacks, hon. That one there'd flatten your hind-end." He sighed heavily.

"Huh? Whadda ya mean?"

I was obviously not going to be much help. Gene fished out his keys and walked to his truck. "I'm going home to get some supplies. I'll be back in an hour or so." It was a forty-mile round trip, so I took a break and hid from John in the backyard.

Gene came back as promised, not just with the jacks, but concrete blocks and an oak beam. One of the many things he'd insisted on saving, over the years. He was renowned for saying, "Don't throw that away. I might need it someday." I'd never seen it happen before, but it appeared that "someday" had actually come.

He and I jacked and supported as we went, moving further under the house, but couldn't reach the middle of the faulty room unless one of us went in that hole. Gene looked at the space and announced, "There ain't no way I'm gonna fit in that hole. I'm likely to get in there and not get out." He patted his belly for emphasis.

There was no choice. I lay on my back and shimmied backward under the house, praying the jacks would hold. Gene shoved concrete blocks through the hole, and I dragged them the rest of the way—working, bracing, and hammering until the joists felt solid again. Hours later and the outside hole was ready to be filled in again. We were too tired to appreciate the milestone.

Gene barely bothered to say good-bye. He climbed slowly into his truck, arched over the steering wheel with exhaustion, and drove away. I stood blinking at the unaccustomed light, waiting for John to come see our handiwork.

Laying belly down in the dirt, he looked into the hole, evaluating our job. I'd been watching expectantly, waiting for the praise I knew I deserved and crowded near his shoulder. He finally rolled over and onto his feet, brushing the dirt off his shirt. He found the least soiled spot on my face, leaned in to give me a kiss, and said, "Good job, Hon," and promptly went back in the house.

I stood there with my jaw dragging the ground and arms hanging. *Good job?* "That's it?" I was near to screaming. "Good job?! That's all you can say? I've crawled, hauled, jacked and shimmied myself into all kinds of places today, and that's all I get?" He had to be kidding. I picked up an old brick and heaved it toward the pond. "Damn you. What do I have to do around here?" I looked around for more bricks to kick or throw and settled for a few of the rocks Gene and I had moved out of our way earlier.

The Old Woman shook her head at me. While I was ranting, she was celebrating. "Oh, that feels better. It's been a good long while since I've been able to put weight on that leg." Although it hadn't been pleasant—holes punched in her side, pieces added, jacks turned—she knew it had been worth the pain and settled herself more completely.

"The foundation is fixed, girl. You did a good thing." She watched me a while more and tried to remember something she'd heard years before. "No one can make you feel inferior without your consent—Eleanor Roosevelt said that I think. Yes, that's who it was, good old Eleanor." Pleased that she'd remembered, she continued, "You should think on that, missy. I mean it! It's not John that needs to tell you you're alright, it's you." She shook her head at me.

"Just for the record, you haven't been telling him he's doing a good job either."

Chapter 10

How Much Wood Can a Wood Duck Chuck?

I calmed down after the basement fiasco. It seemed pointless to rant and scream when there were so many other things that required my energy. For some reason, throwing things and having a tantrum had given me some clarity of thought. I vowed to stop competing with my husband. We were in a mess together, sink or swim. He was stressed and working as hard as anyone could. In reality, I was probably much easier to get along with having decided I was an equal partner—accepting ownership and not trying to assign blame.

My attitude adjustment allowed us to share whole minutes of enjoyment inside the old house. One of our favorite things to do became treasure hunting. Like everyone else, we'd read stories about old houses. There were always hidden heirlooms, a false wall or a beautiful fireplace hidden behind plaster. In between restructuring and fixing, we entertained ourselves by tapping on walls and listening for hollow spaces. We even ripped out areas that appeared to have been tampered with over time. Like treasure hunters, we excitedly followed imaginary trails to dead ends. Despite numerous disappointments, we eagerly explored each new possibility. It would have made everything so much easier if we found ourselves the sudden recipients of a windfall.

"I know the staircases have been redone." I ran my hands over the walls, feeling for inconsistencies. Looking at the ruined walls in the living room, we saw the outline of an old door. "This poor old house has been changed so many times, I can't tell where the original leaves off and the new begins."

The Old Woman sighed. "You can say that again. Seems like every family has to leave their mark—change something and add something."

I joined John at the plastered-over door, "There's got to be something else behind here." He hit the wall with his hammer and, together, we investigated yet another empty hole. Such things continued until we had nowhere else to look. All we had to show for our efforts was tons of insulation, holes marking our hunts, and one very old candlestick that had been wedged between wallboards and forgotten.

The Old Woman, more practical farmhouse than excessive Victorian, had opted for wood-burning stoves on the main level, with pipes pushed through to the upper bedrooms. Sensible and efficient, but not very romantic, to my way of thinking.

The vision of a magnificent mantle in the living room disappeared, and I choked on disappointment. A real log fire seemed appealing and comfortable, and I had so wanted that for us. The one small fireplace, squatting against the longest kitchen wall, would have to do. Thankfully, the mantle had been left behind, and, somewhere along the way, someone had added wood moldings and trimmings to dress up the poor little thing.

It was slightly crooked, but we'd grown used to that. Everything in the old house was tilted or off by a bit here or there. I'd learned to take it in stride and found it charmingly different from our previous cookie-cutter homes, where everything was new and nearly perfect. I taught the boys an old nursery rhyme, "There was a crooked man, who walked a crooked mile. He found a crooked sixpence beside a crooked stile. He had a crooked cat, who caught a crooked mouse, and they all lived together in a little crooked house." The kids and I thought that funny and sang it all the time. John, on the other hand, gnashed his teeth whenever he heard the tune. He was the one trying to work around all those angles and was not amused.

Anyway, despite its listing slightly to the left, I had grandiose visions of how the little fireplace could look. I could see the children at the table doing their homework while a fire blazed and I baked cookies. Perhaps that was a bit carried away; I never baked. A fire anyway. I could see the fire. Of course the kitchen fireplace could be repaired, straightened and a new hearth laid in no time. Making that come true became an obsession. Lord knows, there was no shortage of visions or obsession in the old house. Without such things, we'd never have purchased her in the first place.

John, having been through such drills before, rolled his eyes. "You're making me crazy! We don't have time to clean and fix that thing right now. There are a million other more important things we need to do!"

"I know, but the kitchen's already a mess. I don't want to wait until the room is clean and shiny to fix the fireplace. It'll just get everything nasty again," I smiled at my logical plan.

"We aren't working in the kitchen right now. We're working in the living room. Focus. We finish one thing completely and then move on." He glared, in an attempt to keep me on track.

I just laughed, not impressed at all. "That's the way *you* do things. Me? I like all kinds of projects going on at once. You know how I am. I get bored otherwise."

"Fine. You want the fireplace done, then you're going to be the one to do it." He turned his back on me and went back to measuring the back hallway, where we were pretty sure a tiny bathroom could be added. Two-by-fours were stacked nearby, ready to go. I'd even added a sink to the pile, something I'd found on sale.

Having won the fireplace argument, I decided to see what it would take to get the old girl cleaned up and working. The fireplace, not me. I'd already proven myself. I marched right into the kitchen and began to dismantle the wood-burning stove as if I knew what I was doing. The pipe came off in pieces, spilling ash and soot all over the kitchen and me. Not to be deterred, I began pushing and shoving the stove itself toward the door.

"Michael! I could use some help in here." The boys were playing on the stairs. One would stand at the top of the stairs and drop a bouncy ball. The other waited at the bottom, ready to intercept its crazy descent.

We two skinny people, Michael and me, used legs and backs as leverage on the old stove. We managed to get the stove to the porch and began, literally, to roll it toward the road. Spencer was underfoot and asking what he could do. "Go back and get the pipe from the kitchen. You can carry that." Focusing on the stove and Michael again, I commanded, "Push!"

"I am pushing, Mom. This thing is heavy."

End to end, collecting clumps of grass as it went, the cumbersome, two-hundred pounds of cast iron moved slowly toward the road. I didn't care if it went to a passing trash hunter or to the dump. It didn't matter to me so long as it was gone. Reaching our destination, I collapsed on top of the stove, head hanging toward the ground, and tried to get my breathing back under control. I looked at Michael, who stood beside me, trying to catch his breath too. "Well now, that was fun, wasn't it?"

Spencer had dropped pieces of the jointed pipe along the way but showed up with one piece to pile on top of the stove. He was pleased with himself and grinning. Michael was sweating and thoroughly disgusted. "I'm going out back to play." He disappeared around the corner of the house, Spencer in hot pursuit, yelling, "Wait for me."

I swept up the kitchen as best I could and stuck an honest-to-God aluminum pie plate in the hole left behind from the stovepipe. It didn't look too bad, all things considered.

The Old Woman, on the other hand, stood in the kitchen taking in the scene. "Stove's gone, fireplace looks ridiculous. You're not going to leave that pie plate there, are you?" She was pretty unhappy about things, remembering all the good times spent around the kitchen fire. "I don't think I like what you're up to."

The Old Woman and seemed to cross mental pathways from time to time. I felt the need to reassure the house it would not stay demolished, that everything would be all right. It's as though I could sense the pain and heartache like a presence that wept behind the walls. Because I'd been trying to discern the soul, the history of the house, while trying to restore it to what it used to be, I didn't question my thoughts or the need to speak out sometimes. "This is going to be beautiful. Wait and see," I comforted as though talking with an old friend.

I gave the kitchen another once-over, thinking about what I needed to do next with the fireplace. "There's probably some structural damage," I told myself, remembering the charred beams in the crawlspace. Picturing the multitude of walls, rooms, and plumbing that had been haphazardly thrown together, I decided I should have an expert come look at the fireplace, clean it out and help get it functional.

I looked up "Chimney Sweep" in the phone book. That even sounded appealing. It conjured up scenes from *Mary Poppins*. I didn't even know that the term was still being used. We'd never lived in a house long enough to perform maintenance or call in chimney sweeps. If the paint needed to be touched up or a furnace filter changed, we were out of there, or so it seemed; we had moved about every three years. The Old Woman of a house, however, needed just a little bit more than routine maintenance. It was new territory, a pilgrimage.

Even though we were knee-deep in destruction and restoration, I surely couldn't have the sweeps looking at our fireplace and finding dirt. I tended to be the kind of person who would vacuum right before carpet cleaners arrived or wash my car before service. I knew I wasn't the only one to do such things. I've caught others, mostly women, doing such things.

On the day the sweeps were scheduled, I decided I should open the flue to see what was up there before they looked in there with their cameras and such. I crouched on the cast-iron hearth, my head turned sideways, and shined my feeble flashlight up inside the fireplace. "Look at that! This thing is filthy and clogged." Hands on hips, I stood up and looked at the clock. "We've got about an hour."

Armed with a huge shop-vac and an almost three-year-old little boy, I set out to clean the flue and main part of the fireplace immediately. Spencer thought that was a wonderful idea. He'd been opening and closing the cast-iron doors to the fireplace for months, scaring my girlfriends with stories of mice and spiders. He'd known from the very beginning the old fireplace was interesting and was ready to begin this great adventure.

Never one to turn down the opportunity to use tools, he grabbed the vacuum hose in a two-handed grip and planted his feet like a firefighter ready to put out a skyscraper blaze. "Ready!" He looked back at me and smiled broadly. He was feeling grown up and useful—not a normal sensation for the third child. It almost brought a tear to my eye thinking about the great parenting we were doing, the foundations we were laying, the lessons being taught. I turned on the vacuum and let Spencer lead the charge.

Well, whatever was clogging that hole was not impressed with our industrial vacuum or Spencer's unrelenting attempts to poke the hose up into the flue. Nothing was budging. I should have learned prudence by then, however, as usual, I threw caution to the wind and squeezed my hand into the opening of that little flue.

"Let's see what's in this thing," I announced, purposeful. I looked at Spencer, pushed up my sleeves and bent over to get a better vantage point.

Spencer leaned in to get a better look too, shoving against my legs to get his head in the fireplace first. I wiggled my fingers around and managed to get a hold of whatever white and brown thing was blocking that hole and gave it a tug. It would not move.

Bracing my feet against the old iron hearth, I pulled and yanked. "Come on!" With a final heave, I came out holding one very dead wood duck by its scrawny little neck. If I'd ended up holding an elephant, I wouldn't have been more surprised. The momentum had the damn duck sailing right past Spencer's head. It was left, hanging from my fingertips, limp yet still swaying.

I stood there for a few seconds, blinking and trying to piece the new puzzle together. Spencer, quicker on the uptake than his mom, screamed and ran for cover. There was nowhere for my little guy to hide—no furniture, no boxes. He just backed himself into a corner of the kitchen and yelled loud enough to wake the dead…duck. The whole thing was just too much for me, and I stood there, alternately laughing and wiping away tears. Finally realizing I was the only one amused, I laid the duck on the floor and went to comfort my little Spence-man.

He wanted nothing to do with me and turned back toward the corner, covering his head in defense. So much for all that warm fuzziness, I'd been feeling earlier. This was obviously not one of the lessons I'd hoped to teach. He continued to yell and shake his head no. In his little mind, I had tricked him, murdered the duck, placed it in the fireplace and set the whole thing in motion. Worse, I had stood there and laughed at him, and I was not to be trusted.

"It may have fallen into the chimney from a nest and couldn't get out," I tried to explain, crouching down to his eye level, turning him toward me. "It's probably been there a long time, honey. It's alright."

He was stiff, resisting my hug, and peeking past my shoulder to view the fireplace as though it had somehow come alive and would be chasing him in all his dreams over the next twenty or fifty years. I turned to show him all was well, and wouldn't you know it? Another dead duck was hanging out of the flue. It was the other half of our own dead duck duo and looked like a very bad cartoon. Its webbed feet were caught in the flue, and it hung upside down into the main part of the fireplace. All it needed were little x's across its little duck eyes to be complete.

"For goodness sakes, look at that. No wonder I've been having trouble." The Old Woman stood, looking at the ducks. "Poor little things."

"You said it would be *ooookkkaaayyy*," Spencer wailed and accused, all the while his lower lip trembled.

I tried, really tried, not to giggle. What to do but go ahead and remove that one too? With its release, other treasures tumbled out of the flue to land in ashes and send soot into the kitchen. I looked on in amazement at two small sparrows, also dead, and multiple pieces of nests littering what had been a relatively clean kitchen floor.

Spencer, unable to resist the temptation, edged out of the corner and took in the morbid scene. Because the sweeps were coming at any moment, I quickly wrapped all the dead birds in paper towels and buried them out back. It seemed to make Spencer feel better to see me finally exercise a bit of respect.

As the last of the dirt went back in the hole, he put his pudgy little hands together and prayed, "God bless the ducks."

God and I smiled at that. The Old Woman watching through the kitchen window, added, "Amen."

The sweeps arrived not ten minutes later, wearing dark khakis and matching blue shirts. The kitchen was destroyed, and I was covered in dirt. So much for appearances. All I could do was shrug it off.

The sweeps were a father-daughter team, which amused me. I thought about Shotgun Dave saying I didn't do things normal women did. Here was proof that I wasn't the only such woman. I tried to compare stories with the young woman, but she wasn't overly friendly, and my attempts at small talk faltered.

Also all business, her slightly-built dad went about setting up their camera, which consisted of a tiny lens attached to the end of a long tube, similar to a cable line. The two of them forced the hose into the flue and stood back to watch their monitor. I was watching too and could see all was clear. I was congratulating myself on removing the dead ducks when the two of them started issuing dire warnings.

"You're going to need a brick mason to come in here and mortar this old stovepipe hole shut. You'll fill this entire house with smoke if you use it as it is," Daddy Sweep started in, shaking his head "no" the entire time.

Darling daughter chimed in too. "The flue's pretty small. It's six inches and should probably be eight. Maybe you better not use this fireplace at all."

The Old Woman was feeling better since she could breathe a bit easier now that she was unclogged. "Oh no, I hope that's not really true," she moaned having been looking forward to all of us cozying up in her kitchen—a thank-you for all we had done.

I, too, was momentarily let down about not being able to have a fire. Never willing to admit defeat easily, I nodded at the two sweeps noncommittally. I didn't feel like getting in an argument. I'd simply have to re-evaluate and formulate one of my famous Plan B's. My day had brought such unexpected surprises, incredible messes, and a fair amount of laughter that I moved past the disappointment pretty easily.

Spencer, who'd forgiven me completely as only a child can do, was dancing around my legs and smiling again. By the time the chimney sweeps were sharing their bad news with me, he was glorying in his telling of the ducks: "Two heads came out of there, and mommy laughed and laughed." His little hands were gesturing wildly and his big eyes overly expressive.

Neither the father nor daughter understood much of what he was trying to say. They made a lot of eye contact with one another as if to say, "These people are crazy!" They weren't the first and wouldn't be the last to look at us askance. They rolled up the camera hose, grabbed the check from my outstretched hand, and hightailed it out of there.

They were still raising their eyebrows at one another as they got in their truck. *Let's get out of here!*

"Okay then, bye. Have a nice day." I stood at the kitchen window, arm around Spencer while we watched their hurried departure. I smiled at the looks they were swapping. I certainly wasn't going to go explain things to them. *Treasure is in the eye of the beholder,* I told myself and began to laugh again. That day was definitely going into my treasure chest as one I would always look back on with fondness.

I had no intention of giving up on my dream of a working, fabulous fireplace either.

Chapter 11

Scotch on the Rocks

While living in the other neighborhood, we'd had the good fortune of meeting many wonderful and interesting people. One such gem, Mr. C. He lived a few doors down from Jim and Cindy and usually finagled invitations to bonfires and parties.

He hailed from Scotland and, sixty years prior, had worked his way across two continents as a stonemason, to find work and happiness in the United States. He wore his heritage and his trade proudly, a badge for all to see. He also loved his Scotch whiskey and filled his cup often. Unfortunately, the whiskey made his speech thicker and the stories more difficult to understand. I kidded him about his exaggerations and playfully questioned the validity of every story.

He loved the sarcasm and started peppering the stories with hidden jibes, waiting to see if I would rise to his bait. I did, and he and I often engaged in verbal battles. He particularly loved to tell me how his mother would have done things, painting her into sainthood, and proving me inept. "Me own dear mother..." He seemed to start every insult that way.

We embraced him as a respected elder who had lessons to teach our children: culture, pride, and perspective on what it really meant to be an American. We never considered what he could teach *us*. He asked question after question concerning the work we were doing at the old house. We returned the favor by asking him about his life and beloved stonemason's trade.

If anybody could help me out with the fireplace dilemma, he could. I called him up. "Mr. C.? It's me your favorite neighbor."

He kidded me by guessing I was every other woman he could think of in the neighborhood. After laughing and ribbing, the conversation returned to normal. "Whattcha calling me for, girl? I don't think you've ever called here."

I told him about our kitchen fireplace and how the chimney sweeps had given me bad and unacceptable news. "Do you think you could take a look at it for me?"

"Sure. I can look at it, fix it too, I bet. Tell ya what, you supply a bottle of Dewars, and I'll meet you there tomorrow."

"Dewars? Are you talking whiskey?"

"*The* whiskey girl, my own mother would know that."

Well, it sounded easy enough to me, so I readily agreed and worked time into my schedule to get up to the liquor store.

He showed up as promised. I hugged him and led him toward the kitchen and my problem. Gesturing toward the crooked little fireplace, I started right in, "The chimney sweeps said we can't have a fire because the flue is too small." I removed the aluminum pie plate, pointing and frowning. "At the very least, they said it has to be a really small fire."

Already on his knees and looking up into the fireplace, he disagreed, "No, they're wrong. This can work."

"Are you sure?" I was scared to hope. "They had cameras and everything."

Backing himself out of the fireplace, he speared me with his bright blue eyes. "Who you gonna believe, girl? Someone that cleans 'em for a livin', or someone that builds them?" Spying the bottle of Dewars I'd placed atop boxes and tools, he asked, "That for me?"

I grabbed it and held it behind my back. "Only if you fix the fireplace!"

He grinned and readily agreed. "I'll be here in the morning."

True to his word, Mr. C. knocked on the door, bright and early the next day. He wore a tight little tee shirt and grubby old pants. He was pleased to show me a bucket full of round concrete fillers for my stovepipe hole. He'd filled soup cans with concrete, let them harden, then cut off the cans. The end result were round concrete tubes ready to fill the round hole. Ingenious.

Mr. C. spent hours standing on a little fold-up chair, cleaning out the fireplace. It was a one-person job, so I kept him supplied with conversation. Soot was everywhere, and his hands were gummy from years of smoke and grime. His wiry arms were deep into the stovepipe hole, breaking off chunks of old mortar that had been inappropriately applied to the flue. Once done, he slowly added new mortar, smoothing and shaping.

"Come. Feel in here. Smooth as a new bairn's bottom."

I traded places with him, put my hand inside and was amazed.

The stovepipe hole slowly filled with his soup cans and extra mortar. "There can be no space, or the smoke will come through." He was busy sealing it shut, and I took the opportunity to run back to the old neighborhood to snag the boys. They had to see this, it was amazing. Spencer, especially, needed to know that the fireplace was fixed.

They greeted Mr. C and plopped themselves on the kitchen floor to watch him work. Finally, the stovepipe hole was sealed and the area completely smooth. Mr. C. called each of us over. "Stand here. Put your name in the mortar, afore it dries, so everyone will know who lived here." We happily did as we were told, and I insisted he add his name too.

The afternoon had grown warm. The boys ran out back to play. Mr. C and I went out to the front porch to sit and cool off. I presented him his bottle of Dewars and a grateful hug. "You're the best, no matter what anybody else says."

He grinned and motioned toward the porch steps. "Whatcha planning on doing with these steps? They're crooked as hell. Is there anything in this house that isn't?"

"Nope, that's part of the charm."

He nodded and caught my eye, "Suits you girl since you're such a mess."

I mock punched him in the arm. "Someday, when we're all moved in, and life returns to normal, I'll work on the steps. I've found bricks all over the place, so I should be able to rebuild 'em."

"Oh, and you're a stone mason now? You know just what to do, do ya?"

I shrugged sheepishly, having forgotten I was talking to an expert.

He crouched near the stairs to get a better look. One hundred years of weather and feet had worn grooves in the middle of the stones. Freezing and unfreezing had created cracks and buckling making the damn things near impassable.

"Tell ya what, Missy, for another bottle of Dewars and some Ginger Ale, I can fix these for ya."

"Seriously? Oh my God, that would be awesome!" I hugged him, sure he was a godsend.

"Got some stuff to do tomorrow, but then I can come back out and work on 'em. Don't forget the Dewars."

"I just gave you some."

That was for the fireplace, which really wasn't hard. These steps though…," Mr. C.'s eyes twinkled, "another bottle of Dewars and I'll show you how good I am."

"You've got yourself a deal!" I shook his hand and made a mental note to run by the liquor store again.

John stopped in after work to find me cleaning up the messy kitchen. "How'd it go with Mr. C. today?"

"He fixed it!" I dropped the broom and gushed about how he'd fixed the fireplace, filled the stove pipe, re-mortared. John ran his hand over the now smooth wall and grinned at our names in the mortar. Because they hadn't been there to do it themselves, I'd added his and Deanna's names too. We were, after all, all in this mess together.

Chattering away non-stop and happy, I announced, "He's coming back in a couple days to re-do the front porch steps too!"

John's facial expressed changed from a smile to a frown. "The front steps? We don't have time to be doing that kind of shit right now. Good Lord! Porch steps? For God's sake, look around you. There are more important things to be working on right now."

"Well, sorry," I replied, in a snit. "That's when Mr. C. is able to do it. Take the help where you can get it, Dude. You wanna be the one to fix the steps? We can hardly use the damn things without tripping and stumbling."

After ten more minutes of me convincing him that having the steps done was not only necessary but awesome, he gave up the argument. He didn't have the energy for such things anymore. I vowed I'd work extra hard to keep all the other balls, we were juggling, up in the air. John was not convinced but stayed silent.

Two days later, I pulled in excited, eager. "This is gonna be fun." I carried in some groceries, filled the cooler with drinks and ice, and laughed as I set the bottle of Dewars on the fireplace mantle. "Second one I've bought in three days. The clerk probably thinks I'm an alcoholic!"

Mr. C showed up on time, his sharp, bright eyes lit and ready to go. His buzz-cut white hair standing at attention, also seemed anxious for the day to begin. His smaller frame never seemed to stop moving, and I connected with that energy. It would be fun.

"These are fine, big stones. We'll flip 'em over and start with a fresh side."

I frowned. That did not sound easy or fun. The steps, in question, were four feet long and two feet wide. I looked at his wiry old body and knew I was going to be in for a workout.

Looks can be deceiving. Mr. C. pried those stones loose as if they were no more than pebbles and flipped them with a crowbar and expertise that left me shaking my head. *I hope I can still do that stuff when I'm seventy-five.*

We began gathering our supplies. Things I had never seen before started exiting his trunk. Special trowels, a small hammer, a skinny paintbrush and a strange little tool resembling a long nail file were carefully laid out in order. They were meticulously clean and a showcase of his art. "This hammer belonged to my Da," he said, having followed my line of sight. We piled things near the porch, and he began to paw through the pile of bricks I'd gathered. He tossed aside more than he kept. I watched my pile of bricks grow smaller.

"This is ugly. This is broken. This one hasn't been fired. Me own dear mother woulda had good bricks."

He stood beside my pile of concrete bags. I smiled, pleased I'd thought ahead and drug them from the dungeon. I expected praise. Instead, he shook his head in disgust. "We canna put the bricks together using this. Why did you buy it?"

"I already had concrete. You told me to buy Dewars, not mortar. What's the difference anyway?" I shrugged, "Who cares?"

He wasn't even listening. He was headed back toward his car. Slamming the trunk as he went past, he pointed to the passenger side. "Get in. We're headed to the store."

"Fine." I slammed my door for the hell of it.

Mr. C. sprinkled the entire drive, there and back, with sneaky insults about my inexperience. "My own dear mother would have bought mortar. She woulda known the difference." His eyes twinkled, and I watched him hunch his back, waiting for my reply.

"You lie. You probably had to explain it to her too. No one else would even care." We were an hour into nothing, and I re-evaluated my earlier assessment of a quick and easy job.

Mortar purchased, we tried to get things started again. He demanded a wheelbarrow so we could mix the mortar. That I could do. I knew right where it was and felt redeemed. *Maybe I can do something right after all.* I'd found my wheelbarrow half-buried in the side yard and had rescued it soon after buying the old house. We hadn't owned one, and although the one I dug out of the dirt, was bent and rusted, it was serviceable as far as I was concerned. It had a few holes, but who cared? Free is free.

I squeaked it across the yard as Mr. C. watched my progress dubiously. "Mother Mary, Mother of Saints! What the hell do you call that thing? It's older than me and should be retired."

He walked over for a closer look. "It's got holes in the bottom. How are we gonna get mortar to stay in the damn thing? I'll have to hold the bricks under the holes to catch what falls out." He flung his hands in the air for emphasis.

He marched around; hands on his hips, looking like a mad bandy rooster. "Me own dear mother woulda never have used such a thing. She woulda brung me proper tools." He reached into his trunk again, pulled out a little bucket and began mixing my inferior concrete.

"Thought you didn't want concrete. See? Good damn thing I had some now, isn't it?"

"I didn't know I'd have to fix a wheelbarrow." He mixed and proceeded to fill all of my wayward holes. "We'll have to wait for those to dry a bit before we can begin."

Great. More waiting.

He sat on the stones, telling his tall tales and suddenly stopped mid-sentence. "Where's the Dewars?"

"Dewars? It's ten in the morning. You can't have whiskey at ten!" I couldn't believe what he was asking.

"In the old country, it's served with breakfast."

"Well, that certainly explains some things. You'd better not make my steps crooked."

"They're already crooked. I'm here to fix things, girl. Do you have Ginger Ale?"

Shaking my head in bewilderment, I headed to fill his order. I rummaged in the cooler and pulled out a Ginger Ale, opened the bottle of whiskey and mixed it all together in a sad, plastic cup. I carried it back out to the porch. "Your Dewars as requested, sir."

Mr. C. took a long drink and came up sputtering. "It's cold, girl! Me mother wouldna served me cold Ginger Ale with scotch. It's supposed to be warm."

"Your mother put you on that boat, didn't she?"

Having finally gotten me to fight back, he laughed to himself.

"So, while I'm waiting on your wheelbarrow to dry and my scotch to warm, let's talk about what you're gonna put under the bricks. You need something—a story, a picture, anything."

"What the hell are you talking about?" I smiled though, sure he was up to something.

"Someday, someone else is gonna pull up these stones and bricks. They should find something about you and the house. I've never built a fireplace or worked on a building without putting something personal inside." He expounded, with stories about brandy in fireplace walls, pictures under bricks, and silver under floors.

I sat there, enjoying the sun on my face, listening and thinking. It seemed a truly novel idea. Even then, I'd been flirting with the idea of encapsulating our journey into a story and often jotted my thoughts down while working at the old house. I fetched my legal pad and tore off the first few pages, listing our family, our dreams our passions, and our first encounter with the old house. Mr. C. wrapped it in newspaper, then plastic, then foil, then more plastic. It was our own time capsule. He pried up the big stone, one more time, and slipped our story underneath.

The wheelbarrow was dry, the scotch warm, and it was time for my lessons to begin. "Looka here. Hold the brick." He handed one to me. "Feel the weight. They got to be the same or you won't have good steps."

I nodded. Mr. C. was making sense, and I forgave him his earlier insults because he'd put our story under wraps, so to speak.

He held the brick out in his left hand, grabbed his trowel, dipped it in the mortar and sluiced a solid line across the bottom and edge of the brick. "See here how you push it down the brick, leaving only a small ridge as you go?" He was teaching and talking. I nodded. It didn't look hard, similar to icing a cake.

It was, however, the opposite motion I was used to for applying drywall mud. Mud is pulled toward a person and circular. Mortar is pushed forward and straight. I couldn't get the movement right.

He held another brick out to me. "Do what I do."

I did it wrong.

His little white head was shaking back and forth. He showed me again. I failed.

"Me own mother could do this."

Finally, he stood behind me, grasped my hands and made me follow his trowel and his movements. He tickled me, without meaning to, and I squirmed away, laughing.

"No. No. No. Again! Where are you going?"

His arms went around me again, and, laughing like an idiot, I danced away again. He was disgusted, and I couldn't seem to do anything right. I kept laughing, knowing we made a ridiculous picture there in the front yard.

The Old Woman sat on the porch, watching my antics and listening to Mr. C. "Who is this man?"

"Girl, you're killing me! We need more Dewars."

Mr. C. and I had one brick in place, and he was on his second warm scotch. To better fortify myself, I gave up and pulled a cold rum and coke for myself. I called him into the kitchen and laid out, what I thought was a nice lunch. There were various cut meats, potato salad, and tea.

"Me mother would have offered me bread and butter with my meal."

"For God's sake! Here." I slammed a loaf of bread and a container of margarine on the little card table we used for breaks.

"Me mother woulda used real butter."

"Your mother is a friggin' saint!"

He grinned happily and took a bite of bread. Finishing lunch and hoping the bread would soak up whiskey and rum, I herded us back outside and back to work.

"We need a wee bit more mortar here," Mr. C instructed.

I had finally gotten the hang of applying mortar. Maybe a person needed a good stiff drink first. Mr. C. lay across the front porch, supervising and sipping his third scotch. He was happy. I was happy.

"That one you put in is a bit high. It needs a shiggle."

"What's a shiggle?" I asked, looking over at his tools.

"No, girl. A shiggle." He rolled to a crouch, took hold of the brick and shook it gently, his own behind moving with the motion.

I laughed at him shaking his booty on my porch. "Your momma shiggled didn't she?"

"Aye, that she did."

He and I sluiced, leveled, shiggled and shook, and had another drink each.

Four hours later, the bricks were in place. We carefully hammered them into place to make them level. Mr. C. checked the angle, making the bricks tilt slightly forward so the rain would run off. He showed me how to carefully brush the extra mortar away, and each groove was carefully cleaned and shaped using his file.

We stood back to admire our handiwork, immensely pleased. Beautiful. Drunk.

He wouldn't go home. He'd been there seven hours and seemed content. Deanna had brought the boys over earlier, and they were enjoying an entertaining Mr. C. and a suspiciously giddy Mommy. At Deanna's knowing grin, I snuck inside to make some strong, black coffee.

The kids sat on the new steps, listening to Mr. C. brag about the buildings he had worked on in Cleveland. He talked about the sheer height and constant danger. Listening in through the screened window, I was pleased they were getting a taste of him and slurped coffee.

The Dewars had kicked in, and the brogue was heavy, but having a rapt audience, the stories were growing serious. He was telling my children about a man he knew who had fallen to his death from a tall building. Their eyes were huge, and the details too graphic. I ran to the porch trying to change the subject. *How do you turn off a semi-drunk Scotsman?*

I gave him coffee, some bread and butter, and waited for John to show up to take him home. "I'll be back next week if you'll have another bottle of Dewars, warm Ginger Ale and a good meal with bread."

"Yeah. Yeah. Whatever." I hugged him and smiled as he weaved through the door. I'd learned that art is not just a beautiful painting or classic piece of music. It's something done well and shared generously with others. I vowed to follow Mr. C.'s example.

The Old Woman was pleased. "I like Mr. C. You should listen to your elders more."

CHAPTER 12

Bat Wars Episode I: The Discovery

Despite small victories like working fireplaces and usable steps, it was nearing the end of April and time was not on our side, and we still hit one snag after another. I seemed to be sighing all the time and often blew the bangs off my forehead in frustration. John had taken to chewing on the ends of all his cigarettes and grinding his teeth twenty-four hours a day. Instinctively knowing it would open the door to John's barely tamped-down temper, I never voiced my own anger or irritation. I smiled falsely and made light jokes as though nothing was wrong. In reality, the number of problems and obstacles had left us glazed and functioning at some primal level. Breathe. Move. Fix. Breathe.

As we worked and sweated through repairs at the old house, we became more and more aware of the fact that we had overlooked some rather necessary components during our early evaluation of the property. We discovered them after finally being able to move our work upstairs. John was taking inventory, moving quickly from room to room, when he suddenly spun on his heel toward me and asked, "Do you know there's hardly any heat up here?" He was scowling at the ancient electrical heaters ensconced in each room. Heat, particularly in northern Ohio, seemed an important thing. I joined him in the master bedroom, taking in the frayed wiring and rusted vents. They looked scary and unreliable.

"We aren't using those things, I can tell you that! We'd burn the house down."

"It's pretty dark up here too. Have you noticed?" John continued. He evidently thought it was a good time for him to voice all of his complaints.

I peeked in the other rooms, looked up at ceilings, and was genuinely surprised by what I found. "Well, there's not much overhead lighting is there?" I answered, realizing such things would have been a luxury for The Old Woman when she was originally built.

"No shit." John looked at me as though I'd just decided to join the human race.

We stood, hands on our hips, glaring at the heaters, the missing lights and finally at each other. All of those "No problem" statements we'd flung around in February and March were turning out to be major catastrophes.

"Well, we've got no choice. We need heat and lights up here, and we need them now." John crushed out another cigarette on the old floor and marched us toward the dungeon as if we knew what we were doing. Not to worry with Morgan Construction Inc. on the job. No heat? No electricity? No problem.

We squinted in the basement, taking in the hulking furnace and maze of vents. It didn't make any sense to us. It must have been equally confusing to whoever had installed the stuff. It's the only explanation I could come up with at the time. I mean, why else leave the upstairs unheated and unlit?

With less than two months to finish everything and move in, we were frustrated, by the newest turn of events, to say the least. We were supposed to be doing other major tasks like hanging the rest of the drywall, replacing doors, and installing a whole kitchen. Neither heat nor additional wiring had been in the equation.

In what could only be described as a fit of rage, John took his circular saw to the living room. "We need heat upstairs. Fine. I'm starting here." He fired up the saw and began to cut a wide channel up one whole wall. Dust flew across the room and plaster dropped in chunks to the floor. We'd planned to drywall the room anyway. Thank God.

I offered no complaints and asked no questions. There was a dangerous gleam in John's eye, so, I just smiled encouragingly. No use having him mad at me. "That's great, honey. Really. You just go right ahead and play with that saw." He was having such a good time. I stood out of the way in the foyer and watched in fascination.

As the hole grew wider, hundreds of walnut shells poured out onto the floor. They cascaded into the living room, rolling over and around each other in their haste to hide behind doors and ladders. John set down the saw, considered the latest surprise, and whipped his head around to look at me as if I could explain the situation. I merely shrugged and moved further out of range. He fired up his saw again, cutting further up the wall to see what would happen. More walnuts fell around his head and dropped at his feet. It was a bit like playing a slot machine: Cut a hole, get a prize.

Squirrels had evidently stuffed the walls with their treasures and winter stores for what looked to be a decade or so. "I knew there was treasure in the walls," I called out to John as the saw was winding down.

He climbed off the ladder, shaking plaster dust out of his hair. "Yeah, too bad it's of no value to *us*. I'd love to find a stack of cash. I'd gladly pay someone else to come in here and fix this shit."

We both shook our heads, and rolled our eyes skyward, silently asking for divine intervention. *What else God? Enough, okay?*

"What am I supposed to do about all of the walnuts?" I asked. John had started sawing again and never heard the question. I decided I neither cared nor had the time to worry about them. I swept up our booty and tossed them back outside. We would simply have to accept the remaining shells still stuck in the walls as additional support and insulation. I kept sweeping and flinging. Meanwhile, John was making a hell of a mess.

By the time he put away the saw, there were holes in walls, holes in floors, and holes in the ceiling. It looked like some unknown enemy had set siege to the house, lobbing hand grenades into the living room and each of the upstairs bedrooms. Taking in the demolition, I dropped my chin and conceded defeat. John walked toward me through the filth, covered from head to toe in gray plaster dust, giving me a vivid picture of what he would look like in thirty years or so.

The Old Woman shuddered. "Ow! Careful there. That hurts! What are you doing?" She looked at me, pleading for an explanation.

"Sorry, house," I called out for what seemed no particular reason. I was sad to have caused so much destruction. "We'll fix it, I promise."

John looked at me with an accordion forehead. "What are you doing?"

"I don't know. It just seems sad...all this mess." I gestured wide.

"I'll tell you what's sad. The list is getting longer, not shorter." He dipped his hand into the cooler, cupping water and sloshing it across his face to remove the dust.

The Old Woman listened, still nursing her wounds but content that she and I were finally communicating. She decided, given *that* fact, she'd just have to trust us. "I sure hope all this pain will be worth it. You fixed the foundation. I guess you'll fix this too. I don't really have a choice, do I?"

Seven hours and mountains of plaster dust later, we were finally able to attach new vents from the dungeon furnace to upper bedrooms. I was pretty happy about that, knowing we would all be warm and cozy that winter. "Much better. Now, all we have to do is patch up all your damn holes." I was trying to make eye contact with John. We hadn't exchanged more than ten words in hours.

He kept wandering back and forth from the upper hallway to what would be our bedroom. He was muttering to himself, and I wondered if ingested plaster dust could be the cause.

He shook his head in disgust. "We've got to take this all the way into the attic."

"Why? We shouldn't need to heat the attic." What did I know about such things? It seemed odd.

"It's not heat we have to get to the attic, it's cold air returns. Without them, all these vents are for nothing. The air has to cycle back to the furnace." His hands were circling trying to make me understand.

I frowned, trying to make a mental drawing and decided that, like the walnuts, I didn't care. I shrugged and remained noncommittal. I should have been paying more attention to John's tone and body language.

He stood under the attic access and grinned. Understanding dawned, my head dropped to my chest, and I groaned. I knew what was coming.

"Attic duty, my dear. You promised."

I'd been hoping he had forgotten the attic part. Having done far more than my share in the crawlspaces, I felt I'd lived up to my word and proven myself to be trustworthy. I'd even held out hope that my penance for buying the old house had been paid with the foundation fiasco. John opened the ladder and gestured toward the attic with a flourish, "Ladies first."

Guess I still owe on the debt.

Because I was really the only one who still loved our old house, I couldn't complain, or it would have been "Sold" immediately. At that point in the game, John would have been content to live in the car, a tent or even a cardboard box, so long as the endless work and stress were over. I'd gone back to cheerleading just as I had done to buy the old thing in the first place. Strap on my tool belt, and wave pom-poms. It was a necessary evil to keep everyone on track. I only cried and screamed in private.

"Can't it wait? I want to go home," I whined, slumping into a corner and eyeballing the little hole to the attic. "It's late. We haven't even eaten." I peeked through my hair to see if I was having any sort of effect on him.

"This is the last thing for today. Just go up, look around, and tell me if you think we'll have trouble cutting through the attic flooring to get to the bedroom ceilings." He hauled the ladder over to the access hole.

The Old Woman was standing in the hall. "This isn't going to go well. No sir. Not at all. At least there's no backing out now." She crossed her fingers anyway.

"It's dark up here. The attic's gonna be pitch black."

John having a modicum of concern for my safety, smiled and said, "I'll hold the ladder, so it doesn't slip. Once you're up there, I'll hand you the flashlight."

"Thank you. Really." I snarled from the bottom of my heart as I stomped onto the stupid ladder and headed skyward.

I removed the panel, pushed my head up inside that dark, dark space and was immediately assaulted by a smell so awful I gagged, and my eyes began to water. I couldn't identify the smell. It wasn't musty, it wasn't dead, and it wasn't decay. It was simply the foulest thing I'd ever encountered.

John, still on the ladder, got a whiff of it and raised his eyebrows. "I told you this house stinks." He smiled, smug in having set the attic stipulation and knowing he didn't have to climb any further.

Refusing to back down on my promise or my resolve, I showed my teeth too. I maneuvered into the hole and concentrated on breathing through my mouth. John realized he was going to have to climb further up the ladder. I straddled across two joists and couldn't reach the flashlight he was holding up toward me. He climbed up, stretching the light toward me, and surprisingly stayed at the top.

I snagged it from his outstretched hand. "Just give me the damn light!" I switched it on, waved it around a bit, trying to get my bearings, and was immediately greeted by other beings waving around. Bats!

"Oh my God!" I yelled, trying to keep my balance on the joist and not fall through the hole or into the nasty insulation. The bats did not like my flashlight or my yelling. They were waking up in attack mode and flying in confusion at the light. Myths surfaced, in my head, about those nocturnal beasts being caught in hair. I had no idea whether the legends were true or not. All I knew was they were flying, my hair was long, and I desperately wanted to get out.

John, below the hole, couldn't really tell what was happening as I shouted and waved the light frantically. He just stood there, confused, in the way of my only exit, and asking stupid questions, "What? Why are you yelling? Are you hurt?"

I landed on the frame of the access hole, my feet swinging wildly trying to find a ladder I couldn't see. I was literally stomping at John's head and yelling at him, "Move! Bats up here! Get out of the way!"

I slid down that ladder, missing several rungs along the way, and pulled the panel back in place. I now knew the smell. Bats and bat shit. Guano, if I wanted to be polite, which I did not. The smell was permanently lodged in my brain. I knew I would remember it until the day I died.

The Old Woman's eyes had grown large at my hurried descent. "I knew you wouldn't like it up there. Now whatcha gonna do? They've been there for years, and nobody's been able to get rid of 'em yet." She watched John closely. "This could be the final straw for Johnny Boy. Please don't sell me."

John and I sat together in the upstairs hallway, in the dark in more ways than one, and just stared wide-eyed at one another. I still had my hand clamped over my mouth in disbelief. Finally, a smile snuck through, and we began to laugh. I recounted the jokes people had made about our house. "Boy is my mom gonna love this story! Remember how she joked about us having bats in our belfry?"

John threw his head back, chuckling. "Oh, God. I forgot about that one. You've got to call her when we get home. I want to hear what she says about this."

The Old Woman smiled at us, sure all would be well. She gathered herself together and quietly shuffled away. "You two are good together. Just keep your sense of humor, please."

It *was* kind of funny, and our laughter became a hysterical release of all the things we'd already survived. "Has this been an adventure or what?" I asked, shaking my head and laughing.

"Adventure? Jeez! We've had more things happen to us in the last three months than some people get their whole lives." John continued, "We had things going wrong before we even bought the place. Remember the appraiser falling in the cistern?" John chuckled at the memory, shook out a cigarette and offered one to me.

"Don't forget about the creepy handyman and the dead ducks. God, I can't wait until the next bonfire. No one's going to believe the latest and greatest...bats!" I shared a light with him.

We slid closer together, snuggling in the dark. "What else could possibly go wrong?" We asked each other, believing, for some reason, that we'd truly seen the worst.

It was at about that time that the tired, old house shook with a clap of thunder. We quit laughing immediately, and our heads spun as we looked at each other, wide-eyed again. The rain began to fall, hard and unrelenting. The wind came from nowhere and pelted the windows, trying to get inside. An odd sort of premonition took over, and the two of us started running through the rooms and yelling, "Please, God, don't let it leak."

God has a weird sense of humor. The curved staircase, which, by the way, was no longer charming, had a virtual river of rain running down the stairs to puddle at the base of the kitchen. We followed it back to the room above the kitchen and watched as the rain poured through the sagging ceiling in there. "Great," I said.

"Fabulous," John echoed, deadpan.

The bats would get a reprieve and The Old Woman a new roof. Neither option was acceptable, particularly since those two items had never been in the plan at all. Not knowing what else to do, we put an empty drywall mud bucket under the leak, turned off the lights and trudged toward the car.

"We can't do anything about it tonight." John sighed with quiet resignation. I assumed he was too numb to protest. I, for once, had nothing to say.

We pulled into the driveway of the other house and turned off the ignition, simply letting the dark settle around us. I reached for John's hand, and he pulled me close. I lay my head on his shoulder, and he dropped his onto mine. We sat listening to the rhythm of rain bounce off the car, watching the individual drops slide in haphazard pathways down the windshield. We were each lost in our own thoughts.

We took in the newer house with its working bathrooms, modern kitchen, leak-proof roofs, and bat-free attic, and wondered if everyone else had been right and we'd been wrong all along. Choking back tears, I plodded inside, not even bothering to wipe away the rain.

The Old Woman's face, lit from far off lightning, looked pale and tired.

"They didn't say goodbye." She spoke to herself, unaware a tear had slipped past her guard, to mimic the rain on the window. "The girl never leaves without a goodbye. What can that mean?"

Chapter 13

Fiddling on the Roof

Despite what loomed ahead, a good night's sleep had done us good. We woke up in surprisingly nice moods on Monday morning. John poured a slow cup of coffee and called his boss. "I've got an emergency. My roof's leaking. I'm afraid I need the day off."

My eyebrows went up at that, and I tilted my head questioningly at him. In the twenty years he'd been with the company, I could only remember him taking an emergency day one other time. I settled at the table, enjoying my own cup of coffee and the calm atmosphere. It was a nice change.

Having been unable to spend much time with our children due to work, travel and the old house, John visibly relaxed and enjoyed them. He teased Deanna mercilessly about her boyfriend, ruffled Michael's head and tickled Spencer as he poured out their cereal. They left for school and the babysitter. Deanna was grinning ear to ear, and the boys jumping up and down as though they'd just celebrated Christmas.

Coming back from dropping off Spencer, I looked at John. "They miss you."

"Yeah, I know. I miss the little rugrats too. Damn house." He continued to sip coffee and look through the newspaper as though he had all the time in the world.

"What's up with you? I thought you'd be a bear this morning."

"Can't exactly crawl up on the roof at six-thirty, in the morning, can I? Besides, I need to call my dad. This is gonna be more than a one-man job."

I was surprised by that too. Pride prevented John, or me, for that matter, from ever asking anyone for help. Once the phone calls were made and the situation thoroughly explained, he and I put on layers of work clothes and headed over to the old house to assess the damage.

The kitchen and the room overhead, what we called The Manson Room, were both holding water. We emptied the bucket from the night before and started gathering up tools we thought we might need for roofing. The old adage about preparation taking longer than the actual job seemed very true. We found it to be particularly true for a project we never knew was coming.

The Old Woman stood in the doorway of the Manson Room looking at the mess and watching our activity. She looked at the deep, red-paint handprints and shook her head. One corner of the room showcased the new leak. Old plaster sagged with the weight of the rain and water sat in puddles on the floor, unsure where to head. "This room has been a wreck for years. Probably a good thing this happened. Maybe you'll clean it now." She looked at the handprints again and shuddered.

"Help me get this ladder outside," John called from the upstairs landing where I'd entered the attic the night before. We thumped and bumped it down the stairs and pushed it against the porch. John climbed up on the porch and onto the leaky room. I was right on his heels. Looking at the pitch of the roof, he handed out more instructions, "Go to the barns and find me some old two-by-fours."

"Why?" I knew I wasn't really supposed to ask questions but couldn't help myself.

"I'm gonna nail some on the roof so we can walk around without sliding off."

I climbed down, waved to Gene, who had just pulled in the driveway, and headed off for gofer duty. While Gene and John peeled away shingles and got ready to replace what sounded like everything, I was sent out into the world to buy plywood, tarpaper, roofing nails and shingles. I was lost in a new and very alien territory. It didn't help that the map I was to follow consisted of a soggy list John had scribbled and then tossed down to me. Several hours and a few detours later, I returned with all the necessary materials.

John and his dad were up on that roof, shaking their heads. Whoever had installed our leaky roof had not used tarpaper, but what suspiciously appeared to be cardboard. It came off in long, sodden strips and littered the front yard and bushes.

"The same people who built that piece-of-crap bathroom out back must have put this roof on too," John called down at my puzzled expression. "I've never seen anything like it."

I cleared and hauled and fed. The guys removed and inserted and nailed. It was still raining lightly, having never let up all day, and the three of us were chilled to the bone.

We finished late that night by pulling our vehicles into the front yard and aiming the headlights in the general direction of the roof. I stood back, watching John move purposely across the little roof. I felt a moment of pride, "He's a pretty good guy—most of the time, anyway."

"Yes, he is," The Old Woman agreed, standing on the porch and out of the rain. "A little temperamental, but overall, you've got yourself a good one."

I thought about my favorite musical, *Fiddler on The Roof*, and likened my John to Tevye. We too seemed to be struggling to maintain our balance in a hostile and chaotic environment. I smiled at the image of John dancing on the roof and knew we would survive.

As the last of the shingles were nailed into place, I listened as John and Gene talked. I climbed up and down the ladder to either retrieve tools or deliver final supplies. John looked at his dad. "You know if you hadn't taught me how to do all this shit, we wouldn't be up here right now!"

Gene just laughed. What could he say? It was true. "Well, son, think on it this way. You could be paying someone else to do it."

The guys craned their necks backward to look at the other two roofs: higher, steeper and larger than the one they'd just finished. The house was also covered in lightning rods, which seemed to be a major issue for John. "No way. Not going to happen." They clambered down and called it a day. We were all cold, tired and ready for hot showers and warm beds.

The weather continued to flex its muscles all week. It rained. It was windy. Sunshine flirted and then ran away, playing hard to get. John was growing more and more anxious, "Wonder if the other roofs are leaking too?"

We didn't see any new water damage, but that didn't mean anything. We could have had rain pouring into the attic and wouldn't have known. We both refused to go back up there until the bat problem was resolved. John kept picturing the soggy stuff used as underlayment. After five days flew by, he had had it with wondering. "That's it!" he announced. "I'm going up there, check things out. I'm taking off those damn lightning rods too. They're in the way."

"Hon, that's not a good idea. You're terrified of heights, and it's windy as hell."

He shot me an insulted look. I mentally kicked myself for the choice of words. No *real* man is terrified—ever. He took it as a challenge, not in the mood to be reasonable.

Up he went, while I nervously followed his progress from the ground. If I thought it was windy from my vantage point, I had nothing on John. Facing his fears, he crawled to the top of the house only to be nearly flattened by a gust of wind. Insanity. I wondered if his life insurance policy was up-to-date and how much it was worth. *Would there be enough to finish the house? Send the kids to college? Have a nice wake?*

John called down, interrupting my musings, "This is really not a good idea."

"No kidding! I'm half-planning your funeral. Get down here!"

He ignored me, and lay face down on the crown, one leg straddling each side of the peak, absolutely determined to conquer that roof. Head down and stomach scraping, he stretched out his arms and pulled the rest of his body along behind him. The wind, glad to have a playmate, buffeted his inky, black hair and ran up the back of his shirt. John reached the first lightning rod, tugged slightly while squeezing the roof tightly with his thighs.

"Damn, these things are really bolted in. I need the drill," John yelled down to me trying to be heard above the racket the wind was making.

I turned to get the toolbox about the time I head the thunder roll.

John's eyes went huge. He'd been holding on to a metal rod, for God's sake. Crab-crawling backward as fast as he could, he dropped to the shorter porch roof and made a beeline for the metal ladder and hopefully the ground before being struck down. He missed several rungs landing in the middle of a bush near the porch instead. The poor thing sported a large crater after having a one-hundred-ninety-pound man land there.

I ran to help pull him free. His heart and mine were both knocking by the time he escaped the bush. Pine needles were embedded everywhere. As I hugged him, I noticed our two sets of neighbors were looking out their front windows. The Angells and the Lewis' shook their heads, drawing the curtains closed against our insanity.

We waved and went inside. Like cats, taking a sudden bath after falling off a table, we needed to look busy. We both scanned the front yard quickly, sure someone would jump out from behind a tree brandishing a video camera. "Surprise! You're on Candid Camera!"

We needed help—Professional help, psychological help, financial help. We didn't have the time, luxury or money for all those appointments. Having to choose just one, we settled on hiring a contractor. We were out of time and patience. We started taking bids from construction companies for roofing, eaves, and guttering. The bids were all over the board, of course, and we were having trouble finding a company that would match the short timeline and honor our budget.

We finally found a local business that was willing to meet our requirements, at least within reason, and set up an appointment immediately. The owner climbed up on each of our roofs to get a better idea of the damage and come up with a final estimate. John watched in amazement as the contractor walked around upright on the tallest peak, as though it was a casual stroll in the park. No belly crawling for him.

He called down a list of measurements and materials to his assistant and joked with us as we followed along the sidelines. He was showing off and not watching his footing. Big mistake. About the time he finished assessing the third roof and headed down toward the second porch, his leg simply disappeared. As feared, the roof was rotted, and his leg had gone straight through. He pulled himself free. "Whoa. Add in all new plywood for this roof!" he yelled down to his assistant, who seemed unimpressed by the hole or the leg, and continued to take notes indifferently.

If there had been any doubt or concern over price, it disappeared right into the hole in our roof. The contractor seemed completely unfazed. John and I, on the other hand, were shocked and otherwise taken aback. The contractor smiled—he knew damn well the job was his.

Seeing the hole and looking at the rotted eaves, we decided we would bite the bullet and have his company not only re-do the entire top of the house, but also install vinyl siding on three sides. The paint was peeling like an onion, blistered from the sun and weathered almost to the point of being ruined. We had no idea how to salvage such things. Oh sure, we may have eventually figured it out, but at what physical and emotional cost for us? We admitted, silently, that maybe, just maybe, we'd gotten in over our heads. We were learning though. Everything was going to be more involved and more costly than we had ever imagined.

"Forget about the siding in the back," I directed at the contractor's clipboard, making sure he wrote everything down.

"Yeah, man," John joined in. "We've got two bathrooms to remove first. Just do the eaves back there, and we'll call you when we're ready to add siding." Both of us were striding around, acting like that had been the plan all along.

The contractor, pleased to have gone from roofing and eaves to a whole house job, was enthusiastic and smiling, our new best friend. We hardly blinked when he handed us the estimate and asked for a down payment. We wrote the check and felt relief. We even shared a beer with the guy. We were that happy.

Tipping his can, he wiped his beard. "I'll order the supplies tomorrow morning. We should be able to start next week."

We presented him with large smiles and tipped our own cans. "Hallelujah."

The Old Woman listened and rejoiced as well. She'd been standing there with no make-up on and sporting a new hole in her hat. A total makeover sounded good to her. "I've heard about those," she said and just knew she'd be getting out those dancing shoes in no time. She should have known better.

The last week of April arrived, and, as promised, the workers showed up, ready to replace the outside shell of our house. Three pickup trucks pulled in, one right after another, weighted down with vinyl pieces, wood, and shingles. I was ecstatic and kept putting down my own tools to run outside, check the progress and call John with updates. "They just finished putting the scaffolding together and are heading up!"

Now, to be honest, we never disclosed to the workers that there were bats in the attic. I suppose that was lying by omission. Unfortunately, their senses of hearing and smell quickly brought the bats back into the picture. As they worked on the roof, they heard the shrill chatter our irritated bats made over their slumber being disturbed by hammers and drills. "You got bats up here, lady!" one roofer called down to me, having spied me hanging around on the porch.

I later congratulated myself on my Emmy-worthy acting skills. "We do? No way! What are you talking about?" I even ran out to the front yard, put my hand over my eyes, and looked up at the roof in complete shock.

"We can hear them up here. Sounds like a lot!" another worker yelled down to me.

The workers also mentioned the smell. Bat guano-a-la-mode was wafting out through the hole the contractor had made with his leg. The roofers hammered faster, finished their job and gratefully turned over the rest of the work to a new crew who would be installing the eaves and vinyl.

That group removed one section of the rotted eaves—and promptly backed down the scaffolding and packed away their tools. I frowned heavily, waiting for an explanation.

"There ain't no way we're doing those eaves 'til them bats are gone."

"They're in there scratchin' around, man! I can hear them."

"We open the eaves, and they'll be flying around our heads." They took turns looking at me with accusation in their eyes.

"Picky, picky, picky," I muttered quietly to myself. "Where are all the macho men? The ones not afraid of attics, crawlspaces, bats?" I stalled in the front yard, not wanting to call John with the latest problem. *I've got a bad feeling about this. I'm going to end up in the attic. I just know it.*

I promised the workers we'd get rid of the bats, and they quit looking so hostile. "You may want to start off with these holes in the eaves." They pointed out a huge opening above the second porch and another one in back over the falling-off bathroom.

Later that evening, John and I walked the perimeter of the house, looking at the chasms in the eaves and talking things over. "How are we supposed to fill those?" John asked, craning his neck backward and squinting at the hole.

"The real trick will be the bats. We've got to get them out first." I leaned backward to scrutinize the hole too, thinking along a completely different track than my husband

"Why?" He sounded genuinely confused.

"You can't just leave them in the attic! They'll die." I looked at him. He seemed to have no problem with that scenario. "Hon, you can't have dead animals up there. It's not sanitary."

He eyebrows knit together, thinking of the consequences. "I guess you've got a point."

As we stood there wondering what to do, John watched a full-sized squirrel scurry up an electric pole in the back of the house. It ran across the wire, jumped to the roof and headed for the hole we'd been studying. Just before he zipped inside, he turned toward John and flicked his tail defiantly. He was probably mad about the walnuts we'd uncovered in the living room.

As if he'd just been flipped off, John took the tail flick personally. Despite not having a plan, he declared war, "That's it! The holes are getting filled immediately!"

The Old Woman shook her head. "Honey, you have no idea what you're in for."

CHAPTER 14

Miscommunication

As challenges go, the bats didn't seem like they'd be a big deal. We just needed to get rid of them quickly. It was almost May, leaving our June eighteenth completion date looming very large indeed. More importantly though, in researching fruit bats, we learned that they wake up frisky in spring, mate and have babies by mid-May. We needed to eradicate them before the numbers grew—we had less than two weeks.

We read about bats, asked questions about bats, looked on the internet for bat information, and tried to come up with a foolproof strategy. We had to know what we were dealing with up there in the attic. *How many were there? Were we sure there are only two exits? Could we catch them? Did we need to call someone and have them removed?*

We explored that possibility briefly: We could hire bat catchers, and that would be the end. No real effort would be required on our part except picking up the phone. As it turned out, fruit bats were protected in Ohio. To remove them safely required a specialist and a lot of money. Forget it. Money was flowing out of our accounts at a phenomenal rate, and we did not intend to add a Bat Removal column to our budget.

We didn't leave our name or number with the bat specialists lest they arrive in emergency vehicles to investigate the scene. I could picture the scene quite clearly. Sirens would wail, lights would flash. Our neighbors would come out to see what new thing was going on at the house. Protestors would gather in our yard, hoisting signs and voices.

"Save the Bats!"

"No More Morgans!"

We might even be put in jail for inhumane bat treatment, seriously hampering our renovations and timeline. We had rights too. It was, after all, our house, our problem, and we weren't paying anyone to come in and place our bats in some sort of sanctuary.

The bats remained a huge obstacle, and we talked about it everywhere we went. We couldn't help ourselves. "Bats?!" our friends exclaimed. "You've got to be kidding!" Their mouths dropped open as we explained our situation around yet another bonfire.

Because they all had strong and enabling personalities, they formed a quick think tank to help solve our newest problem. Doug started in, "You need a pellet gun or BB gun or something. Hell, John, my kids have several lying around. You wanna borrow one?"

"Nah, that won't work," Mike joined in. "The BB's will just ricochet around the attic. He's likely to shoot himself." He and Doug grinned and clinked beer bottles at that.

There was always laughter at our expense. Jennifer had been listening and thinking. "How about building bat houses? Have you heard about those?" she asked us and looked around the fire. All of us wore questioning looks. "Seriously. You build them a certain size, and then, I think you put 'em up on poles near water, and the bats live in them."

"There ya go, John. You've even got a pond." Karen smiled and tried not to laugh at his pained expression.

"You've got to be kidding!" I threw my head back and laughed. "Have you seen what he does to spiders and bugs?" I mimed smashing something with my foot and twisting it around viciously. "He isn't gonna build bat condos! Besides, why would the bats pack their things, call movers and change their address? They've already got a great house."

Still chuckling over some of our friend's ideas, John and I continued to brainstorm. We just needed to get our creative juices flowing, and a solution would come.

We came up with terrible ideas. The worst was to feed a long, flexible hose from the exhaust pipe of our car to the attic. "We'll gas 'em." That was one of John's ideas.

I certainly didn't want to kill anything. "We can't do that! Are you nuts? What if the gas stays in the house?" I asked, trying to steer us in a different direction.

"True. That could be a problem." John frowned and offered another possibility. "How about an electric fence around the roof?"

I stared at him like he was an alien. He was smiling and seemed to like his newest idea quite a lot. According to him, we would wait until the bats exited. Near midnight, we would turn on the fence and, upon their return, zap. That seemed cruel, and I pictured fried bat carcasses littering the roof and yard. "This whole mess started because we have no heat or electricity upstairs. No electricity, no fence." I was very glad that the plan had failed. "There's got to be a better way," I declared, not thinking I was backing myself into a corner.

Next, we flirted with the idea of attaching nets to the roof. We'd let them hang down, over the exit holes, effectively trapping the bats as they came out to eat. That seemed a great possibility since there would be no torture or death involved—until I imagined nets full of struggling bats.

"How do we get the nets loose?" I asked not to be funny. We were both dead serious, and avidly exploring all avenues. We would have to go to the roof and undo the fasteners, lower the nets to the ground and haul the cargo away. John was afraid of heights, meaning I would be lowering the cargo to him. The bats would be screeching for freedom, and we would be tugging and hauling a churning mass of fur.

"Could we drag them to the barns next door?" I didn't want them to go too far. Due to the pond, I knew we had mosquitoes. The bats would be a great defense.

"Naw. That's too close, and they'll just come back. We'll need to take them miles from here."

"They are NOT going in my car!"

Desperately watching the calendar, we ordered a super-sonic critter-removal system. We had it Fed-Exed to the old house, anxious to hook it up as quickly as possible. There was no time to spare; the renovations were piled high, and the mommy bats were probably nearing delivery.

The advertisement said it would emit a high-pitched noise that "pests" would hate. They would then leave in droves, flying out the holes never to return. It sounded good to us. A small, rectangular device arrived, looking for all the world like a baby monitor. We plugged in the box using the only working outlet in the upstairs bathroom. The extension cord snaked through the landing and up toward that dark attic hole. I opened the hatch, held my nose and hung the device on a nail that was, thankfully, already there.

Excited, John and I ran outside, expecting to see the bats leaving immediately. Not a single bat flew out of the eaves. "Maybe it takes a little time," we reassured each other, disgusted over the seventy-five dollars we'd just spent.

Two days and nights later, we still saw no bats screeching, floating or gliding away into the distance. "Do you think that box is even working?" Not being critters, we couldn't hear the sound it was supposed to be emitting.

"The instructions said that there was a flashing red light to let the buyer know if it's functioning," John said thoughtfully, looking at me.

"Yeah, yeah, I know. I have to go to the attic again." I grumbled even as John carried the ladder into place.

The box was unplugged and lying face down in the insulation. It was also defaced with piles of fresh guano. "Nope, definitely not working." I screwed up my face in disgust and hurried back down the ladder, leaving the box to lie in shame. I wasn't rescuing it in such a condition.

Evidently, the bats had hated the thing as touted in the advertisement. We could only assume the bats, angry at having their sleep disturbed again, had attacked in anger, knocked the box from the nail and disconnected it in the process. As for the guano, well, it could only be interpreted as a "Take that!" statement from our nocturnal nemeses.

The Old Woman giggled at our efforts. "I told you this wouldn't be easy."

We refused to give in any more than they did. The research projects had taken more than a week. We had to do something soon so the contractors could be called back, and the house finished. The failed plans and ludicrous ideas left little choice in the matter: *I* would have to go in the attic and remove the bats myself. After my last go-around with the bats, I was not excited about the prospect.

"We'll send you up in the daytime, so you won't need a flashlight."

"Oh, thanks. I feel better now."

If I was very, very quiet, they would continue to sleep as I...what? Counted? Bagged and tagged? Was I supposed to shoot them with animal darts? I wasn't sure what I was supposed to accomplish and determined I would simply find out how many bats we were dealing with and check for additional exits, or something along those lines.

The day of reckoning came, and I procrastinated as long as possible. I was, after all, very busy sanding the drywall seams. Two hundred sheets of drywall screwed together leaves many seams and a lot of sanding. I was wearing my face respirator as any good sander would and was completely covered in white dust. John approached cautiously. I wasn't in a good mood.

He tapped me on the shoulder and grinned. "It's time."

Bats beware. Had to count, had to extract so we could finish the roof, the heating, and the electricity. I knew all of that but really didn't care. *Couldn't we use candles? Space heaters? Stretch plastic over the entire roof?* Evidently not or John wouldn't have come tapping.

I pulled my respirator down, leaving it to hang from its straps. I didn't plan to be in the attic long and would resume my sanding in short order. Crawling up the ladder slowly and quietly, I poked my head in the hole, held my breath and waited. Nothing. *So far so good.* Up into the attic I went.

John couldn't stand not knowing and used stealth to follow me to the top of the ladder. Not into the attic, just to the *top* of the ladder so he could peek inside. *Chicken shit.*

I was getting my bearings, adjusting to the dim light when I heard John furiously whispering behind me, "There's one!"

My pulse stopped. John was pointing to a bat directly over my head. Sleeping. Thank God. I started to breathe again. What to do? I didn't see a colony of bats, just that one little guy or gal all cozied up in the rafters. I snuck past and continued with the reconnaissance mission. "One," I called over my shoulder toward John.

The Old Woman leaned against the hall wall and held her hand over her mouth to keep from laughing aloud. *Oh, this is gonna be fun.*

John was furiously whispering again. I had to go back to the ladder, because I couldn't hear a damn thing he was trying to tell me.

"What?!"

He handed me a hammer and acted out bashing the bat. He had to be kidding.

"They're protected," I countered, eagerly casting about for any excuse I could think of.

He made another one of his famous faces that said, "Do this or Else!" He threw in a two-by-four, the hammer, and a towel. I'd like to have thrown in the towel about then too.

I didn't know if I could do it. Bash the bat, I mean, not throw in the towel. That would have been easy. According to John's silent charade, I was supposed to hold the bat in place with the board, bash it with the hammer, roll it up in the towel and dispose of the thing. That was only bat number one. Such a process went against everything I had ever been taught. I was supposed to educate the boys about communing with nature. How could I show up with a bashed bat?

I was stuck between desire and need: Frantic with wanting to get the old house updated yet hampered by the bats that would not leave. They were undesirable tenants who would not pay their rent, refused to let us upgrade their apartment, and ignored our eviction notices.

Desperation does strange things to a person. I was scared. I can admit that and feel no shame. What-ifs began to cruise around my nonsensical brain, making loops and gaining speed. *What if the bat woke up before I could do the bashing? What if I missed? What if it had rabies? When was my last tetanus shot anyway?*

I pictured the critter-removal system lying helpless and humiliated in the insulation and worried I would suffer a similar fate. I doubted John would save me any more than I had rescued the guano-covered device.

The longer I stood there pondering those things the harder it was going to be. I had to act quickly, or my weakening nerves would give way. Having John there was an incentive. I had to be strong. I had to show courage. There was also a certain satisfaction in finding something that I could accomplish, and he could not. *I can bring home the bacon... fry it up in a pan!*

I hopped across the joists, and in one swell move, smashed that bat with the two-by-four. I attacked. It awoke. I shoved the board against the bat and the rafter with everything I had. I was splayed awkwardly across the beams and didn't have as much leverage as I would have liked. Pushing on the board for balance, my legs tap-danced across rafters, trying to catch up with my torso. I loosened the board and took aim.

He'd died without the hammer ever swinging. I must have been pushing pretty hard on that board. He and I were both crushed. I carefully rolled the poor mangled thing in the towel and gently carried it back to the hole. I passed it through with tears in my eyes. John, who was thoroughly disgusted, rolled his eyes and carried it outside for me.

He was back so quickly, I doubted the bat was disposed of graciously. I suspect he flung it unceremoniously into the weeds from an upstairs window, without remorse or tears.

"Keep looking," John demanded, handing me the hammer again.

I stood in place, checking rafters, poking at insulation. Nothing out of the ordinary revealed itself. I seemed to be the only living thing up there. I was comfortable with that scenario.

I was half-way across the first and largest room of the attic, and it appeared to be bat-free. All I had to do was safely reach the far outside wall, and I would be allowed a recess and fresh air before tackling the other, harder-to-reach area of the attic. I slid my right foot across the joists, dragging my left behind. My goal was in sight. Slide. Stop. Look. Slide.

I was getting further and further away from the one and only exit. I turned to make sure John hadn't abandoned me. I could just make out the top of his dark head through the hole. His blue eyes were watching my every move intensely, probably convinced I would walk past any bats rather than attack again. I couldn't see his nose or his mouth; only his eyes and a fast getaway plan.

I explained my hesitation to John. "This is making me pretty nervous. There are a lot of animal droppings and loose insulation up here. I don't think I should do this without a respirator." I hoped my health-hazard problem would result in me being allowed out of the attic. Seconds ticked by, and John had not replied. I turned to see what the matter could be.

He'd been waiting on me to face him. He made steady eye contact, raised his head slightly through the hole and whispered, "There's one on your neck."

You could have heard guano drop. "Are you sure?" I asked, barely whispering.

He nodded, and I froze statue style. I had no idea what to do. I turned toward the opening in hopes of getting away, but it was once again solidly blocked by my husband's fat head.

"I don't know what to do. Do you think it would help if I took off my shirt?"

John's head came through the opening completely, "Sure!" he said eagerly.

"This isn't funny, John. I'm not offering to strip. I need your help!"

He looked a bit disappointed and, I admit, confused. I was in no mood to appease or tease him. I just glared.

"What is your problem?" he grumbled from his safe bat-less position.

"My problem?! You tell me I have a bat on my neck, and you want to know what my problem is?" I was yelling as loud as a whisperer could.

He began to laugh. I couldn't believe it. He was pointing and laughing at me.

"There's no bat! You asked for a respirator. It's on your neck."

Looking down quickly, I saw that he was right. I'd forgotten I'd left it hanging there. I had planned to go right back to work, after all. Well, bats be damned. I didn't care if I woke up the whole colony. I marched over to that opening without sliding, and, reminiscent of our first attic encounter, began to stomp at John's head to let me out. We definitely needed to synchronize our secret-decoder Batman watches.

After chasing John around the house, I finally gave up and calmed down, slightly. It was difficult to stay mad at someone who had collapsed in hysterics.

The Old Woman had given up on trying to be quiet and howled with laughter right along with John. She clutched her stomach and bent over. "Oh," she wiped a tear from her face. "Lord, I haven't laughed like that in ages."

After catching my break, I did go back up, stronger and more confident. I saw a lot of evidence of bats in the form of fresh guano, but nobody else was flying, hanging or sleeping. A lot of guano had to mean a lot of bats. *Where were they?*

"Do you think they're down in the insulation?" I called out to John.

Still unwilling to enter the attic, his muffled reply drifting up into the attic, "Nah, more likely they're in the walls."

How were we supposed to deal with that? Cut holes in the walls? Suck them out with industrial vacuums? That would never work because of all the damn walnuts in the way. I really didn't care anymore. I was simply relieved to be free of the attic rooms, the smell, the guano, and the slippery fear. I gratefully drove back to the other house and took an hour-long shower to wash away such things. I couldn't have bashed or smashed all of those bats anyway.

The Old Woman was disappointed. "How can you just leave? I really thought that if anyone could do it, you two could get rid of the bats," she muttered, anxious to get them out of her hair.

Meanwhile, my parents, who had long since driven away, were getting weekly, sometimes daily, reports on the happenings at the old homestead: electrical, plumbing, drywall, and bats. I called them after my shower, hoping for a sympathetic ear. John was still laughing at me, and I was ignoring him completely. My mom and dad grew more and more concerned as they listened to my tirades.

Afterward, when warm phone receivers had been replaced on cradles, they made plans of their own. Despite the crazy work schedule John and I were keeping, and Gene dropping by to help more and more, we were drowning. My parents agreed on a rescue plan of their own. Help was on the way.

Chapter 15

Calling Up the Reserves

I sat on the porch, anxiously watching the vehicles pulling in and out of the road. Finally, My dad's truck turned the corner, and I jumped out of my chair. Opening the front door, I yelled, "Boys... he's here!" and ran to greet him.

"Oh Daddy, I can't believe you came!"

He slid out of the car, stretched out five-hundred miles of kinks, and hugged me tightly. "Hi, honey! I don't know how much I can do, but I'll help in any way I can."

John rushed in an hour later and pulled him into a man-sized hug. "Bob, good to see you." They shook hands and smiled. John and my dad were great friends and even called each other "Bud." Whether that was a fondness for each other or a nickname for the beer they loved, I wasn't sure. We all settled in for a comfortable evening and semi-relaxed for a change.

We stayed that way until John started talking about the bats. Had my dad sensed, to any degree, what he would be involved in, he would have stayed home or, better yet, packed up my mom and driven in the opposite direction.

John decided it was time to let my dad know what we really had in mind. "Well, Bud, we gotta get the bats out. I sure could use your help."

"Sounds good." My dad smiled, pleased he was to be included in our noble cause.

It had been almost two weeks since the roofers had quite hammering, and I couldn't help but remind Bud I and Bud II that speed was required. "We've got about a week before bat babies arrive!" I exited the kitchen to run baths, check homework, and play with the kids.

There were intense conversations and explanations as John tried to cram all of our bat knowledge down my dad's throat. It was similar to studying for a final exam, and we desperately needed him to pass. He understood the urgency and studied hard.

"We should fill one of the holes and leave just one exit for your furry friends," My dad surmised.

John readily agreed. "Yeah, all of them—bats, squirrels, whatever."

The guys opted to fill the hole in the front of the house. It was much more doable when the two of them could stand on the porch roof and take care of things.

Having come up with a plan, they left while there was still daylight. John pulled into the driveway, and my dad's jaw dropped. "Wow! It doesn't even look like the same house." His head was swiveling to take in the roof, the siding, on one side anyway, and several new, shiny windows. The yard was mowed and tamed considerably since he'd seen it last. "I can't believe it." He shook his head in wonderment.

John grinned and cocked his head to the side, taking in all the changes too. We were on such a fast track, we rarely took time to appreciate what we'd accomplished. "We're almost out of daylight, so I'll let Katrina show you the inside tomorrow."

They retrieved a ladder from the side of the house, and both men were up on the porch in no time. John showed my dad the location and size of the bat entrance, and he began stuffing and sealing the one hole with rags and expandable foam. John tossed bottles and cans of bug spray, Lysol, Comet and bleach to the top of the porch, and good ol' Bob splashed and squirted the rags so the bats wouldn't tear them out in their frantic desire to get back inside.

The combination of chemicals was a Molotov cocktail, and the two men were high off fumes and adrenaline. "Damn, this stuff is strong," my dad said, wiping his eyes and trying not to cry. John nodded, holding his hand over his nose and mouth, trying not to sway on the ladder.

As they climbed down, testosterone filled the air, mixing with the chemicals.

The Old Woman hated the smell. Not at all pleased with their efforts, she wondered, "Just who does this Bob guy think he is anyway?" His first visit had offended her, and now he was assaulting her with chemicals. She watched as he followed John.

The only remaining exit for our bat adversaries was a much larger hole high up in the eaves, on the backside of the house. John and his bud studied and schemed. They drove home, still slightly intoxicated, to formulate a plan.

Celebrating their initial success, the guys sat at the kitchen table, shared a victory smoke and a beer, and began to talk through the next phase. "This is the deal, Bob. The bats don't eat every day. One group leaves to hunt and eat. The rest stay to sleep or babysit until it's their turn the next night," John explained. "This is gonna take us a day or two." He paused to make sure my dad was listening. "We've got to control the flow of bats in and out of that hole."

Bud II nodded knowingly as if he understood. "We'll stuff it closed during the day and open it at night to let a group out."

It was a great and well-thought-out plan, and I was duly impressed. The only problem I could see was the height of that remaining bat door. "That hole is way up there—twenty, thirty feet. How are you gonna open and close it in the dark?"

They scowled at me for interrupting and throwing off the momentum. I seemed to be the only logical one and stood, hands on hips, waiting for an answer.

"You've got a big extension ladder, don't you?" Dad asked reasonably.

"Yeah, but she's right. The hole's pretty far up there. What if bats come out while you're on the ladder?"

My dad wrinkled his nose at that, not noticing John had placed *him* firmly on the ladder and not himself. I knew John wouldn't admit his fear of heights to his bud, and I snickered to myself. "Maybe you could build something?" I smiled knowingly at John, who beamed at the notion immediately.

So began a complicated process of designing a special bat-fighting staff. Dad and I sat at the table and listened to John, who was doodling as he spoke. "It needs to be about thirty-feet long to reach that hole." He drew something quickly, and my dad and I leaned in to watch. "I think we can put a hook on the end and stuff the rags in the hole. Then, the next day, we grab the rags and open it up." More numbers and doodles showed up on the paper.

Dad and I nodded our encouragement, and that's all it took. Affirmation is a powerful thing. Particularly since we'd received so little support concerning any of our grandiose plans. We weren't thinking clearly at that point but didn't know the difference. Being overly tired and overwhelmed, logical solutions were beginning to elude us. John finished his detailed picture, and a long list of supplies emerged so that his clever new pole could be constructed.

Friday morning came bright, and John drove to work, confident the latest plan was a winner. My dad and I, equipped with a sketch and a well-used Visa card, headed to Home Depot. My dad chuckled over the fact I seemed to know most of the staff, and even stopped to talk with a few.

"I'm here no less than two times a week, Dad. It's getting so that they're asking *me* where things are."

Standing in the plumbing aisle, we began to gather the necessary supplies. I laid PVC pipes, angles and connectors, in sequence, on the floor to ensure I had everything on John's stupid list. No one, including the workers who knew me, was able to resist that aisle, and we were drawing a crowd. My dad shrugged and smiled at them, effectively removing himself from the strange behavior being exhibited. At their curious glances, he warned, "Trust me, you don't want to know."

We drove everything over to the old house, and my dad once again expressed his amazement. I reached over for a hug. "Thanks, Daddy. I'll show you around inside before we build John's pole."

We wandered from room to room, and my dad seemed genuinely shocked. "This is beautiful. Wait 'til your mom sees this—incredible."

My forehead wrinkled as I looked at drywall dust everywhere, tools in every room. Like John, I hardly had time to notice the changes. I tended to concentrate on the long list of things yet to be completed. It was nice to see our progress through someone else's eyes. "Unfortunately, there's still a lot to do, Daddy, and I guess we'd better start on that pole."

We gathered our supplies and set them in the backyard, far from prying eyes. I didn't see any value in alarming the neighbors. We fit and glued pieces together until the world's first official bat-fighting staff had been assembled. Eyeballing the thing suspiciously, I looked at my dad and turned my head to the side. "Does this look right to you?"

"I think so. Maybe we should practice, make sure the pieces stay together."

We learned that holding any object thirty feet overhead is not an easy thing to do. The PVC pipe was simply too flexible and kept bending. Even with both of us trying to direct it, the pole wobbled, bent itself backward and refused to go where we wanted.

"Let's let John handle this," my dad suggested, disgusted with our wasted time and effort.

"Sounds good to me. He's the designer, after all." I piled things near the house, and we went inside. My dad and I spent a comfortable and companionable afternoon, painting and sanding. Details, not always revealed over the phone, were shared and explored. We laughed a lot and left feeling quite satisfied with our day.

At dinner, John eagerly asked, "Did you get all the supplies?"

Dad and I nodded. "We already glued the pieces together for you. We had a little trouble holding it in the air though." I winked at my dad, who only nodded.

"Well, let's go over there and see what we can do." John was already out of his chair and heading upstairs to change into jeans. He was excited, sure his plan would be the answer to our bat dilemma. Dad and I didn't bother to tell him how much we had fought with the pole. He was so determined, he wouldn't have listened anyway.

We piled into cars, including the boys, and set off for the old house immediately. Michael and Spencer raced to the pond, eager to throw sticks or chase frogs or whatever it was that little boys did around water. They were oblivious to our trials and errors.

Ever confident, John decided he would handle the pole. Although he didn't say so, his body language indicated we'd probably just done it wrong. Together, Dad and I had struggled, trying to hold and maneuver thirty feet of PVC pipe. John, by himself, was a sight to behold. He stumbled around the backyard trying to hold the thing over his head and remain superior. It was waving, John was weaving, and it absolutely would not go where he wanted it to go.

"I told you it wasn't easy." I felt vindicated. It wasn't that Dad and I had failed. It was the pole, not us, that had serious engineering flaws.

Because it was his design, he was slower to admit defeat and continued to try to muscle his shiny staff toward the hole. I yelled out warnings, trying to save the few new windows we'd installed, "Watch out! You're too close to the house. It's going left."

John turned to shoot me a pained look just as the top of his weapon bent in half, showering pieces of PVC down around him.

John let loose of the pole to cover his head. I let out a cackle. My dad, who had been trying to hide his own laughter, gave up trying when I snorted. The two of us leaned into one another for support and howled.

The boys came running toward us, excited by the sounds of laughter. "What's so funny?" Michael, The Literal, asked. He watched his dad's progress and frowned.

I laughed again. "Dad's trying a new bat toy he made."

"I wanna try. Can I try, Mommy?" Spencer thought it all looked like a game and was always eager to take on something new.

"No, baby. I'm sorry, but Daddy's invention isn't working right now."

My dad faked a cough to cover his laughter, and both of us started all over again. John shot looks to kill and glared at his much shorter pole. He tried to get the pieces back together and finally slung them away in disgust. "I guess that leaves the ladder." John hung his head in shame and headed toward the barn. He came back, lugging our extension ladder behind him. He angrily threw it against the back of the house.

"Hey, Bud, we can do this." My dad moved closer to John, lending the moral support I seemed unable to provide. I was still giggling and helping the boys catch fireflies.

The men decided they'd lean the ladder against the falling-apart bathroom for stability and use what remained of John's staff to push the rags in the hole. Resting a thirty-foot extension ladder and one adult male against that building seemed kind of stupid to me, but, as I've said, we weren't thinking clearly, and I couldn't come up with a better plan.

Having thoroughly enjoyed the evening and a full belly laugh, I headed for the car. "You guys are on your own." I knew that hanging around would only result in my involvement. I was no dummy and made a fast getaway, both boys in tow. I was sure things were going to get out of hand and didn't want to endanger Michael or Spencer.

"Looks like we're gonna be here awhile," my dad said, looking at his pack of smokes and trying to determine if he had enough.

"'Fraid so. Let's go get some beer." John was already reaching in his pocket for keys. My dad perked up and off they went to the store for supplies and a case of their beloved Bud.

Initially, there was nothing to do. The hole was already open, and the bats could come and go as they pleased. They each drank a beer, smoked a cigarette, and gathered the supplies they needed. Gloves, rags, a flashlight, and the remaining chemicals were piled near the ladder. Thinking, thinking, always thinking.

The yard grew darker, and they watched the hole apprehensively. "There's one!" John yelled out. "Two, three, four! Shit! They're all coming out at once!" He jogged backward, away from the house, as the bats dove gracefully and glided toward the smorgasbord pond.

Dad was moving backward too, eyes wide and surprised. "Creepy little things!" He spilled part of his beer on his shirt. "Maybe we should sit in the car!"

"Great idea. I'll go get it—damn, there went three more. You keep counting."

John pulled in to the backyard, and Dad quickly jumped inside. "I saw five more," he reported, and opened the window, just the tiniest bit, to let out his cigarette smoke.

It was getting darker—the utter blackness that can only occur in the country swelled and swallowed the light. Despite the fact no more bats were flying out, they continued to sit safely and quietly in the car, sipping at their warm beers.

Dad broke the silence. "I saw twenty-two. That what you came up with?"

"Yeah. I got the same thing," John answered and settled more comfortably in his seat. My dad looked at him and frowned thoughtfully.

"Someone probably needs to go up that ladder," John commented casually but didn't budge. Silence descended again. They drank another beer.

My dad looked at John. "This is bullshit," he announced and opened his door.

John followed suit, and the two stood under the ladder like gunfighters at noon, glancing at each other out of the corner of their eyes, waiting for the other one to make the first move. Bud shook his head, grabbed the much-shortened pole and stepped on the first rung of the ladder.

John smiled his thanks. He'd secretly hoped he could outwait his father-in-law, and it had worked. Never mind his partner was almost twenty-five years his senior. Never mind that it was our mess and not my dad's. What are Buds for, after all, if not for climbing ladders in the dark and filling up holes in eaves?

John let out a relieved breath. "Don't forget the rags." He tossed them to his bud and held the ladder, showing his support for the project.

Bud rearranged his supplies and marched up the ladder toward the exit. As he moved further up the ladder, it began to shift toward the right. "Look out!" John called too late, as my dad took a ride sideways into the side of the old bathroom. The crash echoed across the yard, and two doves whooshed from the rotted and rusted guttering.

"Shit!" My dad's brain registered the flying objects as bats, and he waved his hands for protection. The rags, pole and flashlight rained down around John's head as he tried to hold the ladder steady.

John jumped out of the way of the supplies and one surprised man who was heading down the ladder with purpose. "Oops. Forgot about those doves." John snickered once. Revenge was ever so sweet. My dad had laughed at his thirty-foot- pole, and John was settling the score. "They flew out at me too, the first time we looked at this place. I kicked this room just to see what would happen—and whoosh—doves just like tonight."

"Anything else you forgot?" Bud asked, frowning sternly and re-establishing himself as the respected elder.

"No, sir. I believe that's it. I'll hold the ladder tighter this time."

Bob/Bud scowled but was determined to continue. He retrieved his weapons and ran up the ladder. He stuffed the hole, snuck past the guttering, and dropped the last foot to solid ground again. "Man, I'm glad that's over."

"Great job! Let's go home. I'm tired." John was heading for the car and missed the look Bud sent in his direction.

On the way home, John declared, "If you can do the ladder, so can I."

As a team, they took turns going up and down the ladder, being ever watchful of doves. Two days, three nights, a case of beer and seventy-two bats later, we believed ourselves to have been successful.

I waited up to see what the result would be, pacing and watching the clock anxiously. It was almost ten when the two marched in the house, chests puffed importantly.

"Well, that should do it."

"Nothing else came out tonight, and we sealed the hole."

The guys were ready to celebrate and settled in to swap war stories, featuring themselves as mighty conquerors. The enemy had proven to be weak and insignificant.

"You can call the roofers tomorrow, Babe," John called out while rummaging in the refrigerator. He came back with a fresh round of beers for everyone, ignoring the fact he had to go to work the next day. "If the bats are gone, your trip will be worth its price in gold." He raised a beer in a salute to his best friend. "I couldn't have done it without ya, Bud." Glasses clinked all around.

The Old Woman changed her mind about my dad. "Anybody willing to give that kind of effort can't be so bad."

CHAPTER 16

This Aint Gonna Work!

Monday arrived, and we crashed through the morning in our usual style. School lunches were packed, book bags hunted down, and kisses handed out to each person entering the kitchen. We were on the second pot of coffee and dishes were piling quickly in the sink. Deanna rushed through, grabbing things as she headed out the door. "I've got to go to work right after school," she reminded us and flew out the door, late as usual.

John left for work, still smiling over the handling of the bats. Michael and Grandpa tramped down to the bus stop, chattering the whole way. I walked Spencer through the backyard to my friend Mary's house. I'd hired her to babysit full time. The renovations required my full- time attention, and there were simply too many dangers for a small boy.

Finally arriving at the old house, Dad and I poured a cup of coffee from the thermos and headed to the dungeon. On the drive, I'd explained, briefly, what we needed to do that day. "It's time to set jacks under the kitchen, Dad. We can't even work in there until we level the floor.

Still feeling euphoric after evicting the bats, my dad smiled. "Hey, no problem."

I knew he had no idea what that really entailed but didn't bother to enlighten him. Turning on the one bulb in the dungeon, I led the way down the stairs and stood at the bottom, wrinkling my nose at the damp, musty smell that clung to the walls and floor.

Dad followed more slowly, watching his step in the dim lighting. Reaching the bottom, he sipped his coffee, glanced around and asked, "So, where do we put the jacks?"

The Old Woman tucked her skirts underneath her legs and settled on the steps, interested and listening.

I walked over to the crawlspace window, retrieved a flashlight I kept there and switched it on. "Let me show you." The beam flickered once, twice and went out. "Stupid thing. Batteries must be low." I banged it in the palm of my hands, tightened up the cap and tried once more. A thin but steady beam came through and I shined it up and into the access window.

My dad stood on tiptoes behind me and peered cautiously inside. The light, barely able to penetrate the thick, black interior, illuminated two, maybe three feet of the cave-like hole. Dust particles stirred and danced across the yellow glow.

My dad's eyebrows lifted, and I looked inside with more perception. I'd forgotten just how bad it could seem. Old, dirty spider webs swayed from vent work, and I saw the remains of one translucent spider suspended in such a trap. Bits of insulation hung from rafters, and the dirt floor was riddled with rock and stone that had crumbled away from the foundation wall. A messy pile of newspaper strips and pieces of paper towel indicated a mouse lived just inside.

My dad stepped back from the window and shook his head. "You've got to be kidding me. How far in do we have to go?"

"All the way to the back." I swung the flashlight sideways and concentrated the light on the block foundation to the fireplace. The flashlight flickered again, and I shook it.

He looked inside again, squinting to see what I was talking about. "How the hell do we even get in there?"

"It's easy—I do it all the time." Full of confidence, I marched over to the opening, stepped up onto the rickety contraption I'd rigged, stretched out, and pulled myself up and into the crawlspace. I turned, all smiles, to look at my dad.

His eyebrows were pasted to the top of his forehead, and his mouth was hanging slightly open. "There ain't no way I can do that." He frowned at the round drink cooler and crumbling concrete block, I'd used as a stepping off place. "It's gotta be a two or three-foot stretch to get in that hole."

I looked at his face, noticing, maybe for the first time, the gray in his mustache. I was suddenly struck by the number of birthdays he'd celebrated and realized maybe the crawlspace project wasn't going to be as easy as I'd thought.

"Just do what I did—step on the cooler, grab the window, and pull yourself in."

"Easy for you to say. Your legs are longer" He climbed aboard anyway and began to teeter crazily. He fell over, and I giggled.

"Hey, don't worry about it," I called as encouragement. "Happens all the time. You're going to have to move quicker that's all. The floor's uneven."

He grabbed the sides of the window, bounced up and down for momentum, and stretched his right leg up toward the opening. I'd entered head first, so I watched his approach with interest.

"Come on, almost there."

"I'm doing the splits already—I can't get higher!"

I reached over and grabbed the back of his shirt, pulling and yanking him toward the entrance. He wobbled again, and his shirt traveled up his back and over his head. I had nothing in my hands but a fistful of cotton. I threw my head back and let out a very unladylike laugh. I hastily re-dressed my father, who was still hanging on for dear life outside the hole.

He continued to bounce, jump and try to get at least one of his feet into the hole. His hair was messy from losing the shirt, and he was starting to sweat with all the effort. The well pump, located directly behind him, chugged to life. The clanging pipes started him, giving him the extra adrenalin to clear the windowsill. His heel was firmly wedged in the frame. I heard him mutter, "Ungrateful kid, telling me it's no big deal."

I reached for his hands and tugged him inward. His shoulders were through, and we were almost to the finish line when he announced, "Hurry! I'm getting a cramp!" He let go and dropped out of sight.

I leaned out the window to find him hobbling around and massaging his leg. "Come on, Dad, you can do this!"

"I need a minute. Let me walk this off." He limped over to the stairs, retrieved his cup and frowned when he saw it was empty. I hopped out to join him for our impromptu break. We sat on the steps, evaluating the situation and waiting for his cramp to subside.

"Okay, Dad, we've got to get you in there. How about you go first, and I'll give you a boost if you need it?"

He took a big breath and climbed back on the cooler. I bent, linked my hands together so he could use them as an extra step. I began to boost him higher, grunting slightly with the effort. He was partially in, and, feeling victory was finally near, I gave one more mighty shove.

He was face down in the dirt, screaming at me to stop, "Quit pushin'! I'm stuck!" His voice was muffled, and he sounded curiously in pain.

"What? What's wrong?" I repeatedly asked, moving closer to the window to hear him.

"I'm hung up on something."

Checking the situation, I started to laugh, "Your belt…it's stuck in the wood." I hooted aloud. "I think the metal prong gouged a hole in the window frame! I carefully lifted his hips free, giggling the whole time at the embarrassing situation in which he found himself: butt and legs hanging out into the basement, face stuck in the dirt.

The Old Woman slapped her thighs and laughed too. It was turning out to be a great show. "This is almost better than you in the attic! This where you get it from, girl?"

My dad reached back, undid his belt and pulled it free, tossing it back into the dungeon. He slithered the rest of the way inside and sat in the dirt, relieved to have finally made it into a place he hadn't wanted to go.

I was still laughing, tears streaming down my face as I climbed, effortlessly, inside to join him. I crawled past him, stopping briefly to kiss him on the cheek. "Follow me." I grabbed the flashlight and belly crawled under a vent. "Get down low. There's a wire here." I pointed it out with the flashlight. On and on I went, as we worked our way further into the damp, dark area.

We reached our destination, under the kitchen, and I showed him where the five holes would need to be dug to place the jacks. He was nodding. Everything was going to be all right. I handed him a very small garden trowel for digging.

He raised his eyebrows. "Jeeesssuuusss Christ! You've got to be kidding!"

"Nope, no joke. Shovels don't fit down here," I stated, all business. "You start on that hole, and I'll work over here."

I dug in silence while my dad mumbled about his inferior working conditions. It took a while to dig through the packed dirt and rock. I worked out a shovel full and flung it sideways. It landed on the flashlight, which flickered once and went out. Immediate darkness descended. "Shit." I scooted over, feeling around in the dirt blindly. Finding it, I banged it a couple of times. "Batteries are shot. I've got to go get more from upstairs."

"Great," my dad said. "I'll just wait here."

We heard a mouse scurry past us. "Don't be too long," my dad pleaded, listening and watching me crawl toward the faint light filtering through the window.

I ran up the steps, rummaged through boxes of tools, found only one battery and tore through the house looking for more. "Hang on, Dad! I'm coming!" I yelled as loud as I could.

He sat in the dark, waiting.

I switched on the flashlight and triumphantly climbed back inside. "You okay in here?"

"Yeah," he replied, "I'm just thinking up new names for John. 'Bud" doesn't seem fitting anymore."

We laughed and went back to work. Within ten minutes, all five holes were finished.

Looking more than a little relieved, my dad began to move toward the exit.

"Wait!" I called to his back. "We've got to get the concrete."

"Where's the concrete?"

I looked at him apologetically, "Outside."

"Are you telling me we have to go back out that hole?"

I nodded.

"No way. It ain't gonna happen." He sat in the dirt like a petulant child.

We agreed his getting in and out of the hole while dragging concrete was probably not the best move. I did have him hostage, though.

"I'll go out the hole, bring in the concrete and hand the bags to you through the window. Okay?" What could he say, No? I would simply remove the exit cooler until he was more acquiescent.

We were, at that point, months into our home renovation, and during that time, I'd hauled and lugged more than my fair share. Although skinny, the work had turned me wiry and muscular. I was stronger than I'd ever been. My dad wasn't privy to that piece of information.

Now, concrete comes in three sizes: forty- pound bags for wimps, sixty-pound bags for most men and eighty-pound bags for Schwarzenegger types who build skyscrapers for a living. Because I neither a wimp or Mrs. Universe, I'd purchased sixty-pound bags for the basement project. I grabbed one from outside, worked my way down the crumbling steps of the storm cellar door and over to the crawl-space window.

I shifted the concrete to my right shoulder, stepped on the cooler, grabbed the window frame one-handed and teetered crazily. My dad squatted inside the window, reaching to take the load.

I knew I didn't have much time before the cooler went over. I locked my knees and heaved the sack up into the hole. I was straining and not really in the mood for conversation. That was unfortunate because I hadn't given sufficient warning to my father. He had no time to brace before being hit with sixty pounds of concrete squarely in the chest. As predicted, the cooler keeled over about the same time my dad did. I heard his "OOF" just as I lost my balance and fell to the dungeon floor.

I fared better since my landing was into the dirt. My dad fell back into the rocky path of the crawlspace and had a newly bruised knee to go along with a sore thigh. I righted the cooler and peered cautiously inside. I was scared. He was going to quit. I just knew it.

The Old Woman had much the same thoughts. "You better ease up on him, or he'll never help you again."

"Well, that was fun now, wasn't it?" I asked cheerily.

He did not look pleased and had begun muttering again. *Does dementia run in the family?* All the muttering was a concern.

The bad news was that we needed more concrete. We were both moving considerably slower but were better prepared for the second bag. We hoisted and pulled rather than tossed and tackled.

My dad, bless his heart, thought we were done with the hauling and bruising. I quickly relieved him of that assumption. "I hate to tell you this, but we need water to mix the concrete." I grimaced and looked at him through one squinted eye, sure the news would be his undoing.

He sat down among the rocks and hung his head. "Do you at least have a hose?"

"Uh, no. We haven't brought 'em over yet."

Using empty buckets, I lifted water into the hole. We lost half of it but managed to save just enough. Muddy, grubby and grumpy, we mixed, poured and set those holes, anxious for our three-hour term in the dungeon to be over.

Despite our appearance, we left to go buy lunch. The hell with what anyone else thought. Exhausted and spent, we sat in the backyard, munching Quarter-Pounders. We tried to decide what else to do with ourselves. Although we would have liked to, we couldn't quit. The list was still too long. We needed something that wouldn't require much effort or thinking.

We noticed the huge fiberglass ladder was still leaning against the back of the house, a reminder of the weekend bat war. "How 'bout if we take the ladder down, put it away for John, and then maybe we'll paint or something," I offered as a possibility.

"Sure, sounds good," my dad agreed, crumbling up his trash and putting it in the bag.

Why in heaven's name we thought that would be an easy task is beyond comprehension. We could barely get in and out of a hole. Engineering marvels we were not. My dad and I knew the logistics, but the weight of the ladder took us by surprise.

I peeled it away from the house, realized my mistake, and let it fall back with a resounding crash. I half-expected Mr. Angell or Mr. Lewis, or our other neighbor, who lived across the street, to come tearing around the corner of the house to see what I was doing. I could just hear them, demanding an explanation.

I shook my head. "This thing's heavy as hell!" I explained to my Dad and wondered how John had carried it by himself and flung it with such ease.

Dad and I began to fling around instructions.

"You stand behind it and push. I'll grab it from the front."

"Hold it upright!"

"Hang on, it's slipping again."

The feet of the ladder were walking one way while we were trying to go another. It seemed to be getting heavier by the minute, and my arms were beginning to shake. I was having trouble but, being Wonder Woman, I didn't want to admit to having inferior strength. *Just a little longer and we'll be done. Hang on, girl, almost done.*

I never gave a warning, never expressed my actions in any way, or stopped to consider the consequences. I simply stuck my head through the rungs closest to me. I needed to support the imprudent ladder with my back and shoulders; they were stronger than my fatigued arms.

The Old Woman had been watching us from an upstairs window and saw what I was doing. Screaming out warnings, she raced down the stairs and out the back door, stumbling across the crippled back stoop.

The hooks let loose at precisely the same time my head went through the rungs. The ladder began to collapse, quickly shortening upon itself until it encountered my neck and stopped abruptly. I let out a loud grunt.

My dad, who had been holding on to the ladder with one hand, spun at my strangled voice and encountered my head stuck between ladder rungs. He practically dropped the ladder and recovered just in time. "What the hell are you doing?"

This is not good, I told myself. *In fact, this is not good at all.* Unable to speak due to the ladder crushing my neck, my eyes bulged, and I silently pleaded for help.

"Hold on, Baby! We've got to get this thing to the ground. Work with me!"

The Old Woman rushed around, unable to help.

I nodded, glad that at least one of us was able to keep his head. Trapped, I looked at the backyard, fully appreciating the privacy it afforded. I did not want anyone to see my newest mess. We'd promised entertainment, but the ladder ordeal seemed a bit much, even for me.

"We've gotta get this thing on the ground." He locked his legs, straining to hold the ladder upright. I was of very little use at that point.

He amassed super-human strength, surprising even himself, and the ladder remained steady. "Wherever the ladder goes, you go."

I was unable to tell him I had very little choice in the matter. Of course I had to go where it went. We were one, the ladder and me.

His hands walked down the side of the ladder bringing it closer and close to the ground. My neck was stretching, my feet dancing along behind. I made it to my knees, giving my neck a break. The lower we went, the less pressure was on me. The ladder and I eventually got horizontal, lying together in the yard.

I could finally talk. "Uh, Dad, I'm still stuck here."

"I know, I know. I've got to loosen the ropes." He slid the rungs apart and freed me. I was finally able to separate myself from the ladder. Despite our intimate encounter, I wasn't sorry to say goodbye.

We sat in the grass and shook, understanding how close we'd come to disaster.

"You still feel like painting?" I ruffled my dad's messy hair and smiled at his torn shirt, crooked glasses and dirty hands.

"Hell no! I need a beer!"

"And a Tylenol," I answered, rubbing my neck, and turning it from side to side to make sure everything was still working properly.

We headed to the car, ready to go, just as John came around the side of the house. He'd stopped in to check our progress. "What happened to the ladder?"

Dad and I shook our heads, made eye contact and silently agreed we would not be sharing all the details of our day. "Just getting it down for you," I quickly explained.

He took in our grimy faces and headed down the cellar steps to see how our holes and concrete had fared. He emerged dirty but also discontented.

"What?" I demanded, sure that I didn't like the look he was wearing.

He looked at us and made a face, afraid to tell us what we had found. "I'm sorry to tell you this, but the holes for the jacks—they're in the wrong place. You're off by about four inches per hole."

I plopped on the dirt floor and hung my head like my dad had done earlier. And, echoing his words announced, "No way! It ain't gonna happen today."

The Old Woman walked away, leaving me time and space to adjust. It had been a tough day. She could see that. "At least she's not throwing bricks this time. Find the humor, honey. It'll be alright."

Chapter 17

Enlightening

Tuesday arrived, and my dad packed his things and headed westward and homeward. His eyes, surrounded by dark circles, were glazed and staring. Everyone who worked with us at the old house ended up wearing a similar expression. As his taillights disappeared, I felt my enthusiasm and momentum fade away too. It was back to solitary working conditions, and I was already feeling lonely.

It took a few days and a lot of sweat, but I managed to get the stupid jacks re-set under the kitchen. Every time I entered the crawlspace, I would stop to remember my poor father's attempts to get in there and then giggle all over again. The laughter renewed my spirit, and I began the painstaking process of slowly raising the kitchen floor. It would take a week because the jacks could only be tightened a quarter turn each day or I'd run the risk of lifting the old house off its foundation. The things I didn't know I didn't know.

While working through the leveling process, John and I moved on to other jobs, desperately trying to knock out our "To-Do" list. We'd lost sixteen days to bats and crawlspaces and had a little over four weeks on the calendar before the big move.

"So, what do you want up here?" John asked on yet another Saturday morning. He was standing upstairs, looking at ceilings.

"Well, I think we should have at least two lights in the hall, don't you? And overhead lighting, in every room."

John nodded and continued to stare at the ceiling in the hall—wondering, perhaps, how he was going to get up there to do any wiring since they were quite high. "I think I'll put ceiling fans in all of the bedrooms. It's hot as hell up here." He was talking more to himself than to me.

The Old Woman nodded her encouragement. She was tired of squinting and making her way in the dark. The fans sounded good to her too.

We headed to the store and carted home eighteen lighting boxes, enough to outfit the entire house. I'd enjoyed choosing the lights and making decisions again. It had been a while since we'd had any semblance of control.

John began to measure the rooms and mark the centers by drawing x's in the middle of each ceiling. I went back to priming walls as fast as my roller would go. Our lives seemed to be on constant fast forward. We jogged everywhere, talked like auctioneers and wasted no motion.

Lights and fans were being assembled in each of the upstairs rooms, and I ran up occasionally to check John's progress. On one such journey, I entered our soon-to-be bedroom to see what could possibly be taking so long.

"What are you doing?" I asked, bewildered. He was at the top of the ladder with his entire hand up inside a hole he'd cut into our ceiling. He resembled the Dutch boy with his finger stuck in the dike.

"Bring me a towel or something, quick!"

"Why?" I asked, hurriedly rummaging through the mountains of debris in there. I'd recently demolished the old closet and hadn't cleaned up the mess yet.

"I need to clog up this hole, so no bats come through."

"They're back? Oh my God!"

"Nooo. I'm just being careful. Just get the damn towel." His brow furrowed, a silent demand that I quit asking questions.

I rolled my eyes, found a rag and tossed it up to him. He stuffed it quickly and thoroughly into the hole. Climbing down, he shook circulation back into his hand.

How long had he been standing there like that? Unbelievable.

He picked up a square, metal junction box used for holding the wires, grabbed the drill, and struggled and juggled up the ladder again. I watched apprehensively. *Would bats fly out of the hole when he unstopped it?*

I needn't have worried. In what seemed one swift motion, John ripped out the rag, slammed the box in the hole and drilled the screws into place. He reached for wires that were already measured, cut and stripped, punched out a hole in the box using the tip of the drill and fed a long length of wires up and into the attic.

"Okay, I'm confused." I tilted my neck back to see him and the ceiling better. "Why are you putting in junction boxes and wires from down here? I thought you had to go to the attic and work your way down." I'd watched him wire lights and fans before, and he'd never done it from below. It looked completely bassackwards to me.

"I am *not* going to the attic until I absolutely have to, and I'm not staying any longer than necessary! I'm measuring and cutting everything down here where it's safe."

"Oh. Okay." *What a chicken.*

Hours slid by, and John still hadn't gone to the attic. I knew he'd never venture there without coming to get me first, so I painted and waited, then painted and waited some more. *What is he doing? We don't have time for stall tactics.* I went upstairs to push him faster.

The halls and bedrooms all had wires hanging from the ceiling, and more rags had been inserted into any extra openings. It didn't look like we were putting up lights at all. In fact, it looked as though someone had come in, yanked every single light fixture down and left all the wires to hang naked and unused.

"Do we have a ski cap here?" John bounced the question off me as I sprinted by.

"Uh, yeah, I think so. I used one when I first went to the basement to keep spider webs out of my hair."

"Go get it, will you?"

He must be losing it. I'd worried that he would have a nervous breakdown over the old house and here was proof. *Why would anyone need a ski cap in June?*

"Hit the main breaker on your way back up here," John yelled as I headed downstairs.

At least that was good news. It meant the lights were ready to go. I pulled our new electrical switch and went up to be the assistant for John's attic debut. He'd laid out all the necessary tools in precise order at the foot of the ladder and was staring at the access hole in the hall. A sheen of perspiration covered his face.

It might have been nerves or heat, but I strongly suspected that his attire was to blame for the sweat. *Where's a camera when you really need one?* He had on jeans, boots and two long- sleeved shirts. He took the knit cap I'd brought with me, pulling it down to his eyeballs. Over that entire ensemble, he draped an old blanket that hung around his head and body like a cape—Super Morgan. He secured it under his neck with a clamp, donned gloves and headed north.

"It's not that fun heading into the attic now is it, Darling?" I raised my eyebrows for effect, hoping he got the message loud and clear.

The Old Woman snickered. She was in a wonderful mood, understanding that all the piercing she'd just tolerated signified that earrings and shiny new jewelry were on the way. "Lord Son, you are something else, you know that?"

I snickered too. With every rung, John stepped on his safety blanket, causing him to cuss and sweat more.

Step.

"Damnit."

Step.

"Son-of-a-bitch," His tirade and irritation grew as he climbed.

"Damn, Hon, you're gonna sweat to death in the attic. Take some of that off."

"No way! If I'm going up there with bats, it stays on." He was obviously afraid we might have inadvertently left one or two up there and that they would be fluttering around his head, pecking at his eyes and caught in his hair.

"The bats are gone. What's your problem?"

I had to wonder why I'd been sent to the attic without such armor. He hadn't given me a hat or a cape. In fact, I was sent up there with very few safety precautions at all. He must have been more pissed off about the house and me than I'd realized. Maybe he'd been hoping I'd give up on the whole project, or that something horrible would happen to me in the attic.

He could, no doubt, feign surprise at his wife's demise: "I don't know how she died, Officer. Had she only listened to me, this would never have happened."

Shaking my head, I handed tools through the opening. How he functioned in the heat and in those clothes, I do not know. He clenched a small flashlight in his teeth as he connected and moved with lightning speed. It was surely the fastest electrical job ever completed in all recorded history. Three bedrooms, the hallway, and the landing were all wired in less than thirty minutes. My sweaty hero had said, "Let us have lights," and so it was done, and it was good—except that another whole weekend had passed.

I walked into the old house on Monday with the intention of doing more sanding and painting. Enjoying a moment with my coffee first, I wandered through the rooms admiring the new lighting. I'd found several reproduction pieces in antiqued, scrolled brass and loved the way things were coming together. We'd modernized the house yet maintained a sense of age. *Perfect.*

As was becoming normal, the exuberant thinking quickly disappeared. By the time I'd gotten to the fourth or fifth room, I was disgusted instead. Bits of stripped electric wires were everywhere. Empty lighting boxes, pieces of drilled-out ceiling plaster and drywall tools littered the floors. "Why the hell can't he put anything away? How is all of this *my* job?"

To make matters worse, I was leaving a trail of boot prints everywhere I went. The continual drywall sanding had resulted in a thin layer of white dust covering every surface. "I can't work like this. This is awful!"

It shouldn't have been important, but I couldn't concentrate or even appreciate what we'd done while that mess reigned supreme. I rounded up brooms, heavy-duty trash bags, and piles of rags. Deciding to work my way from the top down, I hauled out the trash and wiped plaster dust from the walls and window ledges. I carried up an empty drywall bucket full of soapy water and a sad old mop I'd found out in the shed and started washing floors

It was very quiet in the house that day; just the house and me. There was no scratching of sandpaper, no ladders walking across plank flooring, no hammers banging or drills whining. Enjoying the silence and the instant gratification that comes from clearing and cleaning, I found myself humming my favorite songs.

I finished upstairs and took a moment to appreciate the new picture. Standing in each room, I marveled at how much brighter and bigger they appeared. The ceilings and walls gleamed white with their fresh paint, fans and pretty lights adorned each room. Even the closets were fresh and waiting to be filled.

I began to picture the rooms with color and our belongings. When John and I had initially looked at each room, we'd only noted the mess and what needed to be done to rectify the situation. Now, I saw what the house would be as a completed home.

Spencer's furniture is barely going to fit in here. I mentally compared wall space from one house to the other. *I'll just have to make it bright and fun to make up for lost space.* Stepping into the other room, I walked toward the front windows. *Michael's going to love having three big windows. He'd better not try to go out on this porch roof though.* I frowned at the possibility, knowing, as a teenager, I would have tried to escape that way.

Still musing and consulting myself, I took in the little landing we'd completely redone. *This is a great rainy-day spot.*

Suddenly, I was no longer alone. Someone or something else was there. The hair on my arms was charged, and I swung around to determine the cause. "Hello?" I walked down the hall.

"Is someone here?" I asked, with my left foot in mid-air, not sure if I should go down the stairs or not. Not hearing anything, I investigated, hurriedly looking out the front and side windows for cars. "Huh. That's odd." I stood, hand on hips, unable to pinpoint what had set me off.

I sat on the bottom step of the curved staircase where I could see the majority of the house and out into the yard. *Maybe a delivery person? Or worse, the scary handyman returned?* My radar was humming and searching the air for the source.

Slowly, tentatively, I became conscious of The Old Woman. I closed my eyes and opened them quickly, just to be sure I wasn't seeing anything or losing my mind. I saw nothing—and yet the presence I'd felt earlier enveloped me. She was there.

Not an apparition, I sensed her and her comforting presence. The Old House was not framework and plaster at all, but a compilation of all who had lived there: the joys, the tears, the work and the day-to-day living of lives. The old house still held the spirit, the emotions, the echoes of those who had come before. Here, finally, was the soul of the house, the thing I'd known we had to find in order to restore and rebuild. The silence and the solitude of the day had brought past and present into focus.

Elbows on knees, fingers laced together below my chin, I took a deep breath, experiencing her, her essence, and how we would fit together. There was no fear. I simply accepted and understood. It pleased me to be able to put personalize the house I loved so much. She and I were going to get along just fine. As much as I would have liked to, I couldn't just sit there all day. Reluctantly, I went back to my task of mopping and cleaning, talking to the house, the old woman, the spirit, whatever it was, as I went. "We're almost done, but I guess you know that, don't you?"

As the day wore on, I sketched a mental image of my old woman—the caretaker of the house. She seemed to follow me around, and I imagined her cane thumping as we moved from room to room. She was probably a little bent with age and arthritis, and the cane helped her keep up with me, but it was more an accessory than a necessity.

Excited by the woman's picture, but equally concerned about my mental capacities, I searched for my cell phone and called my mom on a whim. *Am I losing my mind?*

We moved past the basic small talk, and I launched into the real reason for the call, "I had the strangest experience at the old house today."

"Oh…what's that?"

"Well, it's hard to explain, and truthfully I'm a little freaked out right now. Do you remember the first time you came to see the house?"

"How could I forget that day? I thought you'd lost your mind!" I could hear her smiling over the phone.

"Yeah I know—and maybe I finally have. On the way home, though, I was telling you that it sometimes felt like the old house was waiting, watching. Remember?"

"Yes." She drew the word out, obviously wondering where I was going with the conversation. "What about it?"

"Well, I think I met whatever that was today." I launched into a lengthy explanation of how I had perceived the house to be an old woman, and what I thought she must look like. "She's not fancy, no white gloves for her. She's used to working hard, but she's still dignified, you know? I can picture her—flowered dress, sensible shoes. I think she has a cane too."

"Is it scary?" my mom asked, concerned. "Maybe you shouldn't stay there."

"No, that's what's really weird. I'm not scared at all. It feels safe, like someone or something watches over the house. Do you think something like that's possible? What's going on here, Mom? I'm losing it, aren't I?"

There was a long silence at the other end of the line. "Hello?" I asked, not sure we were connected any longer. I twisted my hair around nervous fingers and looked around for something to drink.

"I'm here," she answered. "I'm just thinking. Our family has had some odd things happen over the years, so, yes, I guess I do think what you're saying is possible. I'm just having trouble rationalizing it all. Give me a minute."

"You're telling me! I may need more than a minute! It just feels so real."

"I don't know what to tell you, honey. I do believe houses soak up a certain amount of atmosphere into their skins, like paint, a part of all the people who have lived there must seep into the walls."

"Sounds good to me." I found a warm Coke and popped the top, chugging a mouthful. "A house as old as ours has just had more time to soak up laughter and memories. I like to think of them as echoes, earlier people and emotions leaving their voices, their mark in a house."

"Well, I see no reason why your echoes can't belong to an old woman."

My mom and I smiled across the miles at each other and went back to our separate days.

I put away my supplies, locked the doors and bade her farewell. "I'll be back tomorrow! I've got to tell John!"

The conversation with my mom had gone better than expected, but The Old Woman was not so sure about John's reaction. "I'd love to be there for that one—a fly on the wall when Ol' Johnny hears this one! Let's just hope he doesn't get too radical, though." She worried the rest of the evening, half-expecting John to race into the driveway, slam through the door and demand that she leave.

After dinner, John and I sat at the table as I explained what had happened that day and my thoughts about our old house being like an Old Woman. I rushed to explain I didn't think the old woman was real—painting what I imagined her to look like, instead. "It was the most amazing experience."

He shook his head a bit but seemed to accept The Old Woman, at least at face value. No doubt he chalked her up to my imagination or some sort of weirdo, psycho, chick thing. He chose to indulge rather than argue. We had no time for such things. He didn't ask questions. I didn't elaborate. It was safer that way. Besides, I knew he'd eventually meet her—feel her too.

Chapter 18

We Are Not Alone

"So, is it haunted?" they would ask, eagerly stepping back to peer up at the old house more fully. Everyone, friend or curious stranger, asked that question. It just seemed to go without saying that an old pre-Civil War house like ours might host a ghostly resident or two.

"Has anything weird happened?" They wanted to know all the details.

"Other than bats and dead birds in the fireplace, you mean?" I replied with a laugh. "How weird do you want it?"

"No, not animals. Creaking steps, strange sounds, stuff like that," they would ask breathlessly, hoping for creepy details.

I personally had found the bats plenty creepy but understood where the questions were heading. Everyone loves a good ghost story.

I had heard my share of those. I remembered being twelve and eavesdropping one evening while my aunt and uncle told my parents about the odd occurrences taking place inside the house in which they'd just moved. I was skulking around corners, as adolescents do, listening, anxious to grow up and be included.

They were expressive, intelligent and well educated, yet completely convinced they had a hostile ghost living in their house. Gesturing wildly in an attempt to convince my folks of the truth of their story, they told of a previous owner they'd learned about, Mr. Cox—an unhappy, angry man who had died in the house. They suspected it might be him who was turning pictures to the wall, slamming doors, and knocking things off shelves in the middle of the night. Lights would turn on and off, bulbs would be unscrewed from their sockets. It was disconcerting, to say the least, and my aunt and uncle were looking for reassurance. I'd stood listening with goosebumps for company.

Tired and more than a little spooked after many nights of interrupted sleep, my aunt and uncle persuaded their pastor to come and say a prayer for the soul of Mr. Cox. Sure enough, the noisy pranks stopped. A strange story, but coming from two people I trusted completely, I had to believe in the possibility of ghosts.

Years later, my parents had their own brush with the slightly supernatural. During a high windstorm, a huge tree had fallen through a section of their home. A reconstruction crew worked for many months repairing the extensive damage. One day, the construction supervisor, an Egyptian, took my mother aside and told her he felt something malevolent in their house. "If you don't do something about it," he told her as he packed away tools for the weekend, "you'll see more bad things happen. You must go into every single corner of this house and pray," he said, firmly. "Invite God into your house, and you'll be safe." He closed the toolbox and left my mother bewildered.

Because she had gotten to know and respect him, and because months of reconstruction were not something she ever cared to repeat, my mother decided she had nothing to lose and followed his advice. She rather liked the idea of placing each corner of her house in God's hands.

When the contractor returned on Monday, he stepped into the house, paused and grinned happily. "You did it!" he exclaimed. "I can feel the difference."

My mom nodded, and the two of them never discussed it again. She did, however, tell us the story. "It was the most freeing experience... really something," she concluded.

John and I had listened to her tale years before we'd bought our old house. My mom was a modern woman of faith and not given to flights of fancy. She was well read, articulate, and intelligent, someone we both admired. *She believed a near stranger and then prayed in corners? No way.* We'd stood there like two idiots: eyes huge, jaws hanging, not sure what to think.

So, thanks to my relatives, I had two weird stories tucked away in my memory bank. I thought about them as I worked at the old house and answered questions about hauntings. Did those memories somehow fuel my overactive imagination? Or were we to find out that we had something else, something sinister, at work? Would I be praying in corners?

Spending hours at the house by myself, I would occasionally sense something unkind and menacing. The hair at the nape of my neck would stand at attention. I would stop, look, listen, waiting for …what? I had no idea; I just knew something wasn't right.

There were no spectral visions, no unexplained cold spots or unpleasant smells. It was akin to being watched, and my skin would break into goosebumps for no reason. I was reminded of the old phrase, "Someone just walked over my grave." I shivered, remembering the bones I'd found in our dungeon. Like so many unwanted cobwebs, I hurriedly brushed my uneasy thoughts aside.

Why did I think I had some psychic awareness of these things? Perhaps it was because I'd already felt something at the house. Maybe women are genetically geared toward such a ghostly sixth sense. I don't know. I only knew we weren't being haunted in the traditional sense. Sharpening my senses, I tried to understand what I was feeling in the old house. It wasn't The Old Woman who was causing the niggles of fear. I grew to recognize the difference between her and that other, less-friendly presence that seemed to linger in the air. Whatever or whoever that was didn't feel feminine either. "Who are you, Mister?" I would ask, "And, what do you want?"

Although I continued to talk to John and some of my girlfriends about The Old Woman, I didn't mention the other sensations I was experiencing. They would have all thought I was certifiable if I'd two or three imaginary people running around the old house. Besides, saying it aloud would have made it real.

I may not have articulated my thoughts and my fears to the living people around me, but I did talk to the old house more often. I likened it to talking to plants. We've all heard that plants thrive on such personal attention. There is no conclusive scientific proof that such musings are helpful, but what could it hurt to try the same philosophy on my house?

"Hello, it's me again," I would call out from the back door, greeting The Old Woman and whoever else seemed to be in residence. I stood in the doorway, like a wild animal, on alert and scenting the air for danger.

"We're gonna caulk molding today and do some sanding, okay?"

Maybe other inhabitants, awakened by the constant noise of tools and drills, were watching and trying to determine what we were up to and whether they approved. Maybe our frenzied activity led our resident spirits to connect with our own disjointed lives. On the other hand, perhaps our madness in taking on such a project had opened a doorway long forgotten and better left undisturbed. I had no way of knowing and tried to be as positive as possible, but it wasn't easy with such uncertainty swirling around the rooms.

I imagined the matriarch, The Old Woman, calmed their fears and suspicions so thrilled was she to be on show again. "Just wait and see, it'll be alright," she soothed. "It's almost done." They would then fade back to wherever they'd come from, passive and content. Well, almost. *He* never seemed to disappear completely.

I continued to verbalize our design and vision. I knew The Old Woman was on board and approved. I just needed that other thing to agree too. It was a slow, personal claiming of ownership. I envisioned myself as Scheherazade, telling stories and weaving tales until he became so engrossed, he too would fade away and leave us alone. The conversations seemed to help in that nothing scary happened, but my hair still stood on end, alerting me to his presence.

The move-in date was growing near, and the apprehension was growing. I decided it might be wise to take some precautionary measures. I needed to purchase a supernatural insurance policy. Drawing on my family's experiences with the Twilight Zone, my mother's particularly, I thought I would try the same process, on behalf of The Old Woman, and assure our safety. Prayers seemed necessary.

I called home. "Hey, Mom, it's me again!" I started in a singsong voice.

"Bob, Katrina's on the phone!" she yelled in my ear before even saying hello.

I held it away from my head until I heard him pick up a phone. "Hi, Daddy!"

We went through the normal small-talk routine. I looked at the clock and jumped to the meat of the matter. "Remember how I was talking to you about the time the tree fell on your house?"

"Tell me that hasn't happened!" she groaned, thinking we'd hit another physical problem.

"No, but I do need you to tell me more details of how you prayed in the corners. Something isn't right here at all."

"The Old Woman? Surely she's not giving you trouble!"

"What Old Woman?" my dad demanded, annoyed that she knew something he didn't. I could visualize him frowning and looking at the phone.

"Shh. I'll tell you later," Mom quieted him.

"I just need to know what you said in the corners. Be specific."

"Just speak, talk like normal…tell God what's going on and invite him to your house."

It sounded too easy, and I wondered if God really felt that way. "I'm afraid to admit it, but I'm a little out of practice and rusty on this end."

"God doesn't care. He'll probably be glad to hear from you again." My mom sounded pleased.

My dad rejoined the conversation. "We know you haven't been to church in a while. Tell you what, though, prayer isn't something you forget. It's like ridin' a bike. Just jump on and start peddling." Always reasonable and easy-going, he explained the situation calmly.

The two of them agreed through their matching phones, and she began to fill him in on what had been happening at the old house. "Hey, guys, I hate to interrupt, but I'm going to let you go. I need to do this before I chicken out!"

"Let us know!" They hung up, still talking to one another.

Trying to do things in order, I started downstairs, hitting my stride as I moved from room to room, corner to corner and praying aloud just as my mom had done. I even went into all the closets, just in case.

The Old Woman was following me around curiously. As I backed out of the coat closet, she quipped, "I've heard of people coming out of the closet, but this is ridiculous." She waited for me to smile. When I didn't, she cocked her head to the side and went on high alert. Her eyes grew wide with sudden understanding.

I talked about us as a family and explained that we believed in God. "God, please keep us safe here. Let our love flourish." With such pleadings, I invited God into our home. It was a wonderful experience, and I wished we'd done such praying and inviting in the other six houses we'd owned. Maybe we wouldn't have gotten so off track, caught up in the materialistic. Interestingly enough, what I said in each room varied. I simply spoke what came to mind.

The Old Woman was quiet and watchful. "Prayers are a good thing, girl. I see where you're going with this. Keep 'em coming."

I even went to the dungeon. Why not? It couldn't do any harm, and I sure didn't want to leave areas un-done. I didn't climb into the crawlspaces, but had aimed prayers into each opening, talking louder so the words would drift all the way inside. Satisfied that I'd finished the lower level, I stood at the bottom of the curved stairs, took a breath and squared my shoulders before moving upstairs. I definitely wanted to spend time in The Manson Rooms.

I thought about our children living in the old house, and the two awful rooms, at the top of the stairs, worried me. It was, truly frightening. Tucked away in an alcove as they were, we'd done little to improve its appearance. We'd removed the swinging saloon doors, and that had helped, marginally. Despite my having thrown a thin coat of primer on the walls, the red handprints had bled back through again.

The rooms were, however, a novelty, and John and I were like naughty children when it came to showcasing those two areas. During tours, we always saved that area for last. We'd usher new visitors through the lower level and then the second, using the back staircase so we could save our surprise. Thinking the tour finished, guests would pick up speed as they headed toward the curved staircase and foyer.

"Wait, there's more," and we would beckon our guests to join us. Surprised to see another room, they would literally step into, and then quickly out of, the nightmare housed inside the hideaway. John and I waited expectedly for their reaction. We were never disappointed. Appalled, scared, and shocked—their emotions ran the gamut. We loved it all, laughing at their expense. Eyebrows would climb, hairline high, and our guest would look at us strangely. "Is it haunted?" We had always brushed the question aside. Now, I wasn't so sure how to answer that question and set off to rectify the situation.

Standing at the threshold of The Manson Room, I looked around cautiously. The Old Woman peeked around my shoulders. "I sure hope you fix this up soon."

I was anxious to cleanse it of whatever hateful thing resided there. It had to be something awful. What else would possess someone to slather red paint around like that? Even the air in there seemed stale, dead.

I was, therefore, surprised to find that The Manson Room didn't seem to require much prayer. I didn't sense Mr. Malevolent watching or waiting. It seemed empty, and I vowed that I would never call the room by that dreadful name again.

Where is the strange feeling coming from? I'd been sure I would have found it in that room. I moved on toward our bedroom and bathroom, shaking my head. *Girl, your imagination got the best of you this time.*

Shrugging my shoulders, I decided I might as well bless everything anyway. While finishing up near the tub, I heard John. Not good. He'd come home early and was heading up the stairs.

"Hello?" He was already in the upstairs hall. I started talking faster and faster, trying to get to the Amen part.

It was important John not know I'd been praying. He was not nearly as religious as I was, even though I hadn't been to church in ages. He believed in God but not much else regarding the church and its' beliefs. He also knew the story of my mom and dad's house, and I didn't want to have to explain why I was suddenly standing in corners. He'd put two and two together, and that would be the end of the renovations, the move, everything.

"Katrina? Who are you talking to?" He poked his head into the bathroom just as I was scrambling to get out. I even bumped into him lightly and got him moving backward. I was doubly paranoid, knowing it wouldn't take much more to shove John over the proverbial cliff where the old house was concerned.

Scrambling out of the bathroom to intercept him, I offered up a lame excuse. "Just me, Honey, talking to myself." Thankfully, he bought that story, probably because I'd been talking to myself for years. I often joked that I was the only intelligent person around to converse with and he would just smile.

He and I shared a quick lunch together, finalizing our final attack plan for the old house. We had only three weeks to try and finish plumbing, painting, flooring, and installation of a complete kitchen. I talked continuously to fill any voids and draw suspicion away from the bathroom. I needn't have worried; he was more concerned about the deadline.

In my haste to get out of a potentially volatile situation, I forgot that I'd left my prayers unfinished. The upstairs landing by the back stairs, and what would be Michael and Spencer's rooms had gone unblessed. That omission would come back to haunt us, literally, months down the road. As it turned out, The Old Woman couldn't keep everyone quiet after all.

CHAPTER 19

Stop the Ride, I Want Off

We were down to three weeks and a few days. The fact that there was still no kitchen or a place to do laundry was cause for serious concern. Unfortunately, our other life and the people in it kept vying for our attention too.

In between sanding walls and endless trips to the hardware store, I ticked off mental lists of guests to invite, decorations to buy, and food to stock. Deanna was graduating soon, and I desperately wanted that to be a wonderful celebration. "Honey, make sure all your friends come to the party, okay?" The party was imminent, and I wondered if I had the energy to pull it off with any sort of success.

My mom, hearing the near hysterical pitch in my voice, volunteered to drive in immediately to help with party preparations. "You've got enough going on out there. Your dad and I can watch the kids, clean the house and get food ready."

I practically sobbed my relief. We'd been leaving The Old Woman each evening, exhausted and strung out after our twelve-hour days. We'd drive back home only to find ourselves spending more long hours at the kitchen table discussing Deanna's future, her college choices and her dreams. "What do you think of this school?" she would ask, laying out yet another brochure.

The grandfather clock in the hall would tick loudly, and we parents tried not to yawn. It wasn't that her needs weren't important to us. We were just that tired. As we calmed and encouraged, her beautiful smile surfaced again. Having at least semi-resolved one child's problems, we sighed our relief and dragged ourselves off to bed.

"Will I know anyone at the new school?" Michael asked, just about every morning over cereal and toast. "Can I still come back and see my friends here?"

He was trying to be brave, but we recognized the alarm bells he was ringing. He needed to be reassured that all would be right with his world too.

"Of course you'll still see your friends, and they'll come to see you too. I know you'll make lots of new friends when school starts," I explained in words that were automatic and memorized.

"You're going to love having all that space to play. You can hit a baseball as far as you want, buddy," John promised and mimed a home-run swing.

As we tried different promises and propositions to ease Michael's fears, he looked at us with serious doubt. Our physical appearance didn't help. Why would he want to move from all that was familiar to a place that was obviously draining his mom and dad?

We felt guilty at having spent such little time with the kids while working on the old house and worried Michael wouldn't make the transition easily. Then what? Guilt and worry made for a bad combination.

Michael was also playing baseball and had two, sometimes three games a week. At almost nine years old, his athletic abilities were improving rapidly, and he dreamed, as young boys do, of playing professional baseball someday. He was pitching and had even made the All-Star team. Busy as we were, we had to take time to attend his games and cheer loudly.

We madly tried to schedule our renovation projects so that we could finish in time to drive to Michael's games. I wasn't very good at that and had two speeding tickets in three weeks to show for my efforts. I would slam into the parking lot, let Michael out and try to get the dust and paint out of my hair before the first inning got started. *If my mom were here, she'd tell me I look like something the cat dragged in.*

To this day, I could not tell you the score of any of those games. Embarrassed by my disheveled appearance, I would tuck my boots under the bleachers and try to hold normal conversations with the other parents. Even as I yelled and clapped for Michael, I continued to fret and stew.

John and I discussed it, lying in bed late at night. "He's too quiet," I would state, stifling yet another yawn.

"I know," John would sigh and agree. "Do you have any ideas?"

"Well, he does have a birthday coming up...." I let the thought hang in the air a few seconds. "Maybe it's time to bite the bullet. What do you think?"

John propped himself on pillows. His eyebrows rose slightly at what he knew I was suggesting. "Maybe. It just might work." We shared a secret smile and relaxed into one another. If things went well, another one of our children would be alright

Two days later, Michael opened his gifts, frowning at what he found: a rubber bone, a divided plastic dish and a long leather strap with a snap at the end. Their meaning sunk in and his eyes opened wide with wonder. After all the hints, all the whispered wishes made over previous birthday candles, and all the unanswered requests to Santa, Michael's dream was about to come true.

Happily, we stuffed crumpled birthday paper in the wastebasket and drove off to the Humane Society where Michael finally got his dog—a big dumb lug he named Scooby-Doo.

John and I hoped he'd see how things would work together; an old house with lots of acreage, a new puppy with plenty of room to run. He did not recognize the correlation but sure loved that dog.

When I had dreamed up the splendid scheme, I'd managed to overlook the fact that puppies weren't hassle-free. I'd forgotten about the constant chewing and endless trips outside for potty training. I yanked a pillow over my head to drown out the mournful howling from a lonely Scooby-Doo. John tossed and turned. "Please, make that dog shut up!" Michael, kid number two, was smiling though so we would make it work.

We knocked off work early on Friday and met up with our friends as they congregated around the cul-de-sac. Tony shook his head as he watched our new puppy rollicking through the backyards. "What? Did you guys wake up one morning and say, "We don't have enough going on in our lives, let's go get a dog?"

I didn't have the time or energy to argue the pros or cons of our decision. Watching Michael and Spencer chase after Scooby, I just smiled and mentally chalked one up for my husband and me. We could keep working without feeling so damn guilty.

Of course, we had *three* children.

On Monday afternoon, I hurdled over a snarl of tools and a bucket of paint trying to reach the phone before it stopped ringing. "Hello!" I gasped, harassed and breathing hard.

"Mrs. Morgan, are you going to make your appointment today?"

Damn. I did it again.

I'd been trying to get Spencer enrolled in pre-school and was not earning any points with his prospective teachers. I'd missed two appointments, either having forgotten entirely or not allowing enough time to get to school.

The teachers wanted to assess Spencer's abilities before accepting him into their classes. Unbelievable. To my way of thinking, assessing learning skills prior to pre-school seemed ridiculous. *He's not even three yet, for God's sake!*

On that third attempt to enroll Spencer in school, I jogged us toward the car, buckled us in one-handed and hurriedly reversed out of the gravel drive. I'd brought Spencer with me to the old house that day, to avoid the drive back to town to fetch him.

We practiced counting to twenty and sang our ABC's as we drove. Triumphantly, I pulled in for his testing on schedule. *I'm gonna do it this time!* I finger-combed Spencer's hair into his preferred "cool spike" and held his little hand as we walked inside.

Since I was not allowed to sit with him during the evaluation process, I waited in the hall, pulling out my hair one strand at a time, not at all surprised to find a grey one. I concentrated on slowing my breathing and went over my mental lists: pick up the graduation cake; schedule vaccinations for the puppy; go get more paint. *God,* I caught myself thinking, *I hope this doesn't take too long.*

Being a mother and, therefore, a Mistress of Guilt, I felt horrible I'd spent so little time preparing Spencer for school. I'd dedicated hours to priming Deanna and Michael for their foray into school. *Poor little Spence.* The teacher came out of the testing room, beaming at Spencer's abilities, and let me off the hook.

"He has a wonderful imagination. He told the funniest story about a duck and a fireplace."

I just smiled, not bothering to fill her in on that one. I agreed to bring Spencer to class in the fall, paid the tuition and peeled out after checking for hidden police cars. *Child number three accounted for.* Three kids and two houses would have been enough, but other people and other events would continue to crop up and demand our attention as well.

John's dad had been asked to take what was called Reverse Seniority Layoff. He was going to be sixty-four and could certainly use some time off. He should have been at home enjoying the time with Nancy. Instead, he regularly showed up at the old house ready to lend a hand. Like everyone else, he was growing more and more concerned by the volume of work left undone, our pinched faces and hurried speech.

Most mornings, Gene would stroll in, coffee cup in hand, and whistle his greeting from the back door. Donning well-used overalls he kept at the old house, and a smile, he was always ready to get some things accomplished.

I came to appreciate those musical tones greatly. It meant an extra set of hands during the day. He and I were making huge strides in priming and painting. In addition to his tools, Gene also brought his new puppy, Sugar Bear. He would coddle her and make her a bed among the shelves in the upstairs landing. "There you go, my little Sugar," he would coo as he wrapped her in her favorite blanket. John swore the dog was treated better than he had been when growing up, and that was saying something.

After nosing around a bit and barking at the gear lying around, the little terrier would settle in for long naps in her cozy bed, rousing herself occasionally to look for food, which Gene generously and immediately provided.

I began to pack lunch for two and a half. I added to our break area by dragging over an old microwave. A cooler was permanently available, and the grocery bill grew. I also added a small clock as a subtle reminder of the timeline. We were a non-union shop—long breaks were not allowed.

As the move-in date loomed larger, John's mom, Nancy, began to come to the old house too. She'd drive out to see what was happening. "How about you two guys going out to dinner with Grandma?" she would ask Michael and Spencer.

It was a welcome break for them—and for me. We were working most nights with The Old Woman. When school let out, I would speed back to town to pick up the boys from my friend Mary's house. She was always good for a laugh, and I welcomed the ten-minute release she afforded me. I drove the boys back to the old house, stopping along the way at some fast-food place, throwing burgers and fries to them in the backseat. Deanna was working part-time and learning to fend for herself where food was concerned, further evidence of our sub-standard parenting.

On days when Nancy came, I knew the boys would finally get a decent meal in a stress-free environment, and I could get some serious work done without having to supervise kids. In addition, it helped save on babysitting costs—another expense we'd failed to factor into our budget. I figured I could use the money saved on meals towards Deanna's looming graduation celebration.

John was traveling extensively during this harried time and even had to attend a five-day convention in Memphis. "Can you believe the timing?" he groaned. Consumed with anxiety over our deadline, I doubt he heard a word that was said during that week. Meanwhile, I slept less and worked longer hours, trying to make up for his absence.

Back home from the convention, John was trying to insert himself back into the frantic routine when a woman riding her bike rammed his car. Yes, I said a bicycle hit his car. According to John, he was pulling through a drive-thru lane when the woman winged around the corner and crashed into his car. Although she toppled across the hood and landed hard on the pavement, she was relatively unharmed. The car and the bike were not.

Naturally, everyone pretended to doubt John's version of the story. "I swear, she was ticketed, not me," he insisted, as our friends and I laughed and generally gave him grief. Regardless of who had hit whom, it meant he wasn't paying any more attention to the world around him than I was.

There were three days until graduation, thirteen until we had to move. We finally started on the kitchen, the final frontier. Gene and I were in there priming the ceiling when we received a bad-news phone call: His mother had just been diagnosed with a very progressive form of cancer. The prognosis was that she had only weeks to live. Shock gripped us both and settled quietly around us.

A beautiful, earthy person, she had raised thirteen children. They'd lived off the land on their little Kentucky farm. She'd never driven a car in her life and doubted NASA had really sent a man to the moon. She rarely had a dime to her name but was one of the richest people I'd known.

Wiping tears and dust off his face, Gene cleaned up as best he could, hanging up his coveralls and peeling enamel off his hands. Nancy pulled in, and Gene got in the car. "We're gonna miss Deanna's graduation," they wailed.

"She'll understand," I assured them. "This is more important. Be safe and tell Grammie we love her too." I waved goodbye as they headed south toward a different kind of celebration—of a life well lived.

John and the kids and I stayed behind and suffered the guilty emotions of that. We simply couldn't go. Graduation, the move and the long list of things to complete was simply too long. Selfish though it was, I also mourned the loss of my fellow sidekick and painter, Gene.

Meanwhile, the other house was still calling my name. While cleaning and decorating for the party, I decided, for some inexplicable reason, that we should have a yard sale. During eighteen years of marriage, we had collected and saved the usual piles of stuff. The Old Woman had a total of three closets, a damp dungeon, and one guano-laden attic. Therefore, all the extras had to go. I stuffed bags and towed them to the curb for pickup. I cleaned, priced and stacked the remaining items into two piles: one labeled Move, the other Sell.

As promised, my mom came in town early to help clean, organize and layout things for the graduation party. She pulled in, tired from the drive and reaching for a hug. "Oh, Momma! I need you so much!" I squeezed her tight and lay my head on her shoulder, ready to be a child again. I would never have made it alone. I would have keeled over, at some point, while guests stepped over me to get their food and drinks. My organizational skills come directly from my mother, so I happily let her take over.

Unfortunately, Deanna was not the sole center of attention on party day. The old house and our work there took the cake instead. Everyone wanted to know how we were coming along with the house. Not very fair to our girl, but we had to go with the flow, and answered questions and provided details. We could only hope she'd understand. She hung out with her friends, smiling throughout.

Michael's last day of school with his Outdoor Olympic Games opened without me in attendance. I packed him a special picnic lunch and a note from Mommy:

"I love you, Michael. I promise things will get better once we move. We'll play and explore, okay? Have a great time today! Love, Mom."

He proudly showed me the blue ribbon he'd won in the tug-of-war, and I staggered at having missed such an important event. I tucked him in, trying not to cry. *What have I done?*

Yard sale day came and went, and, with it, all that stuff I'd carefully priced. We had only eleven days left before the move, and I began to drive slowly past Dumpsters, eyeing them for empty boxes. Quickly, yet carefully, I packed up our dishes and towels for a move we weren't ready to make.

I would have loved to have climbed up on The Old Woman's roof and shouted, "Stop this ride! I want off!" Of course, the way my luck was running, I would have either been struck by lightning or sideswiped by returning bats. Months earlier, I had imagined our journey would be like a roller-coaster ride. In that, at least, I had been right. The whole experience had been similar to living in a perpetual amusement park world. We careened out of control on harrowing rides, evaded and dodged bullets like ducks in the shooting arcade, experienced nausea from bad food, and looked into empty wallets with surprise.

I swore if one more person looked at me and said, "God never gives us more than we can handle," I would scream like a banshee and throttle them. Whoever came up with that cliché was not knee-deep in a quagmire.

I set aside the last of the boxes and headed toward my bed. I brushed my hair, my teeth, and ignored the mirror. Despite the recent experience of praying in corners, I didn't say any good-night prayers. I should have. Maybe the roller coaster wouldn't have been so frightening if I'd had a partner, someone who would have sat by me and held my hand when things got scary.

Chapter 20

Crow Pie

I sat at my desk, balancing the checkbook and paging through emails that had piled to the point of being ridiculous. I glanced at the calendar. *Ten days? My God, we'll never make it.* I rolled my head back on my shoulders, and, running a hand across my neck, tried to ease the tension. *What are we going to do?* Acting on a whim, I quickly composed, what I hoped to be, a clever little poem, using Dr. Seuss as my model. Across the top, I copied and pasted a cartoon of crows on a telephone line, added a bright border of tools down both sides and sat back to study the flier I had just completed.

This is not easy for us to admit
But we're gonna need help with our old money pit
There are dozens and dozens of things to be done
We're not laughing and it's no longer fun

The clock is ticking and the deadline is near
"We're not gonna make it" is our constant fear
We're thin and frazzled and falling apart
The horse is dead and we have no cart

We're swallowing our pride and eating crow pie
Can you possibly help as the next week goes by?
Assembling, fixing, sanding and painting

We can't get it done without croaking or fainting

Assistance this Saturday would sure make us smile
It can be any time, anyhow, any while
We'll take any form of help you can spare
We'll get over the hump and come up for air

We'll greet you and feed you and ply you with drinks
It might be more fun than anyone thinks
We'll owe major favors, which we'll gladly repay
If only, if only you can help us that day.

It may have been clever, but I despised the stupid thing with its begging request but felt I had no choice. I printed off copies and waited until dark had fallen and no one was out. I briefly considered using Deanna's car instead of mine but decided that was ludicrous. If I wore dark glasses and scrunched down behind my steering wheel, I should be fairly inconspicuous. Driving slowly, I slunk through the darkened streets, stuffing the hated fliers into the mailboxes of our friends and neighbors.

John and I had no reserves left in our tanks. We were shot, empty and completely out of options. I was close to tears and flooded with shame as I distributed our call for help.

I dreaded the response. I worried there would be laughter and jokes at our expense and many an "I told you so." I worried everyone would speak scornfully about us, and about how out of our minds we were to have taken on The Old Woman in the first place. I worried what everyone would say about our inability to complete the house on our own. I worried no one would come on Saturday. I'd only given three day's notice. Stuffing the last flier in the final box, I drove home and worried some more.

Had I only known what was really happening, I would have rested much easier over the next few days. As fliers were retrieved, a collective sigh could almost be heard in the neighborhood. Our friends had known we were sinking and were helpless in knowing how to offer assistance. For months, our pride had flashed in their faces: "Stay Back. Stay Back.

We can do this." Sending out that simple request had let loose a logjam and conversations began to buzz from house to house. They met at the end of the driveways and discussed our predicament, deciding who could go and who could not.

John and I, oblivious to all those conversations, arrived at the old house early that Saturday morning. The boys were with one their aunts for the day, and Deanna was safely at work. Despite having the place to ourselves, neither John nor I got a thing done. We spent our time worrying and wondering instead.

"Do you think anybody will show?" John asked, looking out the kitchen window for maybe the tenth or eleventh time.

Standing behind him, I spotted a small miracle. "Yes!" I shouted, sloshing coffee out of my cup in my excitement. "There's a car pulling in now!"

We ran out onto the old porch to see which brave souls had answered our cry for help. "Look, here comes another car! We've got four people."

"Oh my God! Here come two more cars!" Once again, we danced on the old porch and high-fived each other, just as we had done when we met The Old Woman four short months and a million years ago. The Old Woman stepped onto the porch too, following the sound of our voices.

We three stood there in wonderment as seventeen fresh, beautiful faces emerged from their respective cars, carrying smiles and tools. They filed toward the house, already joking and laughing with one another.

"About time you admitted you needed some help!" Mike shook John's hand.

"No kidding. You've helped us, over and over, it's our turn." Tony pulled me into a hug.

We learned those who couldn't come that day were babysitting and feeding the neighborhood kids while their parents came to our aid—everyone doing more than their share.

Tears of gratitude slipped down my face. I didn't bother to wipe them away as there were more where those had come from. I was overcome by our friends' generosity and humbled to the very soles of my boots. John, too, was deeply affected. He clutched my hand tightly as he hugged and shook hands with each person coming through our front door. It was one of those moments where you know people are inherently good, and a world that had tipped off its' axis suddenly righted itself.

There was plenty of laughter that day, but no derision in the sound. There were jokes too, but not at our expense. There was music, talking, and wonderful, sweet chaos, all of which, when combined, made a beautiful symphony. The Old Woman swayed softly to the music of our friends. "Just look at all of these people! You two are very lucky, you know that?" Oh, yes, we knew.

Before starting work, we shared a quick meal together, which somehow made the picture complete. It wasn't anything fancy—just cans of soda, chips, and sub sandwiches. It was, by far, one of the best lunches I've ever had. We sat on coolers and floors and spilled over each other on the staircase, passing food and camaraderie back and forth. Breaking bread with a group of people you care about brings a sense of community and oneness that is nothing short of holy.

Once the remainder of lunch was packed away, quick tours were conducted with an overall explanation of what needed to be done. Skills were assessed and crews assembled. "Who can do what?" John and I asked the group.

One man, a pilot who was often gone, ambled toward us, with his wife in tow, and confessed, "We have zero talent. We know nothing about any of this, but give us *something* to do, something easy."

We didn't even know him that well and were amazed to see him there. He often missed the bonfires, jetting off to some other part of the country. We took him and his wife to the kitchen and handed them a crowbar and a hammer, explaining they could remove the old windows.

"Do what? What if I break them?" He looked scared.

"We honestly don't care," we assured him. "Just take out the old ones so we can put the new ones in."

"You don't care if we break them?" he asked again, just to be sure.

"Nope."

"Okay! I can do this." He grinned and said to his wife, Kim, "Ready, honey?"

Laughing, she rolled her eyes at me. "I hope you know what you've just done!"

Tony and another friend Al, who lived near the cul-de-sac, wanted to know where to begin. John took them to the back staircase. "We need you to level each step." They stood, one tall and one short—bookends to John in the middle, their mouths frozen into perfect O's.

"Huh? I don't know how to build steps. Do you?" Al asked his partner.

"Haven't a clue," Tony replied. They looked at each other, obviously wondering what in the hell they'd volunteered for anyway.

John elaborated. "It's not that hard and doesn't need to be pretty. We're gonna put carpet over 'em anyway. Just get 'em level." He quickly showed them how to cut new tread boards, shim with small wedges of wood, check the level, and nail on the new pieces.

"Okay, we can do that. Cut, shim, level, nail. Got it." Saws humming, they started to work and were soon telling each other what to do.

There was the sound of glass breaking and muffled laughter from the kitchen. John and I looked at each other and decided not to investigate.

I began rounding up painters and sanders, overjoyed at the prospect of seven or eight sets of hands. I took a slow circle around my eager friends and beamed. Two men from our street, Jason and Brad, had driven over together and were offering their painting services. Cindy and Jim stood beside me, ready to go, smiling and waiting for direction. "Where should we start?"

Another wonderful couple, Darla and Jim, stood in front of me too. Darla looked at me and gave an apologetic, yet beautiful smile. "I'm a terrible painter. I need something different."

Her husband, Jim, nodded. "It's true. I'm a painter, she's not."

"That's okay. Jim, I'm going to have you put another coat in Spencer's room. Hang on, Darla. I'll find something for you in a minute." Jim followed behind me, waiting patiently, as always, for instructions.

Ensconced in a car seat, on the back landing, a baby slept soundly. Her mother, Jeannine, one of my sanders, stopped periodically to check on her, laughing that her baby girl could sleep through all the racket. "Why can't she sleep this well at home?"

I stepped quietly past her sweet, drooling baby and into the master bedroom, to find my babysitter-friend Mary lying on top of the closet ledge, painting the ceiling Michelangelo style.

"Girl, you've got already got paint in your hair!" I climbed up the ladder and laughed at the white enamel streaking her short blond-brown head.

She didn't seem to care. "I needed a haircut anyway."

"I love you guys," I called out to the house in general, and climbed off the ladder to finish delegating.

Darla was still waiting, and Karen had jogged up the stairs to find me. She and Mike had been talking to John downstairs. "Hey, Girlfriend! I don't really want to paint. What else do you need?"

I hugged both women. "Can either of you run a drill or use a level?" Karen said yes, and Darla said no, but quickly added, "I can follow instructions though!"

I rounded up the new shelving for the closets and showed them how to find the studs, set the screws and level the shelves. "What do you think? Can you two put these up in our closet?"

They nodded their agreement. I was ecstatic as they started to fuss and cuss things into place. "Watch out for Mary up above you!" I called over my shoulder, "She's messy as hell!"

"I heard that," a muffled voice answered from the top of the room.

"Does anybody know how to do drywall mudding?" John asked the dwindling pool of potential workers downstairs.

Doug stepped forward, nodded and grabbed a trowel. John practically kissed his feet. We were way behind in that department, having lost Gene to Kentucky. I could do mudding but wasn't very fast, so John was thrilled to have speed for a day. The two of them opened a bucket of mud and started plastering and smoothing, working out a rhythm that made me feel a bit jealous.

The remaining three were given their choice: assemble a bathroom vanity or lay the sub-flooring in the kitchen. The newcomer to our group, Dave, volunteered to put the vanity together. "As long as there's some sort of instruction sheet, I should be okay." He worked with John and had heard about our push day. Bless his heart, despite not knowing any of the other people there, he'd introduced himself during lunch and then sat back to enjoy the show. I reached over to give him a bear-sized hug. "Thank you, thank you, thank you."

The only woman left, Jennifer, volunteered to be in charge of clean-up and gofer duty instead. "I can't do the other stuff, but I'll keep things clear and moving along. Hand out drinks, if needed."

"Great," I said, "that's usually my job. I'll help lay the kitchen floor with Mike instead." I laughed at his expression which clearly said, *'Oh no, I have to work with a woman.'*

"Chill out, dude. I promise I'm a good carpenter. Call out measurements, and I'll do the cutting for you!"

Hours went by. Still they stayed, working to the end of the day to make sure everything was done. As the day wound toward a close, bodies were tired, and spirits lagged. Several of our friends went from room to room to goad each other into working harder.

"Is this all you've gotten done?"

"What? Are you on break in here?"

"You certainly got an easy job! Want to trade?" The ploy had been successful, making everyone work faster.

Night dropped a dark blanket over the house. Tools were gathered, and our friends prepared to leave. John and I stood arm in arm on The Old Woman's porch, waving goodbye to each one. I'd found one of my fliers, folded and lying in the foyer, and clutched it in my free hand. I'd re-read my request for help and thought about the day I'd reluctantly typed it out on the computer.

I'd tried to mimic Dr. Seuss in general and wondered if maybe I should have used his Grinch as my model instead. John and I had certainly been grumpy and grouchy, stressed and unhappy at the turn of events in our lives. Perhaps our schedules had been too tight or our hearts too small. On that day though... our hearts grew ten sizes in all.

Dusty and tired but smiling, John and I put the rest of the tools away, settled the house to rights, and softly bid her a good night. For the first time in many months, we had hope, and I wondered if our chests could expand wide enough to take in the events of the day.

The Old Woman lingered in the foyer, looked in the rooms and marveled at what had been accomplished. All that laughter, the ringing of tools, the joking conversation, the cooing of the baby, the soothing voice of the mother had relaxed and pleased her. "It's been too long since there's been a baby here. And would you just look at what those folks got done today!"

On the ride back to town, John and I talked fast, trying to remember all the details, the conversations and comments. With people working all over the house, we'd each missed individual moments of the day. "Did you see John and Kim's faces when we walked in the kitchen and saw all that broken glass?" I laughed, remembering their big eyes.

"God, that was priceless! They looked like two little kids caught with their hand in the cookie jar!" John shook his head at the picture.

"You need to write everybody's name down on the back of that flier," John tapped the flier I still held. "I don't want to ever forget who was there to help us today."

I smiled at him and agreed to take care of it as soon as we got home. "I guess swallowing crow pie wasn't so bad after all, was it?"

"No, it didn't taste as bad as I thought it would. We're pretty lucky you know?"

"Blessed. That's the word you're looking for. We're blessed with a great family and wonderful friends." I took his hand, and he squeezed back.

I thought about those thumbprints and echoes I'd imagined, those of persons long gone who had perhaps left a bit of their spirits behind, lingering and whispering within the old house. I knew there had been many more such signatures and voices left behind that Saturday in June.

I would never again walk my previously crooked back staircase without remembering the two who had fixed them. Now, when I put my clothes in The Old Woman's closets, I would hang them on memories. When I admired a new vanity, I would remember a friend. When I looked out kitchen windows that were clear and bright, I would see smiling back at me the faces of those who had sweated them into their frames. The walls, dry-walled, painted and bright, would echo with the sound of our friends' voices. Even my kitchen floor, still crooked despite all my efforts, held the imprint of a neighbor's hands and knees.

Thumbprints—echoes, all of them. Maybe, someday, long after we were gone, newer owners would become aware of them too. Maybe a sudden smile would light their faces for no discernible reason. Maybe a feeling of connectedness and at-oneness would wash over them and make their skin tingle. God, I hoped so.

CHAPTER 21

Who Else Has a Problem Today?

Thunder punched an angry fist against the window, waking us up on day eighty-five. We groaned our way out of bed, trying to ignore the aches and pains brought on by yet another weekend of demanding work. Our friends had made it a successful one, but our muscles ached anyway. John slowly pulled on dress pants and a crisp shirt. I eased my way into shorts and a tank top that should probably have been thrown away. We shuffled downstairs for coffee.

"What's on your schedule today?"

"Me?" John peered over the top of the sports page. "God, nothing but meetings today. I've got one at nine, eleven and four. How 'bout you?"

"Me?" I copied. "Did you forget? I get to supervise carpet and vinyl-flooring installation! Too cool. We've got a bunch of inspections scheduled today too. I can't believe we're almost done, can you?" I bunched my shoulders up and grinned all over myself. "We did it!"

"I can't believe we're this far. Honestly, I don't remember half of what we've done. Thank God for friends and family, huh? You and I would be dead in the backyard about now."

We waved goodbye as we prepared to approach very different jobs.

Despite the rain, I was excited. There were still things to do, but I allowed satisfaction to surface that morning. I turned up the radio and held a loud and boisterous car concert, making up my own off-key verses.

The roofs are done. Yeah. Yeah. Yeah.
The siding is on. Boom. Boom. Boom
We've got heat now. We've got lights now. The bats are gone now.

With my hair flying around and my shoulders moving to the beat, I made it to the house in record time. I finished with a great drum solo, tapped out on the dashboard, just as I pulled into the old driveway. Had I known how the day would actually unfold, I would have stayed in bed with the covers pulled high. I certainly would not have been singing or doing drum rolls.

I walked in ready and, thankfully, oblivious. "Hey, house! It's me," I called out my greeting. "Wait 'til you see what's going on today!" Still dancing to my own song, I puttered around for an hour or so. I sanded the kitchen, the last room to do, while waiting on the legions of workers to show. Two vans pulled into the drive and my pulse quickened with anticipation.

A crew of five hauled in roll after roll of carpet, padding, tack strips and the paraphernalia which goes with such things. I directed traffic, trying to save the work we'd done by blocking off areas and laying down some plastic. Materials were hauled into every room, and the noise was deafening.

The vinyl-siding contractor and his assistant walked into the kitchen. The contractor carried a clipboard and a thermos of coffee. He needed to make sure everything was completed correctly before the guttering could be hung. Over the course of six weeks, three roofs and all new siding, we'd gotten to know one another and chatted and joked easily.

"Girl, you look worse than Pigpen!" He laughed at my drywall-dusty face and clothes.

"Careful or I won't give you your money!"

It was nearing eleven o'clock when the carpet installers approached with what was to become the first of an onslaught of problems. They couldn't install the carpet until all of the doors were taken off their hinges.

Not willing to let anything spoil my mood, I simply asked, "Why? They've all been cut to make room for the carpeting."

"It's not the height. We can't get the pad and carpet stretched underneath the doors while they're hanging."

"Oh, that makes sense. Go ahead and stack 'em in the halls or even on the porches. Whatever works." I assumed they'd simply needed permission. I turned to steal coffee from the contractor's thermos.

Feet shuffled, and I turned around. Their eyes were downcast. "You don't understand. We can't remove the doors. There's a liability clause."

Not one of those again. As there was no shortage of doors in the old house, I was stunned. *Shouldn't we have been told about the removal of doors before the arrival of installers?* I stood there in the foyer staring at the nine-and-a-half-foot, solid doors to the living room and knew I was in trouble.

"I can't remove those two doors by myself! They're too heavy. Can you at least help with those?" I pointed at the offensive doors, sure there must be a compromise in there somewhere.

They looked at the doors and then at skinny me. Finally comprehending, they answered, "We can't remove the hardware, but we could probably catch the doors, so they don't fall." They were nodding at each other and proud of themselves for their concession.

"Well, that's good to know. Glad you can help." I was getting ticked.

Five men were going to stand around while I climbed up a ladder and worked out one-hundred-year-old hinges and hardware. I shoved the ladder into place and slung around tools, just in case there was anyone present who was unaware of my mood. I hoped to guilt them into activity, but it didn't work.

My siding buddy had followed me into the foyer and had been listening to the exchange and watching my expression. He was equally pissed at the carpet people, and stated with disgust, "You've got to be kidding, man. I'll help."

I was feeling more than a bit self-conscious up on the ladder in my shorts. The five men had gathered around in readiness to catch the doors, and, I was convinced, a glimpse or two while they were at it. I held the drill in one hand and tried to yank my shorts longer with the other. I was grateful for one chivalrous man and anxious to speed up the process. I gave him, and only him, a smile.

We moved through the house, taking down doors and shooting daggers at the lesser life forms moving in behind us to install carpeting. However, even my hero abandoned me, when he saw the two gutter guys pull in. Reminiscent of my father, I muttered to myself as I removed the last two doors.

The rain was pouring, and I was steaming. As I stacked my last door in the hallway, I saw yet another car pulling in. Before I could race downstairs to stop him, the water inspector stepped past people and tools and tracked across my hour-old kitchen floor. *Unbelievable. What a jerk.*

With hardly a "Hello," or "How are you?" he jostled bottle onto available space, poured water from the faucet into little tubes and added various chemicals. He left them on the card table I'd just shoved into a corner. The tubes bubbled and turned colors. He studied them with a frown.

"Hmm," he said, "there's a lot of Sulphur getting through."

"What does that mean? Is it harmful?" I asked, leaning around him, trying to see the bubbles.

"Don't know yet."

He tracked more mud across the kitchen and headed to the basement to set up his science experiments down there. Just what I needed—a surly alchemist in my midst.

A knock at the door brought the gas guy into the picture. He wanted me to sign off on paperwork and went on to explain the new meter and how our "free gas" actually had a yearly limit.

While I was trying to take in that bit of information and decide if we were being screwed, a strange man approached and asked where I wanted the cable TV lines run. Both my hands landed on my forehead with a smack. "Oh, man, I'm sorry. I totally forgot you were coming today. Obviously, there's a lot going on. Follow me."

More than a little flustered, I stepped over rolls of carpet to get this newest issue resolved. The Cable guy kept apologizing, so I must have been in an obvious snit.

Incredible though it seemed, one more truck entered, jockeying for position on the disappearing gravel. The electric company had arrived. He wanted to be directed to the electrical box for *his* inspection.

Fine. It required the electrician to stand on a roll of new carpet currently occupying the space, but I didn't care anymore. I needed to sign papers for him too. I bet my neighbors loved all the action going on at the old homestead. Personally, I wished I'd charged admission. It was an absolute zoo, complete with wild animals and trainers.

The electrician's arrival took the number of service people, installers and contractors to twelve. I made number thirteen and knew it wasn't a good number. Hammers and staple guns were running, cell phones were jangling, chemical reactions were bubbling, and questions were being thrown at me no matter how hard I tried to escape. I was fisting my hair and running my hands across my face.

Trying to take a much-needed break, I stepped out onto the front porch and walked right into a heated discussion between the contractor and the gutter guys. They stood in the yard and in the rain, gesturing wildly.

"What's going on?" I yelled over the din of tools and thunder.

The contractor, relieved his ally had shown up, yelled back at the porch, "They say we need to put guttering and downspouts on the porches. I say we don't. It was never in the contract. There's no allowance for the extra stuff he wants to do." His thumb jerked toward the gutter guy—the source of the problem.

The contractor looked at me, sure I would save him from the guttering imbecile. He was relying on my memory of the way he had helped me earlier with the doors.

The gutter guy shot back his defense, "You gotta have it. We always do porches. He knows that."

I looked at the water pouring off the porch roof, drowning the bushes and making safe passage to my front door virtually impossible. My barely tamped-down temper snapped.

I glared at those men, representing yet another problem, and stepped purposefully off the porch. I stood on the top step and let the water pour down on my head. I waited until I had their full attention. Slashing hair out of the way, I sputtered, "I think we definitely need guttering here, don't you? I don't care who forgot it or overlooked it. The guttering is going up, and the downspouts are going down. The two of you can work out who will be subtracting the cost from his bottom line. I won't be the one paying for lack of communication."

The contractor frowned heavily. So much for me being an ally. I suppose he wished he'd never volunteered to help take down doors, but that was already done, and it was too late. I stomped back inside, slammed the door closed and just dared something else to happen.

I didn't have to wait long. Everyone seemed to be packing up to leave. I was agreeable with the cable guy and the three inspectors heading toward the door, but where were the carpet people going? *That can't be right, can it?* There was no way they were done. I ran through the house and, sure as hell, only half of the upstairs was carpeted. I stopped them at the door, throwing my arms wide, barring their exodus. "Where are you guys going?"

"To lunch." They looked at each other as if I was stupid. Wasn't it obvious they needed to eat?

"You're kidding, right? You've only been here two hours and part of that time you did nothing because I had to take down doors."

"We can't do anything else until the landing is fixed, so we figured we'd go to lunch." They explained this to me as if I was a slow child.

"What are you talking about? Who broke the landing?" I demanded a confession.

Obviously, I had failed to understand. The crew leader, taking pity on me, led me up toward the questionable landing. It looked all right to me, and I was greatly relieved.

He pointed to the top step of the back staircase and to a kick plate area at the bottom of the landing. Both were evidently missing something, but damned if I could figure it out. I stood there looking and waiting with hands on hips. "What?! I don't see anything."

"These two areas don't have any sub-flooring on them. It means there are a different heights and thicknesses from the top step to the landing. It has to be consistent, or the carpet can't be laid out," the supervisor patiently explained.

"Let me guess—you guys can't cut the sub-flooring, right?" I was starting to get the picture. I was certainly ready to lay something out all right, and whether it was sub-flooring or installers, it didn't really matter to me at that point.

"Sorry." He backed away.

I ran a hand through my hair for what felt like the hundredth time that day, finally just holding onto a section near the top of my head and letting my chin drop toward my chest.

Deciding I was nearer to tears than violent behavior, the carpet guru graciously said, "Look, I know it's been a tough day. So, we'll take a two-hour lunch break to give you time to add the wood pieces, okay?"

"Oh. Ok. That's great. I feel better now." I lifted my head and glared at him while a deep groove formed on my forehead.

I watched from the upstairs bedroom as the driveway emptied. I registered, barely, that the porches did indeed have guttering and wondered when that had happened. Tired and dejected, I knew I had to do the flooring. There was no choice. It wasn't that I couldn't operate the saw or do the measurements; the problem was that the pieces weren't square. I recognized I wouldn't be cutting easy, forty-five-degree angles, but twenty-seven-degree polygons instead. It would require geometry, and I tasted imminent failure.

I thought about the hours I'd struggled in geometry class years before. I'd wondered then when I would ever use the stuff. As I stood there looking at the polygons needed, I found myself wishing I'd paid more attention.

Slogging down a Coke and three cookies, I went to measure, think and attempt to draw a template for the step and landing. I cut four pieces, none of which fit, and had to start over. Twice. The allotted two hours flew past, and I was scrambling. I need not have worried. The installer's two-hour lunch turned into more like three, and my own stomach protested loudly at its meager meal. Although not pretty, I got one of the kick plates done and nailed into place.

John called on the cell phone, sounding cheerful and upbeat for once. He was in between meetings, having lunch, and checking in on me. "How are things going, Hon? Is the carpet in?"

My sudden sobbing no doubt confused him. I hadn't cried in front of him about the old house and all of her problems during the whole process.

"What's wrong? Are you hurt?"

With hitching breaths, I told him about my completely miserable day and the fateful events. "Everything is a mess. I can't take it, anymore!"

He turned cheerleader. *Wonder where he got that idea?* "You're doing great, babe. I'm so proud of you. We're going to make it. Hold on a little longer."

Those words did wonders and gave me new determination. I finished the last of the carpentry and cleared the way for the carpet installers. There was nothing left for me to do but scrounge for more food. I was afraid to leave. If I did, the installers would return, find me gone, and call it a day. We didn't have a day.

They were a bit surprised I'd done the work, and I lorded it over them haughtily. There were no more excuses, no more problems allowed. "Put in the damn carpet!" my stance shouted.

I was going to be there a while, no doubt about that. At three-thirty that afternoon, I called Mary and explained the situation. "Can you keep the boys a little longer today? Deanna will be home around 5:30."

More than three hours later, the house was completely carpeted, the vinyl was laid, and I was systematically removing all traces of the worker, installers, and inspectors. I checked our little clock in the kitchen, stunned it was already seven. *What happened to my day?*

"Hey, Deanna. It's Mom. Is Dad home yet?"

"No, he just called, said he got stuck in a meeting and should be home around eight."

I closed my eyes. *Breathe. Come on, girl, breathe.*

"Honey, I know you've had the boys awhile, but I need a couple more hours here, and I'll be home, okay?"

"I got it, Mom, no problem. I made 'em eat grilled cheese. They're both in the bathtub right now."

"I'm so sorry to put you through this. We're almost done though, just a little longer. Thanks, babe. You're a life-saver." I hung up and found a package of crackers. I started to put the phone in my purse but hit redial instead.

"Hey, Deanna. It's me again. I forgot to tell you I love you. Please tell the boys Mom's almost done and she'll be home to tuck them in, okay?"

"Mom, it's ok. I'll tell them. Oh, and by the way, I love you too."

Snapping the phone closed, I looked at it for a few seconds more, absorbing my children through a wireless connection.

Knowing all was well at the home front, I found some sort of energy reserve and joyfully vacuumed up pieces of carpet fuzz and scrubbed the bathroom floor, neither of which were chores I had ever enjoyed until that day.

I was semi-dazed by the day, the time and the energy exerted. I'd been there almost thirteen hours but took time to wander through the house one more time. I shut off the lights as I went. "We did it! I can't believe it, but we did it! You look wonderful!" I told The Old Woman as I walked out the door. Miraculously, it had all gotten done.

The Old Woman kept looking at herself, amazed, turning from side to side to see better. She stood there in a new dress, hat, and shoes. She heard music, old and new, echoing from upstairs and down. "When does the dance start?"

Chapter 22

Ready, Set, ~~Move~~ Stop

J ohn and I got up early, showered, shaved and chose nice clothing, for a change. "I can't wait!" I yelled from our bathroom while applying mascara and lip-gloss.

"I know, me too!" he agreed, tucking in his shirt and looping his belt.

He'd taken a vacation day, and the two of us laughed and joked as we made our way to Lowe's. It was time to choose the cabinets and counters for the kitchen, our final frontier. Everything else was finished. Well, almost. There were a few closets to build, but that seemed a small thing compared to what we'd accomplished.

"We're gonna make it. I can't believe it." John turned down the radio and smiled at me.

"Four days…we move in only four days! Who would have thought we'd be this far?" I sat back, a smug smile in place as I thought about the old house so transformed.

All two hundred sheets of drywall were hanging proudly on the freshly primed and painted walls. New windows had been scrubbed and gazed out toward a semi-trimmed and almost crispy yard. Flooring gleamed, and carpet squished softly underfoot. One bathroom was functioning. The other, a tiny afterthought in the mudroom, had been scrubbed free of grime and rust, enough to be used in an emergency. All lights were suspended from ceilings, and fans turned lazy circles in the middle of most rooms. Three full, industrial-sized Dumpsters had been removed. Even the doors sported shiny brass locks, waiting only for us to turn the key.

"Unbelievable," I responded to my thoughts. John nodded, leaving me to believe he'd just taken a similar trip down renovation lane.

"We finish the kitchen, and we're in!" John stated, and his face actually flushed.

"Ha! Take that!" I yelled our victory at Fate, Murphy, and Mother Nature. All three had tried to thwart our schedule. I cranked the radio back up to the volume I preferred.

Once at the store, we held hands and playfully tugged one another towards fabulous finds. Having agreed on beautiful, scrolled cherry cabinets with antiqued knobs, I squeezed John into a hug and proclaimed, "These are going to be awesome! Just what we wanted."

The proverbial shoe, the one we should have been expecting, dropped out of the sky and struck us on the head. "These will be delivered in six to eight weeks," the sales associate smiled triumphantly, having just typed in our order.

"What?!" John dropped my hand and glared at the clerk.

"Six to Eight weeks? We need these today!" I pleaded, and I'm sure, pouted.

It had never occurred to us that we would need to order our pretty cupboards. Our smiles slid off our faces, and our heads dropped. Swallowing disappointment, we chose lesser, but available cabinets and carted the boxes back to The Old Woman. We didn't laugh one time.

Each cabinet required assembly and a precision fit to connect them all together. While John started on that project, I headed back to the store to purchase countertops and appliances. We'd never gotten around to purchasing them either, knowing they'd only be in the way. Besides, we had to keep waiting for payday. The checking account definitely ran low at times, and we knew the kitchen would not come free.

I carefully maneuvered my truck and Gene's large, flatbed trailer across The Old Woman's yard. Ever mindful of how the trailer was positioned, I got fairly close to the porch and decided it would have to do. Jumping out, I headed through the door, eager to see my new kitchen.

I skidded to a stop when I got inside. John was sitting in the middle of the floor, surrounded by unopened cabinet boxes and tools. He had assembled one corner cabinet during my absence. *One cabinet?* I spun a quick circle, trying to understand. I wasn't sure how to approach him as he looked dangerous again. "What happened?" I cautiously asked. I would have liked to have screamed, "Is this all you got done?" but bit my tongue.

"Nothing happened. Can't you see that? The damn floor is still crooked, and the cabinets are a son-of-a-bitch to get level. I couldn't go any further until the appliances are in place, so I've just been sitting here staring."

"Hon, I've been gone almost three hours," I wailed.

"I know." He threw his hand up in exasperation. "I can't help it. I'm shot. Did *you* have any luck?"

I had been through a series of small irritations in getting cheap counters cut and the appliance crates loaded, but they all seemed small when I looked at his face.

I forced a pleasant tone. "Yep, sure did. Everything's outside." He was ready to crack, and I was ready to crumble. We had no choice but to stumble forward.

We hauled, opened, and assembled all I'd brought home and timidly tried on smiles as the room finally began looking like a kitchen. Pushing and sliding the stove and dishwasher into place, we had at least one corner finished— and a place to begin building the damn cabinets.

"Your hand is smaller. See if you can reach up here and tighten that nut." John was lying on his back, head inside a partial cabinet, working up a sweat trying to maneuver the socket wrench.

"You put the door on upside down," I announced, standing back to look at what we'd completed.

The clock said seven p.m., and the day, which had been no vacation at all, was over. John went outside to unhook the trailer. The Old Woman, taking advantage of his absence, wandered into the kitchen. "It's almost done! We'll be dancing in no time."

I sighed and closed my eyes. "We're not going to make it after all." I looked at the one, sad corner we'd finished and the number of cabinets left to build. "I can't believe it's still so crooked." I shook my head sadly, turned out the lights and left.

Honey, Honey, Honey. The Old Woman's heavy brows lifted at my tone. *The foundation is solid, you know that. The rest...well, think of it as character. Dance with me. Celebrate. It's gonna be fine. You just wait and see.*

Stressed again, we spent the next three days in a fog. I moved boxes, toys, clothes and anything small enough for me to lift in and out of my truck. John spent all day at his paying job, and then came home to more work in the still-evolving kitchen. Anguishing over leveling cabinets and trying to piece them all together, he stayed late into the night.

I made trip after trip up and down three levels, emptying one house, only to carry it all up and down three more levels at the other. Bewildered, tired, I shoved boxes into corners and half-built closets. The Manson rooms over the kitchen took the bulk, as no one was willing to sleep there. "I will never buy a stair-stepper!" I vowed, absently rubbing my thighs.

We exhausted ourselves and, despite our efforts, didn't finish the kitchen. Half the cabinets still needed to be built, including a double pantry which would be bolted to one wall. The countertops needed to be glued and the sink connected. It floated, lopsided, in the hole we'd cut in the counter, not fastened into place or hooked to the plumbing. I would simply buy drinking water and use paper plates until conditions improved.

Moving day was upon us. Naturally, John had a huge sales meeting and would not be available. "Right. Sure. I bet he's sitting at his desk with his feet up," I mumbled to myself.

Because we were basically down to the furniture, kitchen utensils, and food, the move didn't seem like it would be daunting. Once again, I rounded up three of our nephews, Deanna and her boyfriend, Dan. Refusing to pay one more dime on babysitting, Michael and Spencer were going to have to help that day too. Gene, who had returned home from Kentucky, was in charge of driving his truck and the long trailer. Thank God. I would drive my truck too, taking as much as we dared each trip.

Already muggy at seven in the morning, the day only promised to get worse. Slowly, furniture, mattresses and mirrors were fit onto the trailer. Instructions and warnings were called to one another.

"Tie that strap down tighter!" Gene commanded his grandchildren.

"Spencer, get off the couch!" I yelled, but then cracked a tiny smile. He was so damn cute. He'd plopped down in the center of the sofa and sat, feet swinging, waiting to be lifted onto the trailer.

Scooby-Doo ran smack through the middle of the waiting boxes and furniture stacked along the driveway. The dog's tongue hung out, and his tail swished at fifty miles an hour. As expected, Michael charged around the corner in hot pursuit. "Michael! Tie him up—he's in the way!" I hollered at him too so he wouldn't feel slighted. At my tone, his eyes grew big, and he backed into a box. I smiled to soften the blow.

Teenagers were assembled into open spaces, on the trailer, and instructed to hold onto things as our slow procession began. It was only eight miles, but we dared not go more than twenty, maybe twenty-five miles per hour for fear of losing furniture or family members. We made five long trips that day, each taking more than two hours to haul, unload, carry and place.

The temperatures rose in direct proportion to our deteriorating energy supply. After load four, all nine of us collapsed in the shade of the huge trees in the front yard of the old house. We were catching our breath and praying for a breeze. Straps, blankets, Cokes, and bodies littered the front yard. To anyone driving past, we resembled fallen soldiers and a battle lost.

It was at that point an old pick-up truck pulled into the drive. A gray-haired, bowlegged farmer strolled into the melee, stepping past bodies to stand over me. His jeans were too tight for a man his age, and his boots were old, the leather cracked and gnarled.

"Seen ya around for a while and been meaning to stop in," he said as an introduction.

I reluctantly pulled myself up from the cool grass to shake his hand.

"I live around the corner from here and thought ya might like to know 'bout your house here." He took off his hat, ran his hand through disappearing hair and grinned. The wad of tobacco in his cheek made his words run together.

What did that mean? Was there something really wrong? Other than bats, of course.

As it turned out, he wanted to share history with me. I really wanted to know but only got the gist of what he was saying.

"Gotcha beat by three years! I did the history check already."

He waited for me to answer, but all I could do was nod. He looked around for a spot clear of bodies and hocked out a long stream of brown tobacco juice.

Oooh, gross!

He transferred excess brown spittle from his chin to his jeans and continued, "See this all used to be one big ol' farm. Over a hundred acres—and ya know what that crazy boy, from Carolina, grew?" he asked, enjoying himself, and settling in for a long story.

"What boy from Carolina?" I shook my head, trying to understand.

"The one who had this farm and built the house. I told ya that." His smile faltered, and his tone grew sharp, reprimanding me for not listening.

I shook my head and offered him a Coke. *Guess I'm not supposed to participate.*

"Now, where was I? Oh, onions. Yep, that's what they grew—onions. A hundred acres of the stuff." He took a sip, spit again.

My warriors were showing signs of life and climbing up from the lawn.

"See no one 'round here grew onions, so they musta had the market cornered. Got rich, I reckon." He rambled on with names, years and his own slant on things. "A second brother came and built right onto your old house here." He spat again.

I knew the house had been set up as an early duplex but had never known why. I was fascinated and had dozens of questions. Unable to catch them as they spun away in my hot little brain, I stayed silent. The trailer was being checked, and people were getting into trucks. I would have loved to have stayed there in the shade and listened to a story, I just couldn't.

"I'm really sorry to cut you short, but we've got to keep going here. Everything has to be moved today."

"Oh. Okay then. I understand." He seemed hurt and began to move toward his truck.

"I really want to hear your story. Give me your name and address, and I'll stop in to see you next week."

That seemed to make him feel better, and he rattled off some name and a group of numbers. "Good luck, neighbor," he called. He waved lazily and drove away.

I promptly forgot his name and the name of the previous owners and racked my mind the whole way back to the other house. No one else could remember either having been too hot and tired. "I'll find him next week," I promised myself. We moved the final load as though in mud, working to move our legs through the humidity and sweat.

"Come on! This is the last load. We can do it!" Deanna called in her exuberant fashion

It was a successful day in that it all got there in one piece and we only made one small tear in the new kitchen floor, trying to walk/slide the fridge into place. Gene, exhausted for the hundredth time that summer, drove himself and the nephews toward home. My kids and I headed back toward the other house for our last night there.

The Old Woman had watched us drive away, excited to find herself filled with belongings again. "One more day," she pinched herself, hardly believing that so much had happened. She wandered through the rooms, taking inventory and getting comfortable with our things and their placement. She ran her fingers across dressers, peeked into boxes and sat on the couch. "This is going to be wonderful. I can't believe there will finally be another family here."

She settled in, letting memories flood her. A car sped by on the road, and she remembered it being quieter; the road had been dirt, and harnesses jangled as horses lumbered past with loads. The headlights from yet another car caught the new light hanging in the living room, and she thought back to her childhood when there'd been no electricity. Previous families had sat together, reading, or talking until the last of the day disappeared. The wood burner would be stoked for the night and tired, farmer bodies followed flickering candlelight as they lumbered off toward their beds.

She shook herself, got up from the couch and looked in the kitchen. Folding arms across her chest, she traveled back to a time when she'd been newer and smaller. Looking at the completely revamped room, she was amazed. *Things have certainly changed.*

Her eyebrows went up at the number of boxes stacked every which way. *You've still got some work in here, don't you?* She admired the new stove and bent down to look at herself in the glossy dishwasher panel. *Wonder what this thing does?* Turning, she smiled at the large table we'd set up between the windows and the fireplace. *Lord, but there have been a lot of dinners in here!*

She climbed the curved staircase, marveling that it was actually the *third* set built as previous families had grown and left their mark on the old house. As she continued upstairs, she thought about the alterations, changes, and additions that had been made, throughout her one hundred sixty years.

Reaching the top, she saw the number of boxes and totes piled in the room over the kitchen. "Goodness, where are you going to put all these things?" She tilted her head to read the labels: Christmas, Easter, and Winter Sweaters. She walked to the desk and gingerly reached out to touch the computer. "The last family had one of these. Strange."

She made her way onward. Looking at the finished bathroom, she shook her head at those earlier inhabitants who had used chamber pots or braved the elements to run across the yard. "Times have changed, haven't they, old girl?"

She smiled at the stuffed animals, toys and books piled in the boys' two rooms. She noted Michael's baseball hats and hoped he would keep the balls outside.

Holding the rails, she made her way slowly down the back staircase. The section had been added when she was nine. "What a mess that was—two families living side by side." The Old Woman shook her head at the memory and crowded living conditions.

She stood in Deanna's room, noting that she'd already hung up a few posters and that bright, near-psychedelic curtains were laid across the bed. A phone was already hooked to the wall, and the stereo had been given a place of honor. "Teenagers...at least they never change!"

Having made a complete circuit, she was breathing hard. "I've turned into a rather large woman," she huffed. Overall, she was quite pleased with our things and us. She'd survived major reconstructive surgery and was ready, more than ever, to join her new family in the celebration. "Guess I'm not too old after all." She curled up for one last, lonely nap at about the time the lights were going down in an almost empty house across town.

After dinner and showers, I puttered around, cleaning empty rooms. The kids were sleeping in the family room on a thick pallet of blankets and pillows. It allowed me to completely scour their rooms, wipe down walls, and vacuum. John and I were to share a similar pallet in our bedroom, leaving the rest of the house barren. I walked to the basement, thinking back on Halloween parties and our friend's ridiculous costumes through the years. Already empty, the basement seemed hollow and sad. I turned off the lights and went back upstairs.

I looked out windows at our darkened yard, shaking my head at one of the largest swing sets I'd ever seen. We'd had so much fun designing and building the thing. "John and I never do anything small, do we?" I asked myself, seeing Michael swinging high in my mind's eye.

I opened the sliding door, stepping outside to admire the deck we'd spent months constructing. We'd added safety gates to contain Spencer. I laughed at the memory of his numerous attempts to escape. I pictured Deanna and her friends congregated around the wrought-iron table, eating pizza and laughing.

Closing the patio door, I tiptoed past sleeping children and one ugly dog. I looked into each room one more time. We'd decorated, celebrated and brought home a new baby to those spaces. We'd had great times, and although I would miss having my friends so close, I wasn't nearly as sentimental as I thought I would be. I tucked the memories away and smiled rather than cried. The move was going to be a great one, one of the best things we'd ever done. I was sure of that. I made a mental note to find the old farmer and grinned at his tobacco-laced words.

John came up behind me as I stood in the living room. He wrapped strong arms around my smaller frame and rested his chin on my shoulder. He nuzzled my neck. "Regrets?" he asked.

I shook my head and leaned further into him. "No. No regrets. Memories—we'll always have good memories of this house, but I'm ready to go." He held my hand and pulled me up the stairs toward our last night in the house on the wonderful Cul-de-sac. A home, after all, is where you hang your heart.

Chapter 23

Bat Wars Episode II: "They're Back"

We'd conquered the ninety-day deadline and physically moved in with The Old Woman. Although she suggested it many times, we did not stop to celebrate the milestone. There were too many things still going wrong.

For starters, none of the children would sleep alone in their rooms. The absolute dark of living in the country and the strange sounds that were part of the house seemed eerie and unnatural. Frogs croaked incessantly from dusk to dawn and cicadas sang fifteen-stanza love songs to one another from neighboring trees. Even The Old Woman creaked and groaned as she regulated herself to our comings and goings.

The days were no less harried. The kitchen was still only half-assembled, and we rummaged through boxes for silverware, plates, and food. Something about the center of the house—the kitchen, being in chaos, made all of us grumpy and short-tempered. I kicked an offensive box out of my way, trying to find room. I was constantly hit with a barrage of questions or requests to help locate dishes or underwear or some damn thing.

There were new rules to establish where Deanna was concerned too. Although she was gone most days, working or socializing, I demanded she enter the house through the kitchen or main front door and not come sneaking in through the door that led to her bedroom. She'd tried it once, experimenting with new freedom. I'd lost my mind.

"Okay. No problem, Mom. Jeez, it's not like I'm going to go weird on you all of a sudden!"

She had a few conditions of her own. "Tell the boys that they can't come down the backstairs! It's not a short cut. They don't even knock; they just crash through my room. It's not fair!" Sounding younger than eighteen with that final statement, I recognized her anxiety over moving and making changes.

Speaking of the boys, those two turned me into a worn, harassed, screaming and blithering idiot. They required constant supervision, and I spent the majority of my day tracking their movements through open doors or windows.

We'd never replaced the kitchen or back hallway's windows. I'd found them too charming with their tiny, foldout screens and multiple panes. The glass was old and droopy with time, distorting the backyard, giving it a hazy appearance. Several panes were cracked, also hampering my perusal of the yard and the whereabouts of the boys. The windows represented my mood; old, distorted, hazy. Emptying another box, I peeked outside anyway.

Michael threw a tennis ball against the large green target John had painted on the shed door. The ball slung back toward him and his waiting glove. The boy was bored most of the time, missing the neighborhood. We'd invented things for him to do to help fill the day. The shed was missing all the glass so he couldn't hurt anything anyway.

Locating Spencer, I sucked in a surprised breath. His naked bottom was out in the middle of the yard, and he appeared to be drawing pictures, midair, with urine. It gave a completely new meaning to "pissing in the wind."

I charged out the back door, careful of my footing on the old stoop. "Spencer! Get your pants on, boy! What are you doing?"

Spencer spun toward me, body parts hanging free. I covered my snort. The boy wasn't shy that was for damn sure.

"Daddy said I could," he insisted and tried to look sorry.

"That was only in an emergency, honey. We don't really do that! Were you born in a barn?"

Michael caught a ball and lazily replied, "No, but we live in one now." He even dared to wink at me as he said it.

I grinned at him and his developing sense of humor. *Smart-ass*, I thought to myself but loved every minute of it.

"I'll be out in a minute to play. Meanwhile," I raised my voice and looked at each of the boys, "Stay away from the cistern....out of the pond..."

"And don't play under the walnut tree." Michael and Spencer finished my sentence for me, half singing the words.

"I guess I say it all the time, huh?"

They both nodded.

Looking at their play area, if you could call it that, I decided I would continue to repeat my dire warnings, whether they liked it or not. The front yard was off limits—permanently. The cars sped by at sixty, maybe seventy miles an hour, and it scared me half to death. A dilapidated, barely-hanging-on, holes-in-the-roof, tilted-to-extreme ancient garage was out there too. I couldn't see it well from the house and worried the boys would be exploring the interior about the time it released its last breath and crumbled.

That left the backyard, complete with a still yawning cistern and a suspiciously muddy and shallow pond. Tree limbs were still strewn every which way and stumps stuck out awkwardly from the ground. I'd managed to hit one of the damn things with the mower, bending the blade beyond recognition. It had required a pipe wrench and a goodly amount of elbow grease to straighten out the blade. I had no doubt the hidden stumps could do serious injury to unsuspecting boys.

The walnut tree in question had been struck by lightning, probably during a tornado that had torn through the area several years before. As a result, it was partially uprooted and in a free-fall toward the yard. It was nearly perpendicular, and there wasn't room to walk underneath the thing without hitting your head on branches. Ants, loving the nutty piquant taste, had hollowed out most of the base, taking advantage of the tree's precarious and vulnerable condition. The tree and the old garage would probably collapse simultaneously.

Sighing at a mess that seemed universal, I took a few minutes to play catch with the boys. I made a mental note to get a sandbox soon, so they'd have something else to occupy their time. Stooping to investigate a glint in the grass, I came up with another reminder. "Don't go barefoot either!" I showed them each the glass I'd just plucked from the ground.

I needed to be everywhere at once. As a result, nothing was getting done. Attempting to catch up with laundry, the first load I ran had the rinse water backing up into the kitchen sink. "Turn it off!" I yelled down the hall. The washer was temporarily sitting in the center hallway until we could build a laundry facility.

"Get the snake," John instructed as he let loose a sigh. I trudged to the shed to paw through three toolboxes to find the long coil of metal that needed to be fed through the drain. As it worked its way back and forth through an ancient pipe, I wrinkled my nose at the black, smelly mess that encased it with each exit.

We resolved the plumbing issue, and still we faltered and failed. Hoping to correct our bad attitudes, I tried to decorate the house and make things look nice. That didn't last long. My knick-knacks soon ended up caked in construction dust.

I gave up on such domestic chores and ordered two tons of stone instead. To my way of thinking, the cistern needed to be filled immediately. It took two days, moving a shovelful at a time from the pile in the front to the hole in the back. As I creaked my rusted wheelbarrow back and forth across the yard, I remembered Mr. C.'s dismay at having to fill the holes in the bottom of the wheelbarrow. Seeing the concrete patches, I gave a rare smile.

The boys helped initially, but they didn't last long.

"I want a turn," Spencer complained, slamming his shovel across the pile.

"Ow! You cut me!" Michael yelled, looking with contempt at his sibling and the new scrape on his ankle.

Between them, they managed to get five, maybe ten rocks on their shovels before dumping them in the wheelbarrow. Waiting for them to take turns made me crazy, and I released them from duty. "Forget it!" I screamed. "Go play, for God's sake. I'll do this." They gratefully ran away with Scooby-Doo, in hot pursuit.

I watched them go and was leaning on my shovel for a quick break when I noticed Mr. Lewis crossing the road. We'd finally met the neighbors directly across from us. It turns out they'd been on an extended vacation in Florida. *You can do that when you're retired*, I thought jealously.

Weeks before, Duane and Terry had shown up unannounced and found us in the back stairway. Having come home to see our chaos and zoo-like activity, they'd crossed the road to introduce themselves. They took a tour and accessed the situation and us. They'd found the house still lacking but seemed to accept us, overall. They were tolerant, even grateful for what we were doing, often yelling encouragement across the yards. They had a good sense of humor, both of them, and we liked them immediately.

Joining me at the pile of rocks, Duane grinned and showed me the can of WD-40 he'd brought along. "That squeaky wheelbarrow is setting my hair on end! Sounds like fingernails on a chalkboard." He bent over and sprayed the wheel. "Are you planning on moving all this stone by yourself?"

"Got to. We've got an open cistern out back and two boys running around."

He shook his head. "Never saw anyone work as hard as you guys. You tell John I'll hire you when it's all done!"

"Duane, we may never be done around here." I went back to shoveling.

As we tried to return to a normal routine, I would catch myself thinking about the old farmer and his unfinished story. "I'll finish my chores, clean up and go see him this afternoon," I told myself almost every day, but before I knew it, the hours slipped past, and I was tucking in the children. "Tomorrow. I'll definitely go see him tomorrow." A week would pass.

I kept finding things to do and convinced myself that free time was not allowed. I had to earn the right to spend an afternoon listening to old stories.

When we turned the calendar to July, I finally set out to find him, relying on the directions he'd tossed my way weeks before. I pulled into a driveway and looked at what seemed a vacant farmhouse—curtains were drawn tightly, windows shut, the absence of cars and a No Trespassing sign pounded into the yard. I sat in the gravel drive and mourned.

In asking around, I learned that his farm was being swallowed in an Eminent Domain battle with the county. Until the legal fight was resolved, he'd moved away. I grieved the loss of such an interesting character and his historical tale. How could my list of inconsequential things have seemed more important?

I promised myself I would be more careful with the opportunities offered to me. I would start each day with good intentions, *and* great follow through. It worked for a week or so, and I was back to my old habits.

Determined to find peace, I began to take long walks in the mornings. I explored our property and acquainted myself with the animals living there. I invited Michael and Spencer to join me on one such foray. "Boys, come outside. I've got something to show you!" I handed them each a brown paper sack.

"There's nothing in here." Michael peeked in his bag, disappointed.

"Not yet. We'll find treasures to put in there. Trust me."

"What treasure, Mommy?" Spencer looked in his bag too.

We headed toward the field behind the pond, side-by-side, arms swinging in unison. As we rounded a stand of trees and brush, I shared my discovery. "Look! Raspberries!" We picked as fast as our hands could move, not caring that our fingers and mouths were purple. "Save some of them! Maybe I can make a pie or something." I'd never made one in my life, but who cared?

They were both filthy but smiling broadly. My heart rejoiced, knowing we'd made the right decision in moving away from normalcy and replacing it with wonder.

They talked non-stop through dinner, explaining their day and showing Daddy their new scrapes and bruises. I smiled serenely.

Two days later, John popped his head into the bathroom to see me scrubbing at my arms and pouring alcohol over the bumps there. "What's up?"

"Poison ivy—can you believe it? So much for the great outdoors."

The rash continued to spread leaving angry tracks on arms, legs, and even my neck. It turned into one of the worst cases of poison ivy I'd ever had. So bad, I welcomed the shots of Prednisone the doctor administered and asked for more.

John admonished me, "You should take better care of yourself. You're a lady."

"What are you saying? It didn't seem to bother you for a *lady* to go in crawlspaces or attics! I pawed through guano-laden insulation looking for bats, and now you want me to be careful? Look where we live." I gestured wildly at the house and the land.

"That's not my fault." He looked at me pointedly.

"What the hell is that supposed to mean?"

The fine-tuning was going to take some time.

Initially, The Old Woman didn't seem to notice. She skipped from room to room watching the kids, listening to conversations, peeking curiously into boxes and still asking, "When's the dance? Is it time yet?"

We couldn't hear her over the din of further construction and the growing arguments that were taking place upstairs.

"It's my turn. Back off!" Michael yelled at Spencer, who was following him.

"Can't you see the sheet's down? Don't come in here!" Deanna screamed at Michael, who hadn't paid attention.

The five of us were sharing one bathroom that didn't even have a door. We'd hung a flannel sheet to afford some privacy, but it wasn't working. Instead, the bathroom became a venting ground for all the anxieties and stresses over the move.

We decided to re-hang the damn door and finish the second bathroom we'd roughed into place on the main level. In fact, if we didn't finish it soon, there were bound to be injuries or worse. To gain peace, we would have done anything.

The fights and chaos were beginning to take their toll on The Old Woman too. "If I had known this is how you were going to be, I would never have allowed you to make alterations," she muttered to herself, wondering how she could have so misjudged the situation—and us.

Although overcome with heat and the sheer enormity of the latest job, we were determined to get a bathroom vent pipe through a ten-foot ceiling on the main level, through flooring and ceilings on the second level, and eventually out the attic and roof. Musty insulation, plaster, and even some of our newer drywall crashed to the floor.

"Thirty feet. It's only thirty feet." We reminded ourselves as we sweat our way to the finish line.

It required both John and me to go to the attic to finish the job. The bats were gone, so all we'd really need to fight would be the heat. We were dripping as soon as our heads cleared the opening. The pent-up heat rolled out, roasting our eyeballs. The temperature also made my irritated skin itch more, and I squatted, in misery, trying not to scratch open the lines of poison ivy that tattooed my arms and legs.

We positioned ourselves in a small corner of the attic and prepared to exit the roof with the pipe. Trying to disregard our discomfort and the exhaustion that washed over us in waves, we heard a squeak. Then another. Our eyes opened wide. It was not the squeak of a mouse, but bats. There was a definite distinction, and one we recognized, having heard their prattle before.

The squeaks set John off. He exited the attic immediately, leaving me behind to fend for myself. He was in the hallway, muttering and even contemplating waiting until the first frost before completing our job. Hanging my head down through the opening, I followed his speech and protested, "No way are we sharing one bathroom for three or four months."

He considered covering himself with a blanket again. We grinned at one another.

"We're being silly."

"There can't possibly be bats up there."

"It's just our imagination."

We discussed the seventy-two bats that we had evicted earlier that summer. We sat in the upstairs hallway in silence and finally tripped over our tongues, each asking at the same time, "Have you smelled anything weird up here?"

As it turned out, each of us had caught a whiff of bat guano since the move. We hadn't mentioned it to each other, because that would have somehow made our apprehension probable. We'd both assumed that it was the attic heating up with summer. *Was it possible that we hadn't gotten all of the bats out?*

Dreading the answer, we chose to ignore the uncertainty. Instead, we concentrated on what needed to be done to finish the bathroom. John outlined the process, briefly, as was normal. He gave me a list of tools, and I scurried away to gather them while he continued to glare at the ceiling.

We crawled up into the attic again, being very, very quiet. Just in case. We laid out the tools in chronological order. I'd even brought up a large pan of cold water to cool the drill bit. We knew it was going to get a real workout trying to go through that roofing lumber at top speed. There was no question that we would be working at top speed. John was in the attic. Bats might be in the attic. Any questions?

It was well-executed, exact and seemingly rehearsed. Once started, though, the project had to be completed, or we would have a bathroom we couldn't use and a semi-hole in the roof. The drill spun and whined, working itself to near exhaustion and puffing smoke. Dunking it in the pan, the two of us watched, mesmerized, as steam filled the attic.

Squeak.

"Did you hear that?" John breathlessly asked.

"No. Keep working!"

Sunlight finally filtered through the hole, and we left the attic to move on to more pleasant jobs, scaling the tallest roof and sealing the new pipe. John hauled out the big ladder for what felt the twentieth time. Positioning it against the back of the house, he climbed the thirty feet necessary without faltering once. Fear of bats overshadowed the fear of heights.

After placing the pipe and sealing it into place, he sat on the roof, contemplating the very real possibility of bats. I watched his actions from the security of the backyard. I wasn't afraid of heights, but John never allowed me up on those rooflines. He was concerned for my safety, which seemed laughable.

Because he was disgusted with the likelihood of more bats, he began to kick at the roof with the heels of his boots. Were they there or not? He demanded answers with his tantrum. Evidently, he heard squeaking, because he called, "Come up here and tell me if you hear them too."

While I hung just below gutter level, John, still perched on the roof, began to kick again and, sure as hell, bats. Not only did we hear them, but, as I watched transfixed, as a tiny hole began to appear.

I yelled over his noise, "The little suckers are making a hole."

I thought he would cease and desist all activity. For some incomprehensible reason, he began to pound the roof harder. The noisy vibrations upset the bats further, and they clawed and chewed their way out in desperation.

As the first one emerged, John froze. I ducked for cover under the guttering as twelve bats screeched and flew over my head. John beat the roof once more as I tensed on my perch. No more bats appeared.

Despite John's warnings, I hauled myself up on the roof.

Together, we crawled the roofline, inspecting each shingle in earnest. We found just the one new hole. We scrambled up and down, trying to locate tools.

"How could we have bats up there?" John demanded. "Everything's new—the roof, the eaves. Damn!"

"Maybe they got trapped in the attic?"

"For two months? I don't think so."

"Well, I don't know. There are spiders and bees up there. I saw mud-dobber houses all over the rafters, so there was food."

John tilted his head back and forth, thinking and considering, "Maybe, water though, there wasn't any water."

I shrugged, having no answer for that one.

Sealing the hole the bats had chewed, we climbed down to glare at the roof, wondering if we should trust it or not. We weren't really fooling ourselves. We knew the bats had returned, but it was self-preservation. Our bodies and our spirits cried out for sleep, food and rest before rejoining the fight. Even great warriors need a break.

The Old Woman sighed and rolled her eyes. "This ain't gonna be good."

"We'll come back up here in a week or so, see if the hole is still sealed," John stated with finality and headed inside.

Catching up, I reminded him, "At least we can finish the bathroom now."

He stopped, mid-stride. "Hell, I forgot why we were even up there! Stupid bats."

"Well, I didn't. Let's go get that done. I could use some peace around here."

We needed peace. We needed quiet. We needed to regroup and gain some fortitude. The Morgans and bats would just have to co-exist for a while.

CHAPTER 24

The Exorcism

Adding a bathroom did not make one thing better. Other avenues provided fodder for arguments and venting; nothing was normal, and I began to wonder if we even remembered what the word meant anymore.

Linens were stacked in corners since they had no closet to call home yet. Cleaning supplies were piled high and out of reach of Spencer's little hands. Tools, necessary to keep us moving forward, were scattered throughout the house. Through all of that, we jostled our belongings from room to room, as we continued to work and renovate. It was embarrassing to be so disorganized. It didn't bother John, but I was crazed.

I kept up a non-stop pace. I was trying to find homes for all the things in boxes, add color by painting rooms and pasting wallpaper. There were also countless trips to the store to buy endless lists of supplies. The kitchen was at least assembled and squared away, which was cause for celebration. I had no time to think about the strange "presence" or ghosts or whatever the hell I'd been so worried about two months before. The possible return of bats was enough.

Summer came to a close, and at the end of August school began. Deanna drove back and forth to college each day, basking in adulthood. Despite his initial worries, Michael inserted himself seamlessly into his new school and made new friends. Spencer turned three and successfully attended pre-school every other morning, minus screeching tires and hastily applied brakes I'd applied before the move.

He and I still spent a lot of time together though. One such afternoon, while sitting at the table having lunch, Spencer stopped in mid-conversation, whipped his head toward the front door and asked, "Where'd he go?"

I was quiet for a moment. "Who?"

"Percy. Didn't you see him?"

My eyes grew larger than normal, and my head twisted around trying to see this Percy. No one was there. I tried to rationalize the problem. *Do we know anyone named Percy? Was the television on and reflecting something in the glass of the front door? Did I hear anything? No, and no and no, to all three questions.* I calmly inquired, "Who's Percy?"

Spencer had gone back to eating lunch and was not in the least concerned or even aware of the havoc he'd just wreaked. He took another bite, munching and talking with his mouth full. "Percy. You know. The boy who used to live here."

He was messing with me. That had to be the answer. He was a smart little boy with an enormous imagination. He'd probably seen something on a cartoon and was emulating that with me. The logical part of me was trying to sort things through while the illogical side cringed. Somewhere in there, a parent was screaming. *Be Careful, don't lead him in the wrong direction here.*

"Spence, I don't know anyone named Percy. How do you know someone named Percy lived here?"

Quick as can be, he answered, "He told me. Some kids make fun of him and call him Piggy 'cuz he's big, but not me. I'm his friend."

"And you just saw him?" I couldn't help myself. I had to ask, to clarify.

"Well, yeah. He was right there a minute ago." Spencer climbed down out of his chair, balancing a plate and sloshing milk. The interrogation was over.

I didn't say another word. It was a situation that was going to get worse the more I explored it. I simply filed it all away for future consideration. Weeks went by, and Percy was not seen or heard from again. End of story. End of discussion. Or so I thought.

Spencer's behavior changed, almost imperceptibly. They were small changes, but he was becoming more agitated, more violent in his play.

Moms notice such things. His imagination seemed to take on the worst, and he would laugh when I explained the potential outcome of such things happening in real life. *How do you reason with a three-year-old?*

He had no remorse, and, despite their being so much older, antagonized his brother and sister constantly. Discipline didn't work either. In fact, when he did something he wasn't supposed to do, he backed up to John or me with his little bottom stuck out. "Wanna spank me? Go ahead," his body language said. As parents, we laughed to ourselves, but I remained troubled.

How much of his conduct was normal? Did all three and four-year-old boys say and do these types of things? I didn't think so; we'd already raised one boy and been around countless others through sports. I began reading parenting books and early childhood behavior articles. I wondered if something else wasn't at work. I watched and listened.

It all went to hell quickly. Spencer started getting up almost every night at or near 3:00 a.m. He would wander around upstairs, talking to himself. Sometimes he would wake us up and tell us he was having bad dreams, sometimes he would simply go back to his little bed. Always, we gathered him up, hugged him close and gently tucked him back under the covers. I listened harder, my heart hammering.

I hung little guardian angels over the children's bedroom doors.

It had gotten to the point where I was also waking up at 3:00 a.m., scared and waiting. *Would everything be all right?* On one such night, the laughter started. Loud. Evil. It was a young man's laughter, maniacal and scary. I sat up in bed, reaching for John just as he jumped out of the bed and flung open the door.

Following right behind him, we headed toward the kids' rooms. Michael was tossing and turning. Spencer, however, was a different story. Although he appeared to be fast asleep, the awful, evil laughter was coming from him. Deanna, who had been downstairs fast asleep, opened the door in the stairway, blinking owlishly, even as question marks dented her forehead.

There lay our baby, oblivious to what we were witnessing. John and I looked at each other, wide-eyed and scared. We woke Spencer, took him to the bathroom and washed his little face, looking for clues. We didn't tell him what we'd heard. Instead, we snuggled him between us in our bed, shielding him. We waited, with breath held, to see if he would go back to sleep peacefully or whether the laughter would return.

There was no way we, the adults, were sleeping. It was inconceivable that the voice, the eeriness, could come from a three-year-old. We weren't talking about it, that much was clear. John had his thoughts, and I had mine. Although it wasn't restful, sleep eventually came. We were irritable and short over morning coffee.

The laughter repeatedly came, always late at night, but louder and more mocking. On the fourth night, we headed for Spencer's room and encountered Michael standing in the hallway, wiping the sleep from his eyes, looking bewildered. Deanna had opened her door and was heading up the back stairs with conviction. Something was wrong, and we couldn't ignore it any longer. We woke Spencer, got everyone readjusted and back to bed. John and I lay in our room, unmoving, watching the fan blades spin, our bodies and minds shaking. The children lay awake wondering if they were safe.

The Old Woman had thumped her way upstairs and stood guard in the hallway, concentrating as we were. "What's going on around here?"

John went to work, his eyebrows up. Another one of his famous faces. Meaning, "Whatever the hell this is better get fixed now!"

I frowned and shrugged. Meaning, "How the hell is this *my* fault?" So began our day. I knew something else was at work, and I needed to confess a few things.

We tiptoed around all evening, trying to pretend all was well. We tucked everyone in, following our normal routine. We read stories and said prayers. We handed out drinks and kisses. John and I practically tripped over each other in our haste to get back downstairs and talk the thing through as adults. No kids allowed. We needed to cuss and get mad. "Go to sleep quickly," we wished in the general direction of our children's bedrooms.

We turned the TV on and settled back. *See? No problems here.* We looked relaxed and content, in case anyone got up to go to the restroom, requested yet another drink or tried any of the other one hundred things they did to prolong closing their eyes. We checked one more time. All was well, and the little darlings were finally out.

John started in right away. "What the hell is going on? I'm telling you right now this house is so for sale! If it wants us out, no problem. You don't have to knock me upside the head. I can take a hint."

"Okay. Fine. Something's wrong," I admitted, not making eye contact.

"What? You think I want to watch all of our time and work go down the drain? I don't, but nothing, and I mean nothing, is gonna mess with those kids! Am I clear?" He chain-smoked his third cigarette.

"Crystal. But, understand—I didn't do this. It's not *my* fault. I don't like it any better than you do. They're my kids too!" I folded my arms and pursed my lips in defense.

We sat in silence, looking at one another, knowing, at some level, that blaming one another would not solve the mess in which we found ourselves. I finally worked up some courage and asked, "Do you remember the story of my mom and dad's house—after the storm?"

John nodded. Gently, I reminded him of the day he had come home early and caught me supposedly talking to myself.

"Do you remember that day? Right before we moved in, you came up the stairs asking who was here, who I was talking to," I prodded.

"Vaguely. You seemed like you were hiding something, now that I think about it."

"Well, I was praying in the corners—just like my mom did."

Johns piercing blue eyes opened wider. He knew exactly what I was implying. "Did you ever finish?" he asked in a near whisper.

"No." I shook my head. "I realized it today when I was thinking all of this through," I found myself whispering too. "I never finished the landing or the boys' rooms."

John leaned forward in his chair, pointed toward the stairs and said, "Then you'd better start fricking praying right now." Only he didn't say fricking.

"Sorry," he quickly amended.

Call it anxiety, but his poor choice of words cracked me up to no end. I couldn't have ever conceived those words together in a sentence, but there they were. I laughed until it hurt. Worried, John tried to determine if I was suddenly possessed too.

Catching my breath, I explained, "I can't just go up there and start praying. I needed to be alone, be in the right frame of mind, you know?"

He didn't understand at all. We did agree, however, that I would take care of matters the next day, and he would not call me hourly for updates.

I had trouble getting into the spirit of things. No pun intended. It had seemed simple before, even innocent, but the late-night laughter had changed things, and I felt very much out of my league. I wasn't sure what to think or believe. I stood in the kitchen bracing myself, trying to relax, and began to pray.

It seemed a safe place to start. More a conversation with God, I let our uninvited guest listen. "God, I have no idea what I'm doing. A little help here, please."

I moved up the stairs, still talking and half-praying as I went. I proceeded back to our bathroom, trying to create the mood. *Maybe I didn't finish in here either.* At least it was half-blessed, and I could hit my rhythm, which was not an easy thing to do while standing next to a toilet. "Please protect us, God. Enter our home."

I worked toward the landing area, a cozy place we'd constructed for rainy-day afternoons. The rebuilt shelves were full of books, games, and puzzles. Big pillows were piled in a corner by the window, inviting the kids to pile up, read and dream. As I looked out the window toward the pond, I told our "house guest" what was on our minds and that we were angry. "Our children are off-limits!"

I was inviting God to the places I'd missed when I felt "him." Even now, it can make the hair on my arms stand on end. It felt like someone, or something had moved out of Spencer's little room and was looking at me as I stood in what should have been a happy child's place.

There was a sudden hotness to the air. Not wind—nothing was moving. It was like a breath. I closed my eyes, afraid to look. I just knew if I turned my head, I would have been looking into a sinister, sneering face, older than its years. I could formulate the mental picture: mean, challenging.

"You talking to me, lady?" he seemed to ask, all the while grinning and breathing on my neck.

I shook but never stopped praying. Instead, I spoke louder, asking for help. "This house is ours now. You're not welcome here! We believe in God!" Like Dorothy trying to get back to Kansas, I was chanting, "We believe. We believe."

Whatever had been there in the landing disappeared. It simply diminished in size and was gone.

The phone rang. There was no way I was going to answer. He was playing games with me and trying to get me distracted. It wasn't happening that time. I'd stopped before, due to an interruption, and look what had taken place.

I hopped down a step onto the landing and chased whatever had been there into Spencer's room. Still talking, still praying, I was really angry. I think God understood. I wasn't mad at him, I was furious that such a thing that would dare touch my child. Once in Spencer's room, I turned a circle. The room felt empty like the Manson room had months before. I prayed in all the corners anyway, cleansing the room where our little boy seemed so affected.

I was the one laughing. "Are you scared? You'd better be you son-of-a-bitch! Don't come back in here. Stay the hell out!" I paused, shocked at myself.

"Sorry, God. I'm cussing, aren't I? Please don't undo my prayers. I'm scared, that's all."

I went on to Michael's room, the last unblessed, unprayed in room of the house. It was there, lurking and sucking up the air. "Did you think you could fool me? Did you think I would believe you'd be in Spencer's room? You're here. I can feel you. It's Percy, right? Well, Percy, you and I both know you're done. There's nowhere else for you to go. All the rooms are blessed, sincerely and completely."

That room was frightening. It was the only place in the house where I felt like I needed to touch the walls. I stood, hands splayed, and poured out my thoughts, my fears, my hopes, and my requests. Sweat rolled down my neck, a slick combination of fear and stale air. I was there a long time; at least it seemed that way to me. I ended and walked each room, each staircase, each corner, and each bend one more time. I knew, in my heart, that it was going to be safe.

I explained it all to John after dinner, whispering again so the kids wouldn't hear. His eyes remained unblinking through the story, and I watched as goosebumps appeared on his strong and normally capable arms. At that moment, he was vulnerable, unable to protect or save. I'd gotten to the part about the landing and following Percy into Michael's room. John was half- convinced but worried just the same.

"We should move!" He stood up as though ready to start packing.

"Let's wait and see, Hon. I really believe it'll be alright."

"How do you know it'll be okay?"

"It's called faith, Darlin'. I prayed with everything I had. God will intervene."

He nodded, noncommittally, wrinkles of concern playing out across his forehead.

We parents went on with our evening and eventually herded the boys up to bed. Spencer rolled over, closed his eyes and fell quickly to sleep. I kissed my fingertips and brushed them across his cheek. I silently asked for angels.

We checked on Michael one more time, thinking he was asleep, but he rolled over to ask, "Mom? Did you change something in my room today?"

The boy hated variation. I couldn't so much as shift his knick-knacks without him being irritated. I knew that. So, why the question? John looked at me and shrugged.

"No, Baby. I didn't change anything in here. I threw out some trash earlier, that's all. Why?" I went closer to tuck in blankets and run my hand through his hair.

"I don't know. It just feels so much better in here." With that, he snuggled down into his comforter and dropped off to dream. I shivered once and looked at John.

We stood a moment in the landing, looking at our boys. "See?" I took John' hand. "God is good."

John nodded and held on tighter while we descended the backstairs to check on Deanna too. At eighteen, she may not appreciate the intrusion, but we didn't care. Not that night anyway.

The Old Woman stomped around; mad as hell that Percy had walked in on her family. She mentally shooed him out her door and offered up a prayer of her own: "Give me strength. I'm old, God. I need your help too." She walked the rooms, checking on all five of us. Noticing I hadn't put a guardian angel over our door, she peeked in on John and me. "Seems to me somebody better watch out for you two as well."

Waking and stretching with the light of a new day, John and I both realized we'd slept soundly. For the first time in more than a week, there had been no interruptions, no laughter, no sleepwalking Spencer.

"I guess you were right," John admitted, with a soft kiss as we met for coffee in the kitchen.

Chapter 25

Bat Wars Episode III: Incoming

We looked around, finally able to focus again. Summer had truly come and gone, and we weren't sorry to see it go. It had been a disaster. The move, the chaos, the construction, and the fear had eaten up our days and nights. We hadn't had the money or the time to take a vacation.

On an early September evening, John and I sat outside, trying to relax. It was a new thing, and neither of us was quite sure what to do. We leaned back in lawn chairs, arms at our sides, marveling at the sensation of sitting still and having a slow-paced conversation. We talked about prospective projects, lazily though and without urgency. We weren't sure what to tackle next. The pond? Landscaping? The old garage? Continue to work inside?

The Old Woman was disgusted. "What is it with you two? We're sitting here, enjoying the scenery. Can't you be still for a while?"

John and I grew silent, sipping beers and watching various colors stretch toward twilight. He flicked a cigarette toward the lawn, and a small, black furry object whirred by to inspect it. Our heads spun toward each other.

"Was that a bat?"

"Yep...think so."

We began to scan the sky more carefully, trying to determine which tree or direction they were hailing from. Spitting out our beers and lunging from our chairs, we looked at each other in shock. We'd watched several bats fly out of the tallest peak of our roof. They were shooting out the ends of the ridge vents. We zigged across the yard trying to get a better angle on the roof.

"Oh my God!"

"How could we be so stupid?"

We'd completely forgotten the bats. It had been over a month since we'd watched them chew a hole in the roof. To be fair, we'd been pretty busy. Between finishing bathrooms and full combat with Percy, our distraction was understandable.

I was sent to the attic to check the situation. *Why is this my fault?* I didn't even care anymore, and, to be honest, I was sick of the bats. As my head and light cleared the hole, I smelled the guano and heard their high-pitched screeches.

I closed the attic firmly, backed down the ladder and stood on the bottom rung, dumbfounded. "They're up there all right."

A whole airport had probably been flourishing over our heads. The rooflines were long and straight, making the ridge vents long and straight. I imagined that some of the bats were employed as air traffic controllers, some handled baggage, others planned vacation packages and rented out cars. There were probably restaurants, bookstores, and kiosks.

I looked at John and noticed his ears had turned red. "Bullshit!" he yelled, "God damn roofers! They didn't do the roofs right. There is no way we should have an issue with a new roof. Jesus Christ! It's only three months old! Call that contractor right now!" He pointed his beer bottle like a weapon.

"It's 9:30, John. He can't do anything about it tonight."

"Well, you can bet *he's* at home, relaxing, having a nice time—while we're here stuck with a half-assed job!" He pounded down the stairs and flung open the fridge in search of another brew.

Following him to the kitchen, I waited. I knew the tirade wasn't over.

"I'm telling you, he's going to fix this shit!" The fridge door slammed. "And, by God, it's going to be at night after the bats leave. They're not going to trap them inside again!"

Disgusted, we went about our business and ignored the bats for a few days. We occasionally watched, checking the nighttime sky to see if we had perhaps dreamt the whole thing. No such luck. They were still landing and taking off with regularity.

During the week, John had calmed down enough to climb up on the roof and inspect things in detail. "There aren't any new holes, so they haven't chewed their way inside. I'm telling you," he shook his head, "the ridge vent isn't sealed. The whole damn colony probably moved back inside." He fastened plastic sheeting over the vent, but the wind or bats soon loosened it and left it flapping uselessly in the wind.

"Don't tell my dad!" Ol' Bud would probably drive back to Ohio to evict the bats again. I imagined the upcoming phone conversation and laughed to myself. John didn't find any of it funny. He'd taken to mumbling to himself, so I stayed out of his way.

We called the contractor, more than ready for him to fix his mistake. He arrived, having no idea we were as crazed as we were. We told him, in quite serious tones, that the bats had returned and that it was his fault. He seemed genuinely puzzled about how the bats could possibly be his responsibility. "It's been months." He refused to be held accountable.

"The ridge vents weren't installed correctly," John and I ranted simultaneously, "You have to fix them! At night. After the bats leave!" We were quite firm on that point.

For some reason, the contractor didn't comprehend. "You want me to send roofers up to the tallest section at night?"

We nodded.

"In the dark?" He clarified one more time.

We nodded again.

"To inspect and possibly repair the vent?"

"Yeah." *Thank goodness, he finally understood.*

There was some talk about darkness and liability. We were left with a vague "I'll send someone up to check it out."

To be honest, John told me he didn't want them to fix the roof during the day because the roofers would trap the bats inside. He then went out of town, and I promptly forgot that conversation. Three days later, the installer informed me he'd gone up on the roof and caulked around the vent. "There was a half-inch gap around the end cap after all."

His conclusion and resultant fix were not especially good news to me. John couldn't believe it. "Are you telling me they sealed the little bastards in the attic?"

"Pretty much." I looked at my shoes instead of him. I knew he was mad.

"Now what are we supposed to do?"

"Well, the way I see it, we've got two choices. A. *We* can go to the attic and round the little suckers up, or B. We can wait 'til spring and carry the skeletons out."

John looked at me heavily, frowned, and thought about the options. "I ain't no cowboy."

We decided to leave the bats to die and rounded up the Lewis' instead. They stopped by often to check on the progress or hear our latest story. Having been made aware of the latest bat saga, they were the obvious choice to celebrate the bats' demise.

Duane and Terry were more than happy to set a date and agreed to come over on Friday night. "I'll bring some wine," Terry announced.

On Thursday evening, however, things began to fall apart. John was outside on the mower, and the boys were in bed. I was working downstairs on the computer. The front screen door opened and banged shut, and I watched Scooby-Doo shuffle past. He'd nosed his way in as the door didn't quite catch. Such things were typical in our crooked old house. Five minutes later, I heard blood-curdling screams from upstairs, followed by the sound of pounding feet.

I raced for the stairs, meeting Michael and Spencer already halfway down. "What's going on? Who's hurt?"

"There's a bat in Michael's room!"

"No way," I informed them sternly and ushered them back upstairs.

"It flew down the stairs to Deanna's room," they both insisted.

That sounded serious, and I couldn't ignore their worried faces. I checked every room upstairs, guaranteed the boys it was safe and put them together in Spencer's room. "Stay in here, okay? I'll go handle the bat." *Yeah, right. There's no bat.*

I snatched my broom from a corner, thinking I might need a weapon. Maybe there was some flying creature in the house. I eased into Deanna's room and closed both doors, one to the back stairs and one to the rest of the house. I didn't see anything.

Meanwhile, Michael had snuck downstairs. He stood at the back door hollering for John, "Daddy! We need you!" John, of course, could not hear this plea for help and kept mowing.

Spencer came down the back stairs and stood outside Deanna's door, yelling at the top of his lungs. *So much for them waiting quietly upstairs.* They'd also blown my cover.

I circled the room, broom ready. I swept, literally, and discovered our little intruder hanging from a silk tree. I jumped backward. "Oh my God! There is a bat!" It spread its wings, preparing to fly. I couldn't allow that to happen and wound up for bat-ting practice. With a smack, the broom and bat collided. I'd hit a line drive single, knocking it behind Deanna's bed. Dropping to my hands and knees, I began the process of ferreting it out from among boxes, shoes and old socks. In the commotion, I dropped the broom just as the damn bat crawled out from under the bed right next to my face. It scared the hell out of me, and I took my turn yelling. I recovered my broom, trapped the bat and called for Michael.

Michael refused to enter the room until I swore the bat was not flying. "Come on, Michael. I need you! Get me a box or something—anything with a lid." There was more shouting of instructions through doors because Literal Michael couldn't understand what I needed. "What kind of box? What are you going to do with a box?"

Spencer, still at the other door to the back staircase, yelled out questions of his own. "What are you doing? How come Michael gets to come in?"

Meanwhile, the bat flapped and shoved against the broom with all its might, screeching and calling for help. It was stronger than I expected, and I concentrated on holding the broom steady.

Hours later, it seemed, Michael cautiously entered and slammed a Tupperware bowl over the broom and the bat. I carefully pulled the broom free, leaving the bat under the bowl. "Good job, Michael! You did it!" Holding the bowl firmly on the rug, I eased the lid under it, moving the bat out of the way. Carefully, holding the pieces firmly together, I turned it right side up and sealed it closed. Bat in a Bowl. I knew Martha Stewart never tried that one.

I coaxed Michael closer and yelled for Spencer, who spilled through the door immediately. The bat cussed and body-slammed itself against the sides of the bowl while we three watched in fascination. John, finally done mowing, followed our voices and stood in Deanna's doorway. "What's going on in here?"

I held the bowl up for him to see and he took several steps backward. Michael and Spencer talked over one another, explaining the exciting events.

John listened hard, attempting to make some sense of their staccato words. I leaned in to see the bat better. Its gritty pink tongue panted. "Poor little thing," I sympathized and carried the bowl to the foyer. I held open the door and set it free.

The men had followed me and stood in the foyer, incredulous. "Did you let it go?" Michael demanded.

"What the hell are you thinking? You gotta kill these things!" John glared and shook his head, pained by my actions. The boys never knew I'd smashed a bat up in the attic, and I made a face at John, imploring him not to give me away.

He swore again. "It's going to go right back into the attic."

Deanna, coming home from one of her night classes, sailed in the back door, called out a greeting and saved me. *Good timing.* Michael and Spencer raced each other to the kitchen to tell her there had been a bat in her room.

"Do what?!" Less than pleased, she peeked in her door, clearly unsure about sleeping there. The boys slept in Spencer's room, and Deanna took over Michael's room for the night— just in case. We promised all three of them it was safe.

John and I lay in our bed, discussing the bat and whispering so the kids wouldn't hear. "Maybe Scooby let the bat in when he opened the front door?"

"I don't know..." John wasn't convinced.

"The light was on—maybe the bat followed a bug toward the light."

John raised his eyebrows. "You shouldn't have let the contractor caulk that vent."

"Fine. Whatever. Goodnight, Hon." I rolled away from his heated tone.

Friday came, and Terry and Duane knocked on the door. Terry, a rather short, lively lady, held out the promised wine and laughed. Pleased, I poured glasses all around, and we trooped outside to enjoy the pretty weather.

As darkness came, the mosquitoes began to whine and look for warm flesh to bite. We moved inside to relax in the living room. Michael was upstairs reading, Spencer in bed, singing, and Deanna was at work. We were enjoying some well-deserved adult time until the screaming started.

We reacted as parents, not hunters. "Go to bed! Lights out!"

The yelling continued, and John politely excused himself to check the situation while I continued to chat.

"Oh, Sweetie...." John called down to me in exaggerated tones, leaning on the upper railing and waiting for me to appear.

"Yes, Darling?" I answered with a grin and walked to the foyer.

"He's so cute." Terry smiled. Duane rolled his eyes.

"Remember that problem we had last night?" John asked, not so nicely.

"The bat?" *Uh-oh*.

"Yeah—the bat. Well, guess what? We have another one in Michael's room."

Poor Michael. That made two bats in two days. John wasn't handling it well either. Following my example, he'd found the broom and was whacking and shooing the bat toward the front door. Both boys followed behind, alternating between cheering and yelling, "Get it, Dad!"

The bat got to the two-story entry where there was plenty of room for flying and turning circles around the chandelier. John hung over the railing, swinging whenever the bat sailed past. Concerned, I yelled from below, "Watch the clock! Watch the light! You're going to fall."

Spencer and Michael stood behind John, clearly disappointed. How could he let it get away like that?

At the first sign of the bat, Duane and Terry barricaded themselves in the living room by shutting the big curved doors. They'd left the barest hint of a crack and were crowded against each other to see what was happening. I saw their eyeballs, heard their laughter. "Sure, laugh all you want. Have some more wine, why don't you?" I yelled in their general direction and heard more snickering.

The Old Woman giggled at the Lewis' holed up in her living room.

The bat was hit and dropped to the foyer floor, fluttering. In a well-orchestrated move, John flung the broom to me, and I covered the bat, without breaking stride. I pulled the broom toward the door, opened it with my free hand, and swished the little creature outside.

John hung over the railing, unbelieving. The boys book-ended him, shaking their little heads, and looking at me as though I were an ill-behaved child. I grinned and shrugged up at the guys. "Sorry." I had moments of insanity, and really, given all we'd been through, I was entitled.

We freed our neighbors from the living room, despite the fact they were still laughing and applauding. They declared it one of the most enjoyable evenings they'd had in a long time. "You two are so much fun!"

The Lewis' stayed, still talking. They didn't seem to want to leave, and I wondered if they were afraid to go out into the yard where I'd swept the bat. We finally waved goodbye from the porch, watching them pick their way carefully across the front yard. Leaning against the door, John and I stared at one another.

We decided, being the good parents we were, that Michael should not sleep in his room but with his brother again, thus protecting them both. "The bat's gone, okay?" we assured them, leaving the hall light on so they'd feel safe. We weren't gone two minutes when a sudden burst of sound, well, screaming really, came from Spencer's room.

We ran in to find both boys buried, under the covers, shrieking their little heads off in time to a bat circling the room. John shot me a told-you-so look, hauled the two boys to safety and slammed the bedroom door shut.

I left John and the boys to trap the bat and went down to the kitchen to pour myself another glass of wine and think. I slugged it down, whiskey style. Looking out the kitchen window, I pondered. *Was it the same bat? No way. It couldn't get inside that quickly.* I needed to defend myself, but the time for logical conversations had passed.

John had had it. I mean *really* had it. He marched past me with the bat in our trusty Tupperware bowl, took it outside and thwacked it on the crumbling back stoop. No more bat. No more Mr. Nice Guy either. We weren't going to set any more free.

We all calmed down and went back to bed. The boys were mistrustful and afraid to sleep, and who could blame them really? John was trying to have a conversation with me as to how and where these bats were getting in the house. I had, by then, consumed most of the bottle of wine and didn't care about bats anymore

"There has to be a hole somewhere in Michael's room," John concluded. We begin to talk about the closets upstairs. We'd repaired them before moving in but had not re-done them completely. Not having dry-walled the closets probably meant there were cracks in the old plaster. *Bats and cracks.* Made sense to me. Having solved the mystery, I rolled over ready for sleep.

John, still sitting up in bed, back ramrod straight, poked me in the arm. "How can you possibly sleep?"

I *was* having trouble sleeping, but only because he kept asking me that ridiculous question. The wine helped though. I wasn't used to so much and slipped off to dreamland while John lay there, staring at the room and watching for bats.

After another less than great night's sleep, we decided it was time for all-out war. It was going to be a fight to the finish, Morgans vs. Bats. We would be victorious.

Chapter 26

Bat Wars Episode IV: B Day

Despite the fact he was supposed to be working, John and I talked on and off the whole next day, trying to determine, once and for all, how to alleviate ourselves of the bats. Being the geniuses that we were, we set about constructing another of our fabulously fool-proof plans. How many such plans had we had at that point? Five? Six? We just knew that we'd be victorious this time. We would be awarded bat combat medals of honor.

"How do we get them to leave the attic?" I started the question-and-answer format.

John pondered my questions and solved the problems. "How about if we open the attic and just the one window right there in the landing?"

"What if they go the other way toward the foyer?"

"We could hang a sheet in the hall. That would keep them upstairs."

On and on it went, each of us volleying ideas. "We'll turn out all of the lights upstairs. I'll move the car out back and turn on the headlights. That should draw them out."

"I think I'll remove all of the curtains and silk trees just in case."

Lest we forget our children, we agreed they would be placed in the living room with the big doors shut, a.k.a. Lewis style. John and I would then be free to coax the little bastards (the bats, not our children) outside by shining car lights toward the one open window.

My truck's headlights would be a bat beacon. The truck would also provide a safe haven for John should all the bats come out at once.

He was to be outside, running reconnaissance, and I was to be inside, herding the bats toward the window. There was always something fundamentally wrong with our scenarios: I tended to get the dirtier jobs.

We felt we had thoroughly considered every angle. Certainly, the bats would feel the cool breeze of freedom slipping through the one open window. Having been trapped in the attic, they would naturally want to leave. As an added incentive, the light from the car would attract bugs, and the bats would welcome the feast we offered. The bats, all of them, would then calmly leave the attic in single-file formation, even thanking us in the process. It was a great plan, and John and I were extremely proud of ourselves. I couldn't wait to get started and paced around trying to find something to do until he got home.

As promised, I removed all the curtains and silk trees, shoving them in the shed outside. Having already discovered a bat hanging from silk branches, I didn't want to provide any hiding places for them. I carried the ladder to the upstairs hallway and balanced precariously while trying to tack a queen-sized sheet across the opening.

John arrived and nodded at my make-shift barrier. "That should keep them upstairs where they belong!" I looked at the narrow opening where the sheet didn't quite meet the floor. I considered it a possible escape route. For me, not the bats. After all, I would be upstairs too.

We proceeded forward as though we knew exactly what we were doing. Scooby was closed up in the mudroom and Fat Cat Chance, our arrogant feline, was sent to the basement. Both animals regarded us with ears flat, clearly not liking their accommodations.

We'd even had the foresight to borrow the boys' walkie-talkies, so John and I could effectively communicate with one another during battle. John got the talkie since he'd be sitting in the car managing the situation from afar. I got the walkie since I was the grunt, the one expected to do hand-to-bat combat inside, armed with a Bat-Minton racket no less. The racket was my only defense should the enemy try to escape down the hallway or back staircase. I went and found my Tupperware bowl as further weaponry. Oh, we also had a beer or two each. That seemed necessary fortification.

To be funny, I smudged mascara under both eyes. "What in the hell are you doing now?" John asked, taking in my appearance.

"Hey, if I'm going into combat, I want to look the part." I laughed and gave him a quick kiss.

He shook his head. "You're really weird sometimes, you know that?" The kids, taking in Moms' strange appearance, looked worried.

Settling into our bat-tle stations, we waited. We joked across static-laced air and shared a long-distance beer. We waited some more, growing more and more disgusted. Nothing was happening.

"We need to re-think the plan," John whispered over the talkie. Crawling, army-fashion under the sheet, I snuck outside so the bats wouldn't eavesdrop on our conversation. We didn't trust them. So far, the bats had proven themselves more resilient and smarter than we were. There had to be a network of bat spies, no question about that. They probably sent their youngest to spy camps and special training facilities located somewhere in our walls. No doubt they'd been educated on how to sneak through insulation and how to move in and out of vents. Maps were distributed in the attic, outlining all possible exit points and, as Enemies of the Attic, our pictures shown to each new member of the bat brigade.

Once outside, I snagged a couple of drags from John's cigarette. I didn't want to alert the bats to my presence by smoking upstairs. We laughed about how ridiculous we were acting yet refused to change our plan or throw caution to the wind.

"Maybe we just need to wait a little longer."

"Probably. We have kind of messed up their routine."

"Want to trade places?" I offered in case John was bored with his station.

"No thanks. I'm fine right here," John replied, smiling, fully aware he had the better deal.

We hadn't checked on the children and went inside to do so. All three of them, including grown-up Deanna, were huddled under a blanket. They sat shoulder to shoulder, butt to butt. They were not watching the movie, or content as they were supposed to be. They were, in reality, scared to death. They'd been through numerous bat drills before and, for some reason, didn't trust their parents to be victorious.

The Old Woman had ensconced herself in the living room, lending her presence to the kids. She was snickering about the walkie-talkies and the sheet. "Lord, you two are a hoot."

The kids sat there together, sure they were going to be attacked by combative bats at any moment. Maybe they feared being kidnapped and held at bat point until we humans left the house for good. Who knew? Ransom was not inconceivable.

"You guys okay?"

"Not really," They each took turns answering,

"Yeah."

"No."

It was not a pretty picture, and we felt bad about that. We couldn't just leave our kids clumped together like that. They were miserable and close to needing therapy. John and I called Grandma and Grandpa Morgan, using the cell phone outside, of course. We didn't want the bats to hear. One had to assume the phone lines were tapped as well.

We were using code speak to keep the bats off balance, and Gene and Nancy were confused and unable to understand a word we were saying about bats, wars, combat, and sheets. They heard enough to know, for some reason, their grandchildren were in danger and needed to come to their house to spend the night. They agreed immediately.

Going back inside, we approached the kids again. "Hey, you guys want to go stay with Grandma and Grandpa tonight?" John asked.

"They said you can, and this whole thing seems to be taking longer than we thought," I filled in the blanks, granting permission.

Blankets were thrown off, and they scrambled to their rooms to pack. Less than five minutes later, the kids ran outside and hurriedly buckled themselves in the car. Deanna peeled out, and they were gone. Traitors.

Having taken care of the children, and feeling better as parents, we resumed our earlier positions. Drank another beer. Listened to static. I was growing bored and stiff trying to stay inconspicuous on the landing. I'd positioned myself on the top step of the back staircase, affording me a view of not only the exit window but the attic access as well. John moved the car around in case the bats didn't like the direction of the light. The radio finally crackled.

"We have bats! Repeat! We have movement!" His voice stuttered.

"Where? Where are they? I don't see anything!" I jumped to my feet, Bat Minton racket raised ready to do battle.

"Downstairs in the den. I can see him flying around."

Downstairs? How the hell had it gotten downstairs?

"Did you let one through?" John queried, indicating, with his tone, I'd failed in my duties by letting the varmint through.

"No! I've been watching the opening, I swear! It didn't come through here."

"Well, you need to get down there."

John was cackling although he was trying to blame it on the talkie, finding my dilemma too amusing for my liking.

I was muttering about how unfair life was. "How come he's not coming in here to save the day?" I wiggled under the sheet again and tiptoed down the stairs, avoiding those I knew to be squeaky.

I rushed into the den, brandished my Bat Minton racket and trusty bowl. Flipping on the switch, I started swinging immediately. John was definitely laughing, I heard him clearly from my walkie clipped to my waistband. The whole battle was outlined through the window, and he watched as an interested spectator, never coming in to lend assistance. I won and handed the bat and the bowl out the back door to John.

"Laugh at me, will you?" I said with a sneer. It's amazing how quickly a person quiets down when handed a bat in a bowl.

I didn't wait around to see how he handled the situation. He could do whatever he pleased. I wanted no part of the euthanasia. This went on for hours. Swing a broom or a bat-mitton racket, trap the bat in a bowl, and hand it to John. The bowl always came back empty.

"Bat down! Bat down! Do you copy?"

"Roger that."

"Bat sighting. Spencer's bedroom."

We removed seven and finally closed our eyes, fully dressed, at one in the morning. A new day dawned and, feeling euphoric over our win, we called our children back. "It's safe now. All the bats are gone." They were a bit dubious, but John and I were very confident as we conveyed the nights' activities and our prowess as soldiers.

We let Scooby out the back door, and he jogged around the backyard trying to determine what we'd been doing out there the night before. He stood beside my truck, head cocked, wondering why we'd parked it there. "This doesn't belong here," he seemed to say.

Chance was released from the dungeon and immediately headed to his food dish. He meowed and complained. How in the world had we thought he'd survive eight hours without food? His tail swished in agitation. He gulped the food we dispensed and then promptly went the middle of the living room to throw it all back up. "Revenge is mine," sayeth the cat.

Gene and Nancy decided they should follow the children home. They had to evaluate the situation for themselves; make sure things were truly safe. Besides, the story was too good to simply share over phone lines. We greeted the kids, who ran to their rooms to make sure their things had not been destroyed in battle. Still unsure of the house, the bats, and their parents, they opted to go outside to play.

Nancy and Gene went upstairs to see the sheet and the battle station. Sitting comfortably at the kitchen table, sipping coffee, they joked and laughed at our expense. "Boy, I'm telling ya, I don't know why you stay here." Gene shook his head.

Nancy and I moved to the computer. We sat side by side, researching and reading about bats, making sure we hadn't missed anything. "It says that young bats can become confused and trapped. They'll follow any bit of fresh air to get outside," I yelled the information to John, who was still visiting with his dad.

"Sounds good to me. We just need to make sure there are no more holes," John replied. "Better start emptying things out!"

I sighed and headed upstairs again. Most of the decorations we owned were scattered, lying in piles, taken down the night before. It had taken months to get us moved in, things put away. It was depressing. To fully declare victory, we emptied every single closet and filled every hint of a crack with caulk.

"What a mess!" The Old Woman declared, walking from room to room. "The bats are gone though. Are you' ready to dance?" she called to us, but we'd already moved on.

"Well, we'll just leave you guys to finish up," Nancy and Gene commented, taking in the growing disorder and mess in each room. They hugged their grandchildren. "You guys can come stay anytime."

For a moment, the kids considered following them home, but John and I shook our heads. "We need your help getting everything put away." In reality, the kids were very little help at all. They were more interested in the contents of the closets. Deanna found sweaters and shoes she hadn't seen in months. Michael played with forgotten toys. Spencer tried on my shoes. Even John forgot what we were doing for a while. I found him sitting on our bedroom floor, sorting through some of his old baseball cards.

"Guys, this is crazy!" I admonished. "We have to put things away!" Recognizing the crazed look in my eye, everyone got very busy very quickly. It took hours, but the house was put to rights, and we were completely and totally bat-free. Liberated. Vindicated. We vowed to celebrate 'B' day every August.

I imagined a huge Bat Mitzvah celebration was going on in the barns. It was probably a well-orchestrated event set in motion by all the veteran bats, trying to save their young P.O.W.'s. They were probably out there drinking bat beer and laughing. "Did you see that crazy woman?"

There may have been long speeches. Some clutched awards, while others shot paws skyward, giving God the glory. I'm quite sure toasts were made to brave spy bats who had kept everyone informed of the situation and even risked bodily harm by brooms and rackets to achieve the goal.

"Hip-hip-hooray!"

Well, they could have their celebration, and we would have ours. In the end, everybody got what they wanted, freedom.

Chapter 27

Silk Purses and Sow Ears

The sun and I both rose eager to start a beautiful, September day—smiles brightly shining, anticipation in our movements. Yanking an old pair of cutoffs and a stained tank top, I hummed under my breath as I headed toward the bathroom. I smeared on moisturizer and swept my hair into a ponytail, clamping it tight and high at the back of my head.

Once downstairs, I dreamed out the kitchen window, glad we had beaten the bats, and eager to tackle something more satisfying, if only for a while. Bare feet tapped in rhythm with the Mr. Coffee drip, drip, dripping.

John startled me, slipping up behind and squeezing me into a hug. "Good morning. You're up early. What's up?"

"I'm waiting on coffee so I can head outside. I've got big plans today- - going to set the bricks around the front landscaping." I smiled and pointed to the pile of old bricks outside the window. "Those are the ones Mr. C. rejected. They may not have worked for steps, but they're fine for landscaping."

"You haven't even showered yet. Don't you want to do that first?" He asked.

Slightly insulted, I frowned. "Nooo." I pulled one syllable into three for emphasis. "I took one last night before bed. I'm just going to get dirty again anyway."

You sure?" He seemed perplexed, and I ignored the impulse to sniff my armpits. There's nothing like someone suggesting you need a shower to put a damper on your confidence.

"Seems like you'd want to start fresh," he added, not leaving the topic alone.

"I'm clean! I slept. I woke up. It's not like I ran a midnight marathon or anything." I turned away. He was starting to irritate me, and I didn't want to lose my enthusiasm.

He shrugged and moved away as though I was offensive. "Okay. Suit yourself."

I gestured with my now filled coffee cup, "I'm going to be working in dirt and mulch for God's sake. Why are you so insistent on me needing a damn shower?"

"Who needs a shower?" Michael, who always seemed to catch the tail end of conversations, wandered into the kitchen. Bed-head stood at attention as he looked from John to me, trying to pick up the thread of the discussion.

"Nothing Honey. Dad's just anal." I smiled and gave my son a morning hug.

"What's anal mean?" A new voice asked.

I turned, shaking my head at my early risers and greeted a spotted-dotted Spencer. "Good morning little man. Don't you two ever sleep in? It's only 7:40." I pulled him into a hug too, lifting his shirt for inspection. "Oh, baby. This looks worse." I ran a light hand across the raised and ugly trails of poison ivy. "We'll get you Benadryl after breakfast. We may have to get you to the doctor today, too." I mentally calculated the time the office would open, when I could get him in, and, selfishly, how it would affect my plans.

Remembering my earlier bout with poison ivy, Spencer's bottom lip plopped forward. "Will I have to get a shot like you did?"

I welcomed my shot, anything for relief, but three-year-olds didn't think that way. "I don't know honey." I shrugged. "I'm sorry. You're allergic like me. Let's just wait and see."

I plunked bowls on the table, hurriedly poured cereal, sloshed milk and patted their little heads. "I'm going out," I called to the kitchen, including all my men in the announcement. Sliding on my comfortable, grass-stained shoes, I ran through the door, avoiding any other interruptions.

I raked and shoveled, creating a geometric design beside the front porch. I was tired of the carful square and rectangular landscaping I'd done at the other, newer houses we'd owned. I wanted curves, and slopes, gently blending from one area to the next-- some semblance of creativity. I stood back pleased with the effect. Little boy faces kept appearing at the window, tapping and making silly faces at Mommy. I waved back and smiled but never stopped working. I noticed Deanna was in the kitchen too. *Odd. She's never up before ten on a Saturday.*

Trowel in hand, I smoothed the edge of the mulch, digging down to dirt, and flattening a six-inch space for my bricks. I heard the grandfather clock bong and sat quietly counting…seven, eight, nine. I'd worked up a fine sweat in the hour or so I'd been outside. I wiped a hand across errant bangs, leaving a smudge across my forehead.

It was at that moment a long, black limousine pulled into our driveway, and my plans for the day changed forever. Trowel and jaw dropped simultaneously. There are *no* limousines in the country. Well, maybe during prom season, but that was an eternity away.

I didn't notice four faces pressed against the kitchen windows. My back was to the house concentrating on the anomaly that had just appeared. I stood like an idiot, waiting for the driver to realize his mistake and back out onto the road again. The sexy, sleek car pulled forward instead, slowly crunching gravel. Wiping blackened hands across my sorts, I sauntered over, as the dark window lowered.

The uniformed driver tipped his hat in my direction. "Morning, Maam." His wide, smooth face reflected the sun.

"Good morning to you. Are you lost?" I smiled sure he simply needed directions. Directions to some fine home and fancy family living in the area.

He tilted his head, looked at the mailbox. "No, I don't think so." He checked a clipboard on the passenger seat. "Says here…" He read off our address.

I took a quick step back and tried to remember if I'd mailed in the Publisher's Clearing House forms. "Are you sure? Why?".

"I've got instructions to pick up a Ms. Katrina Morgan." He smiled benignly.

"What? That's me! What's going on?"

"Not allowed to say, Maam."

I stared, not having the slightest ideas what to do, what to say, where to put my hands.

"Katrinaaaaa...," John yelled from the porch. "You need to get in here!" He waved frantically toward the house like a third base coach signaling me home.

I jogged toward the house; one stride had me looking at John, the next at the limo still idling in the driveway. "What's going on?" I concentrated on John's face, looking for clues. "That guy says he's here for me."

John grinned. Spencer and Michael's heads appeared beside him, and he held a finger to his mouth, indicating they should stay silent.

Having reached the front door, I kept pestering, "Seriously. What's going on?"

"You're going to be gone for a while today. The kids and I are fine."

Deanna piped in, "I'll help with the boys, Mom." She'd come from the kitchen, smiling conspiratorially at her dad.

"What do you mean *I'll* be gone for a while today? Where? Why a limo? How come you guys aren't going?" I peppered the air with question marks.

John dodged them easily and dragged me toward the stairs. "You're just going to have to trust me." He pulled me toward our room. Carefully laid out on the bed was one of my favorite summer dresses—soft green, long, sleeveless. White sandals that had seen better days were on the floor. "Remember that shower I kept trying to get you to take? Well, now you know why." He glanced at the clock. "You've got five minutes, tops, to rinse off the dirt...change," he pointed toward the bed, "and get in that car. No questions either. You'll find out soon enough."

He shoved me toward the bathroom and took off down the stairs.

I scrubbed as best I could, watching dirt circle its way down the drain. Hurriedly shaving my calves, I decided there wasn't enough time to do the entire leg. *No one will know.* I shook damp hair loose from its ponytail and hung upside down brushing it into submission. More moisturizer was slapped on, mascara applied, and a quick slash of lip-gloss. John knocked on the door, urging me to hurry.

Running past my grinning family, I grabbed my purse, slid on my sandals and headed toward the door. "Wait!" I skidded to a stop. "Do I need money?" I fumbled in my purse.

John grabbed a ten, shoved it in my hand and held the front door open.

"What about Spencer? He needs to go to the doctor. Will I be home in time?"

"Quit worrying! We've got it under control." John gave me a quick kiss, patted me on the behind and propelled me outside.

The chauffeur, who was waiting beside the car, tipped his hat again and opened the car door. "Ronald at your service, Maam."

I slid into luxury, acting as though I was accustomed to traveling in style. John and three kids stood on the porch waving. I sat in the back, trying to fix my hair, shuffling my feet. "Where are we going, Ronald?" I talked through the window separating the front seat from the back. "It is Ronald and not Ron, correct?"

"Yes, Maam. Ronald will do just fine. I'm afraid I can't say where you're going. You'll be all right. Looks like you were surprised this morning."

"Boy, is that the understatement of the year."

"How about if we stop and get you a cup of coffee?"

"That sounds great. I could use some caffeine." I half hoped someone I knew would see me in the limo, and immediately rejected the idea. I was a mess. Scrounging through my ill-matched purse, I took a quick inventory; Billfold, ten-dollar bill, three pennies, half pack of smokes, one mostly used pack of matches, a partially wrapped piece of gum and lip gloss. Great. I didn't even have my phone and wondered uneasily about driving off with a strange man.

As promised, we stopped at the corner gas station. It boasted a *Starbucks* that I'd never even tried. Before I could open my door, Ronald had hopped out and was holding it open for me like royalty. Patrons stared, forgot they were pumping gas, buying candy, drinks. I felt a thousand eyes on me and wished I was anywhere else in my scuffed sandals and make-up free face. Taking a big breath, I marched inside;

head held high. "Do you want anything?" I called back to Ronald. He smiled and shook his head. Splurging on a small Espresso, I had $5.47 left to my name but carried myself like an heiress back to the waiting car.

We cruised onto the highway, and I sat in back trying to imagine where we were going. We passed the exit for town, heading further north, and I smiled. "The airport!" I spoke aloud.

"We're going to the airport, aren't we?" The driver said nothing. I composed a quick story of John flying my parents in as a surprise and sending me to the airport in a limo, to fetch them. I imagined their faces, the fun weekend we would have. I sipped hot, bitter coffee and smiled.

The exit for the airport came and went. Ronald grinned in the rear-view mirror. I tried to imagine John sending me to a place in Cleveland but couldn't come up with a decent scenario. I took in the scenery and watched the dashboard clock. Forty minutes had passed, and nothing looked familiar anymore. We exited the highway, took a few left turns and stopped in front of an exclusive spa- -one I'd read about in our paper. I looked at the building in horror, scrambled for more lip-gloss, even considered a quick smoke. Sure as hell, Ronald parked the car and opened my door.

I exited in slow motion. "I don't even know what they do at these places. Look at me, Ronald. I can't go in there!" I whined. "Maybe you'd better take me back home."

If I expected the driver to save me, he didn't. The traitor opened the door to the spa and gestured grandly inside. "Have a nice day Mrs. Morgan. I'll pick you up at four this afternoon."

With that, the door closed, and he headed toward the car.

"Four? What am I supposed to do for six hours?" I stared at his back, incredulous. I stood just inside, afraid to take another step, and looked at the group of fabulously put together people smiling, standing near the counter and calling out a cacophony of greetings.

"Good morning, Mrs. Morgan."

"We're so glad to see you, Mrs. Morgan."

"Did you have a nice trip, Mrs. Morgan?"

Customers were staring, trying to determine if I was a person of import—some local celebrity. I clasped my hands together to hide my fingernails, turned my scuffed shoes into one another and wished I'd listened to John about that shower. Trying to regain some sense of composure, I smiled. "I admit you," I gestured toward the crowd of workers, "have the advantage. I have no idea what's going on today."

They nodded knowingly, sent a few surreptitious glances at my apparel and lack of grooming. An older, regal woman stepped forward and pulled at my hands. "Your husband has arranged for you to be here the entire day. He's taken care of everything, the bill, the gratuity, the driver, and even lunch. We've been instructed to give you the full package—head to toe."

I'm sure she wanted to add, "And, honey, you need it!" However, she was a smart businesswoman and left the obvious unsaid. "Tracey will take you to your changing room."

Tracey stepped forward, and I followed the supermodel down a short hallway. *How can anyone look like that at ten a.m.?* She opened a door and gestured me into a small, opulent room, beautifully wallpapered and furnished with a plush Victorian chaise lounge and fresh flowers.

"You'll need to undress completely and…"

"Naked? I need to be *naked*?" I interrupted, destroying my last shred of dignity.

"Well, yes. You'll be au natural, but we're providing you a spa robe and slippers for the day." Manicured hands pointed toward what looked to be a white shag rug hanging beside the door. I noticed clear sandals peeking out from beneath the lounge and felt my face color with stupidity.

She politely ignored my embarrassment. "This room is assigned to you. Leave all clothing, and personal effects here; your purse, jewelry, including *all* piercings you may have." Her eyebrows rose slightly, suggesting that she suspected nothing less of me.

I snickered. I couldn't help it. *She must think I'm a real piece of work to mention body piercings.*

Tracey resumed the conversation, "The room is locked until your spa treatment is complete. You'll return here at that time. Press the buzzer beside the door once you've donned the robe. Lana will show you to your rose-petal bath." Tracey smiled, perfectly bleached teeth gleaming, wished me a pleasant day, and the door clicked shut.

I stood quietly, taking in the room, and the magnitude of what John had done. I bounced on the chaise and looked at the sandals. After checking for cameras, I undressed, grabbed the robe and slipped into luxury. A pleasured sigh escaped, and I wondered if I got to keep the robe. I pressed the buzzer, pasted a neutral expression on my face and waited for the next experience. *Lead on. Lead on.*

Lana, a small dark woman, led me to another beautiful room. Twin columns outlined a sunken tub. Candles, placed on every available surface, reflected soft light and elegance. The warm, scented water bubbled softly while dozens and dozens of rose petals swirled across the surface, slow dancing to the classical piano piece sobbing softly from hidden speakers.

My newest guide was quieter and simply smiled at my astonishment. "Enjoy. Relax. We'll be back in twenty minutes."

Panicked, I grabbed her arm, "Wait. I hate to ask, but today has been a complete and total surprise. Do you happen to have a razor I can use?" I bit my lip, embarrassed to have asked, but desperate to fix my overall condition of arrival.

She nodded discreetly. "I'll be right back."

Although I was supposed to be savoring, soaking and relaxing, I used my time to scrub away the remaining bits of yard work. I punished my skin with a loofah, something that was probably meant as decoration. My legs were fully shaven, and I let the oils and scents soak into sad, neglected skin. Not knowing how such things work, I pulled the stopper for the drain, dried myself and put the robe back on, feeling more confident, until I looked at the empty tub. *Oh my God!* There, for anyone to see, was a faint ring around the perimeter of what should have been a lady's bath. *Now what?* Frantic, I looked for a solution. All towels, robes, and accessories were white. Grabbing the loofah, I ran it under hot water and scrubbed away evidence of my less than feminine soak. Rinsing it clear, I set the room to rights and waited for whatever other humiliations the day would bring.

A quiet knock at the door, had me following another woman down the hallway toward a full body massage. More nakedness was required, and I mentally thanked Lana for that razor.

"Do you have any injuries or previously broken bones?" The masseuse asked, holding out a small bowl. "We like to lay warm stones on such areas."

I lifted myself off the table to peer into the mysterious bowl. I counted three stones. "Well, for starters, you're gonna need more rocks." I laughed. "I haven't been kind to myself over the years." I then proceeded to list of areas of concern; "Two broken fingers—left hand—Wallyball accident, broken right index finger—car door. I fell down some stairs and broke the left foot. The right ankle area's been smashed." I sent her a smile. "That one's complicated. I managed to run over myself with my car. If you want to make me happy though, put all your stones on my lower back. I've done nothing but lift and haul for the last six months."

Kneading my muscles and placing the stones as instructed, the girl commented, "You're far more active than our other patrons." She sounded relieved, and I relaxed having finally found another woman that worked hard all day.

In another room, the technician asked, "When was the last time you had a pedicure?"

"Never. Not one time," I answered honestly, giving up on pride. "I like to go barefoot."

A massive, two-foot long file materialized, and she began to remove what seemed eight layers of skin from each foot. Toes and fingers were soaked in soap, oil, turpentine, anything to remove the stains, the cracks, the calluses. Soft new skin emerged, shiny and clean. She buffed and polished, cleaned and shaped. Extensions were added to my fingernails, and I watched in fascination as my man hands disappeared. I wiggled red nails, marveling at the transformation.

Lunch, however, was a disaster. A small café, catering to the rich and boring, served ridiculously small portions of salad, tuna and apple slices. My stomach rumbled in complaint. I sat with two swanky women who took turns bragging on their exhausting days spent shopping, playing tennis and attending clubs. "I just *had* to come in today!" one woman exclaimed. "The week's been absolutely crazy."

I gave an accounting of one of my normal weeks— swinging hammers, applying drywall mud, hauling construction material and shoveling rock into cisterns. They were amused by me, and smug in their superiority. I reached into my purse, pulled out my sad five-dollar bill and laid it next to my very empty plate. The attendant slid it back toward me. "That's not necessary, Mrs. Morgan. Your husband handled all gratuities."

Oops. I'd forgotten about that part and simply followed my own habits. How ridiculous is it to have your tip returned? I slid it into my purse and wished I could go home, but trapped, and without means, I had no choice but to endure. I longed to slip outside and grab a quick smoke but couldn't figure out how to pull that off while wearing just a robe.

Next, I landed in a stylist's chair. "Who normally cuts your hair?" the perky brunette asked, holding a section of my hair up for inspection, frowning at the split-ends, and the lack of body.

"I have no preference. Wherever I happen to be when it's most convenient."

The girl came close to swooning. "We're going to soak this in conditioner and give you a new look."

I was less than happy to find my head wrapped in towels and then foil, while they highlighted, cut, dried, fussed and moussed. It took two hours, and to help pass the time, they gave me a damn Glamour magazine to read.

Two more women took advantage of my predicament and moved in, demanding that I sit still while they applied foundation, powder, liners, eye shadow, blush and lipstick.

"Keep it simple." I was getting cranky and had a few demands of my own, "I don't normally wear a lot of make-up. Don't make me look like a clown."

Four o'clock arrived, and although I'd technically not done a single, physical thing all day, I was exhausted. I slid on my dress, gathered my purse and ran outside to smoke while I waited for my ride home. *It's hard work being on display all day; to have people poke and prod, scrape, file, cut and apply all types of chemicals, cosmetics, and paint.* I had a new appreciation for what my poor old house must feel like after one of our long, busy weekends of renovation.

Ronald, my morning kidnapper, returned and ushered me back inside the limo. "Looks as though you had a nice day, Mrs. Morgan."

"Well, it was certainly an experience." I slid gracefully into the car, trying to be a lady. I admired my nails while Ronald climbed in the driver's seat. "I'll be honest with you, Ronald. I don't think country women are cut out for the spa. I spent most of the day feeling out of my element." I swung my new hair around, not even realizing I was preening. "My mom has a saying, "You can't make a silk purse out of sow's ear.""

Ronald barked a quick laugh. "Never hear that one before." Catching my eye in the mirror, he continued, "But if you want my opinion, it's not the outside that makes you a lady."

I smiled my appreciation, leaned my head against leather and closed my eyes. I wanted to remember all the details, embarrassing and otherwise to share with John and the kids. As a result, I paid little attention to the drive until we took an exit toward downtown. "Hey, where are we going?"

Ronald just smiled.

"More surprises?" I groaned. "I can't take anymore!" More alert, I sat up and watched the tall buildings of Cleveland slide past my window. We pulled into the circular drive of a luxury hotel, and my breath caught. There, standing out front, sporting a brand-new three-piece suit and looking more handsome than a man had a right to, was John.

The car had barely come to a stop, and I was out the back door and running toward my husband. I wrapped arms around him and kissed him in front of God and everyone. "Oh my Gosh! What a day! Look at you in a suit. What are you doing here? What's going on?"

He held me away at arm's length, taking in my appearance, turning me from side to side. "Wow. You look so beautiful. I've got more to say, but you need to wait a minute." He inclined his head toward the car. "I think we need to let the driver go."

A bemused Ronald stood by the open door of the limo.

I giggled a little girl's laugh. "Sorry, Ronald. I couldn't help myself."

"He grinned. "I've had more fun today than I have in a long time."

John walked over, shook his hand, and tipped him. *Thank God. My Five dollars would have been an insult.*

Ronald tipped his hat, one more time. "Maam." And with that, he drove away, never to be seen by the likes of us again.

John led me inside the lobby, dangling a room key in front of my face. "I've got the most incredible woman in the city, as my date for the night." He pushed an elevator button.

"The night? We're staying *overnight*? I put on the brakes. "What about the kids? Did Spencer get to the doctor? I don't' have anything else with me. We can't stay."

The elevator opened, and John pulled me inside, stopping the questions with a long and passionate kiss. Marching purposefully down a hall, he scanned numbers while his bewildered wife followed a few paces behind. Having found the correct room, he opened the door with a flourish. "Deanna's babysitting the boys. My parents are on emergency call, just in case. Spencer's been to the doctor and has a prescription." He pulled me inside. A plush living room looked out over the city; a four-poster bed and master bath dominated the rest of the space. I couldn't believe what I was seeing and stood in one spot afraid it would all disappear.

John took off his jacket, threw the key on a table, and kept answering my questions. "As for clothes, make-up and all that girl stuff, we're going shopping right now."

My eyes grew huge. "Oh God! What is it? You can tell me, honest." I walked toward the living room and plopped down on a chair.

John frowned. "What are you talking about?"

"You're sick right? Something is horribly wrong. That's why I got all this special treatment today and shopping tonight, right?" I was half-joking, but the whole day was such abnormal behavior for John, I couldn't quite ignore the tiny voice in the back of my brain that whispered, "H*eart condition, something serious…maybe cancer.*"

John pulled me up from my seat. "Our anniversary is coming. I wanted to do something really special, and memorable. I looked in your closet, and you don't have one new thing in there. In fact, most of your clothes are ruined from working on the house. Your make-up is broken, bits and pieces everywhere. You haven't spent a dime on yourself in months. You've done more, complained less than any woman I know. I've been so caught up in the damn house, the work, and the stress, I haven't even said thank you." He sat on the couch and patted me next to him. "So, today is my thank you. My way of saying I love you. I couldn't do any of it, not the house, the kids, the job…none of it without you."

Tears welled in my eyes. "I love you too." Reaching out to him, I sobbed softly into his crisp new shirt. I was overcome, grateful to be appreciated—cherished.

Hand in hand, we walked to a downtown shopping area and spent hours getting Katrina outfitted and accessorized. Like the scene from *Pretty Woman*, I tried on clothes, loaded John down with bags and smiled non-stop. Back in the room, I poured the contents onto the bed, admiring a dress, slacks, blouses, make-up, creams, expensive shampoos, nylons, shoes. "Look at me! I'm a princess for the day!"

We called to check on the children, changed into new clothes, and headed toward a romantic dinner. It was another thing John had thought through, planned, and orchestrated. Laughing like newlyweds, we crashed back into our room, giddy from wine and conversation. Lights from the city bathed our bodies as we danced in front of the windows. We were lost in the moment and each other. John leaned back, looking at me intently. "Did you have a good day?"

Sending him a siren's smile, I responded, "Let me show you." Soft arms, painted nails, and smooth legs wrapped around him as I led him toward the bed, planning on giving as much as I had received.

Chapter 28

Mired in Mud

"This house is killing me!" John lamented, looking at the list of things to finish. It seemed to grow longer, that list, never shorter. We'd spent a month, following our romantic getaway, tapping crown molding into place in all the downstairs rooms and adding storage closets wherever we could find the room. My nails were chipped, and my feet back to being bare.

"We probably need another year," John said it sadly, ashamed his earlier prediction of finishing the house in a year, had not been true. He's sworn to my mom and dad, way back in March, when everything was shiny, new and possible, that he'd have the entire house done in a year. That anniversary date was just four months away. It may as well have been an eternity since the list of things to do, fix and build grew longer, not shorter.

The Old Woman sighed, found a book to read and settled in to wait. "You two are something else, you know that? You won't even stop long enough to enjoy what you've done. It's always more, more, more."

Sliding the morning's weather report across the table, I pointed to it hopefully. "I'm sick of working inside. Let's head outside."

Glancing at the colorful weather report depicting little yellow sun pictures and warmer temperatures, he agreed, "Sounds good to me!"

Grabbing jackets, we stepped out the back door and balanced on our sad little stoop. We hadn't fixed the back entrance yet, one of those items still on the list. Huge chunks of concrete were missing or lying nearby. One corner had crumbled, and moss grew in the crevices. It was a precarious exit at best, and I should have taken heed. I turned to make room for John and slashed my nose wide open on an old dinner bell hanging by the door. "Ow! Shit!"

The rusted bracket was more bent than ever, and my eyes were watering profusely. I was also bleeding all over myself, and not happy my first chance to get outside had resulted in an injury. I ran to get a paper towel.

"Sure didn't take you long to hurt yourself," John called through the open door. Hearing him snicker, I yelled for him to be quiet, but it was already well-documented I was not known for my gracefulness.

"Let's check out the pond," John suggested

It sounded good to me. I assumed the pond would be easy compared to everything else we'd tackled. Lifting the towel again, I saw that most of the bleeding had stopped and trooped behind John, stumbling over a hidden root and bruising my ankle in the process. I prayed John hadn't noticed.

Michael and Spencer had followed us outside, anxious to see their yard too. At the word pond, they headed for the water, yelling and running just for the sheer joy of doing so. Scooby-Doo bounded along beside them, happy to have playmates. His brindle coat matched the patterns of sun and shadow that passed through tree limbs near the pond.

John stomped through thorns, and we two pushed our way forward, ready to enjoy our first hard look at the pond. Stepping gingerly to the edge of the pond, I encountered deep, slick mud. "This is pretty bad." I slid.

"Wonder how deep this thing is in the middle," John wondered, unaware that the mud was creeping up his shoes toward his ankles.

Taking it all in, our disappointment sank in deep. Nature had marched forward unhampered and, like a naughty child, she'd created havoc while we'd been busy with the house. Thorn bushes abounded, weaving their branches together in dream-catcher patterns. Tall yellow grasses had dried and clumped together, laid over by rain and neglect. I was certain, if left uncut, they'd eventually turn into a metropolis for chiggers and mosquitoes. Storms had dislocated part of the enormous swamp willow along the bank, dumping huge chunks of it into the middle of the pond, leaving them there like forgotten toys.

The Old Woman stood at the edge of the pond. "My, look at the size of those pines." She remembered the day they'd been planted more than fifty years prior.

Disillusioned, I didn't hear her or the wonderment in her voice. "I had no idea a pond could look this bad," I stated, picking up a stick and poking through a thin layer of scum.

"It must be pretty shallow to have all that junk on top," John agreed.

Like everything else in our world, it would require sweat and exertion first. I sighed, knowing our lazy days were somewhere off in the muddy future. We convinced ourselves we could handle the work and concentrated on understanding the dynamics of how our pond filled and emptied.

The boys didn't seem to have a problem with the appearance. They balanced on the rocks of a small, ineffectual dam, tossed sticks into the water, dug along the shore.

Spencer worked something free from the mud and ran toward us. "What's this?" he asked eagerly, sure he'd found treasure.

Michael followed him over to me, jealously hoping Spencer had not found anything of value. Turning it over in my hands I recognized what he'd found. "It's an old fishing bobber."

Spencer frowned, not having the slightest idea what I meant.

John leaned in to see it too. "It goes on the end of a fishing line—when it bounces or jiggles..." John's voice trailed off. He'd not even been able to finish his explanation. Both boys were running flat out for the shed.

"Come on, Spence," Michael called over his shoulder, "let's go fishing!"

"Yeah, fishing," Spencer agreed, his shorter legs pumping full out to keep up with his brother.

Scooby-Doo tripped over himself in his eagerness to be with the boys but threw on the brakes when he saw where they'd gone. He stood at the shed door, quivering, unsure if he wanted to join them in that dark place.

Stupid dog. I said to myself for the thousandth time. I knew why he'd been at the animal shelter. He'd been born without a brain and proved it daily.

John and I could hear things being tossed around in the shed as they eagerly searched for tackle boxes and fishing poles. We looked at each other and grimaced. Neither of us had the heart to tell them there were probably no fish in the water, or, if there were, they'd be pretty small.

We continued our pond discussion. "If we clear the branches, and build up the dam, it will help," John said confidently and headed toward the shed for his chainsaw. We knew not one thing about dams and water, but ignorance had never stopped us before.

John helped rescue fishing equipment, and together, we untangled fishing lines and attached Spencer's new bobber to the end of his pole. They'd found old baseball hats and turned them backward, indicating their seriousness about the fishing idea. They raced back to the pond to see who could put their pole in the water faster.

John fired up the saw and began clearing. I gathered and hauled. We weren't getting anywhere since the boys were hitting serious roadblocks on their fishing expedition. Yelling at one another, they took turns casting, getting their lines ten, maybe fifteen feet across the pond. They reeled in lines full of decayed leaves and slimly duckweed. It meant John and I often stopped to untangle lines and free poles.

Spencer let loose of a decent cast, and his line and bobber landed twenty feet out toward the middle of the pond. The line snagged on the partial tree trunk floating there and wound itself several times around the branches.

Spencer's face fell. "My bobber—" He yanked and pulled his pole trying to save his prize, all to no avail. He sat on the bank and sniffed.

Michael patted his back, in an unusual show of brotherly concern. "It's okay, Spence, maybe the wind will get it free or something."

"Maybe I can get it for you!" Wanting to fix his sad little face, I didn't stop to think about the ramifications. Ever the one to prove her strength and valiance, I waded, uncaring, into bitterly cold water to save the bobber and untangle the line. It was late October, and the temperature easily dipped into the low forties at night. I wished I'd thought of that before taking a swim. The mud pulled at my boots, but I figured it would all disappear once I got five or six feet from the bank. I assumed I could paddle the remaining distance to the middle and reach the branches. Not so.

The further I went from shore, the deeper the mud. I was knee deep and unable to pull my legs free. Panicked, I kicked but could find no solid footing. I was sinking, and called out to John, "Pull me out of here!"

He'd been watching my slow, unsuccessful progress and shook his head as though I was a sissy girl. "Hang on. I'll be right back." He jogged toward the shed to find a rope while I tried to ignore the fact that I would soon be submerged.

He threw the rope toward me while I begged him to hurry. "I'll get you out. Quit worrying! Jeez!"

"Why don't you come out here? See if you like it!" I dared him.

Not being much of a swimmer, he declined gracefully.

I made it to solid ground, which was amazing as each of my boots seemed to weigh no less than twenty pounds. I stopped for the day. I could have cared less about the bobber and patted Spencer's head absently. "Sorry, little man." Freezing, I headed for the house, stripping boots and jeans at the back door. The boys turned their hats around to face the front and went off in search of something else to occupy their time.

As Sunday evening rolled into place, one side of the pond had been cleared, vines chopped from trees, and numerous unsuccessful attempts had been made to haul the branches from the center of the pond. I continued the work on the area throughout the week, reveling in the instant gratification that came from such physical transformation.

The maples had created a magnificent display or oranges, yellows, and golds. Cedars turned rusty, and even the damn poison ivy that thrived on our property had turned crimson, winding itself tightly around every tree. I whacked all those vines at the bottom and pulled them loose. I sawed through thorns, freeing a twisted apple tree from their grasp. My parents were coming into town that week and I couldn't wait to show them the latest changes. We could finally walk around the perimeter of the pond, and I was getting more excited. Now that there was room to see possibilities, the dreams came quickly. "We could get one of those aerators. That would keep the water clear," I mused.

"Maybe we should buy a paddle boat or something," John suggested, getting into the spirit of things.

My parents arrived, and we happily welcomed them into our midst. They seemed shocked by the changes inside and out. It had been almost three months since their last visit, and we'd been very busy. After admiring all the newly decorated rooms, moldings, and trim work, they wandered outside, appreciating the pond and listening to fish stories from the boys. Deanna raced into the driveway, anxious to visit too.

That Saturday morning, we all donned long sleeves and began to clear. John cut, and the rest of us hauled and burned the excess. Deanna, uncharacteristically home on a Saturday, tugged and shoved at what appeared to be a half-buried footbridge. "I can't get this out. I need some help here!"

We all joined her and finally heaved it over the stream. Spencer ran back and forth across the bridge as though it was the first one ever created. We sweated and smiled, knowing the end was in sight. All that was left were the large limbs still in the water.

We built a Flintstone-style fire, with flames shooting fifteen feet in the air and curling the leaves of nearby trees. Grandpa took over fire duty. It seemed to be his thing—fire. Didn't matter if it was a raging bonfire, a cozy fireplace or the outdoor grill, he liked to supervise, coax and build the flames, so they were perfect. We let him be in charge and kept hauling branches and thorns to him so he could feed his creation.

"This is like being a settler and clearing land to make a homestead," I explained to Michael and Spencer, who were not thrilled at the amount of hauling they were doing.

"I'd rather be fishing," Michael complained, not caring about history.

Spencer was chattering non-stop and bringing one stick at a time to the fire. Nana and Grandpa seemed to be enjoying themselves. They watched and listened to their three grandchildren, who lapped up all the focused attention like an ice-cream sundae. John joined us at the fire, taking a much-needed break from the constant sawing and hauling he'd been doing. He listened to the kids for a while, and, I swear, I saw an idea light bulb click on directly over his head. He smiled and gestured me aside. "I've got an idea." I listened and grinned.

We didn't say a word to anyone, just headed to the edge of the yard and disappeared behind a pine tree. Together, he and I rolled an old tire out of a tangle of vegetation. We'd seen it there eons before. John rescued a rope from the shed and began trying to throw it over a large branch of a tree near the pond. Michael and Spencer watched his movements apprehensively, wondering, perhaps, if Dad had finally snapped. Deanna stopped what she was doing, cocked her head and decided she'd better investigate. Nana and Grandpa stood back smiling, having already guessed what we were doing. Understanding dawned for the children when we tied the rope to the tire, and both boys began to hop around excitedly. Even Deanna seemed anxious to try, although she tried to act uninterested, above such childish play.

I stood back, smiling, watching them each fly skyward and back on their new swing. We four adults took turns pushing the tire up and away.

They alternately screeched in delight or argued over whose turn it was next. Scooby ran beneath the swing, getting knocked in the head with each pass, never learning to step back from the danger.

We played and enjoyed the rest of the weekend, having accomplished quite a lot.

November was peeking around the corner, and the pond was not finished. The stupid tree branches and limbs still lodged in the middle were making John crazy. We'd tried snagging the offensive limbs, using poles and every tool at our disposal, but had little luck. The tree remained stuck fast. John frowned toward the pond and announced that we were getting the tree out that weekend. "I don't care if we have to rent a bulldozer!" It was a declaration…a proclamation. I sighed, having grown sick of the pond and its unending demands.

I slogged out to start another fire while he wandered toward the pond, searching for a solution. I watched covertly as he made several trips to the pond from the shed. After my last go- around in the water, I wasn't anxious to offer assistance and kept myself very busy and unavailable.

The Old Woman watched his comings and goings, growing more curious too.

He went by with another old rope he'd found, and I made a note of that as I threw thorns on the fire. He lumbered past again carrying a tangle of roots. *What is he up to now?* I worked my way to the other side of the fire, watching him through my hair. On his third pass, he sauntered by with three ten-foot-long boards and a shovel.

"Alright—I give up. What are you doing?" I called out as I made my way to the pond.

He flashed a bright smile. "I knew I'd get to you eventually." He was giving no clues and enjoying my curiosity.

Looking at his strange assortment, I asked, "What's the plan?"

"I'm going to tie a rope around these roots and use them as a grappling hook. If I can get closer to those limbs, I think I can grab them and pull them to shore."

I wasn't so sure and watched while he built a dock of sorts out of his boards. He laid them across the mud, toward the center, gaining maybe ten feet at the most.

The Old Woman had come outside to watch the proceedings. "Obviously, he's up to something." She walked around the pond, surprised by how much better it was looking.

"Okay. So, I get that you're trying to get closer, but what's the shovel for?" I asked, skeptical already of his strange way of doing things.

"I'm going to the end of the boards to throw the root. I'll hold one end of the shovel. You hold the other. If I start to fall, you can pull me back."

"Got it?" he asked, needing affirmation, as I was uncharacteristically quiet.

"No, not really. This seems ridiculous. Maybe you should practice first."

Going back to the fire, I watched him tie the rope around his roots and start flinging. The root fell off immediately, and he had to fish it out of the pond. I snickered and acted as if I'd seen nothing when he shot a look my way.

He got it back together and was swinging and flinging with some success. My own urban cowboy. He managed to snag a couple of branches. "Are you ready for me yet?"

"Yeah, come on out here and stand on the end of these boards."

I got situated on the bank, holding my end of the shovel. John headed out on the planks, arms spread wide for balance. He held the roots and rope in one hand and his end of the shovel in the other. "Okay, be ready to haul me!"

Balancing one-handed, he had trouble throwing the root, and it seemed to take forever. I drifted off, looking around, trying to identify the trees and not paying much attention. The whole exercise seemed silly. *Who cared if there was a tree in the pond?* He swung, flung and began to falter. Shoving the shovel backward, he screamed, "Pull!"

The primal yell brought me out of my meanderings quickly. Sizing up the situation, I yanked with everything I had. Being slightly chagrined at having been caught daydreaming, I exerted more effort than necessary. One minute John was teetering and the next he was flying through the air, still clinging to his shovel.

He landed with a loud thwack; face down and in the thick mud near shore, and exactly where he did not want to be. He clawed free of the mud and turned to face me. At the sight, I lost my composure, not even trying to act as if I was sorry. He was covered from head to toe with green-black sludge. Only his eyes and teeth gleamed white.

The Old Woman let out a cackle and pointed at John.

Not aware of his appearance, he turned toward me and yelled, "What the hell are you thinking?"

It didn't seem wise to answer his question truthfully, and I bent over laughing, eyes streaming. He sputtered and cussed, trying to find his footing. To make matters worse, I wouldn't let him in the house.

"There is no way you're going in like that. You'll ruin the carpet and new floors." I sprayed him down with the hose, causing more sputtering and cussing. Well water is cold, particularly in late Fall.

During the following week, John had a lot of time to consider the problem because he couldn't talk to me without getting mad again. Every time he tried to hold a civilized conversation, I pictured him covered in mud and started giggling.

He finally talked over my laughter. "I want to get a bulldozer or Bobcat in here to level out the yard and take a look at the pond. We need someone who knows what the hell they're doing."

I kept a very straight face and agreed. The Old Woman snorted and left the room.

Chapter 29

A Little Warning, Please

After a series of phone calls, John settled on a local contractor to help us with the yard. "He's got a Bobcat, bulldozer, dump truck—everything we could possibly need. He's gonna stop by Tuesday night." He seemed to have forgotten the mud ordeal, and I was greatly relieved. It had been tiring walking on tiptoes for a week.

We even managed to get the tree out of the water. It required me wading back out there to get ropes and chains wrapped around the damn thing. Teeth chattering, I was determined to make this attempt at extraction a success.

The Old Woman laughed at me in the pond. "Didn't think you'd be going back in there. Foolish girl, always gotta make everybody happy."

I convinced myself the water was not as cold as I remembered. "It's only October. It's warmer. It's not so bad," I chanted to myself, dragging first one leg then another through the mud. Knowing my enemy, it was easier to deal with on round two. Besides, I would have done anything to make up to John. Things, in general, operated much more smoothly when he and I were speaking.

He stood by the bank, encouraging me. "Just a little further. You can do it!" My truck was parked nearby, waiting for me to loop logging chains around the tree trunks. John planned to hitch them to the back of my truck and pulling the tree free. I made it to land and stomped my boots to get free of the mud and encourage circulation in my frozen legs.

John put the Navigator in four-wheel drive and inched forward, watching the side mirrors to make sure nothing broke loose. "Stay back!" he yelled at me. I moved further away so he could see me, still stomping and shivering.

I watched as the tree began to move. "You've got it, baby! It's coming!" In slow motion, the tree slid an inch, two more. I heard a loud sucking noise as the mud finally let loose. The tree picked up momentum. "Pull, Johnny! Don't stop, it's free!"

I saw him nod, and the truck went faster. Waterlogged and huge, we celebrated its arrival on shore. Three feet wide and twenty feet long, we understood why it had not been moved by poles, ropes, and tangled roots. We left it there to dry and decided we'd cut it up later. We saluted one another with a beer and thought ourselves quite smart.

Tuesday evening arrived, and we eagerly awaited our yard savior. As dusk settled, Dave showed up for his first visit to The Old Woman. He pulled into the driveway, an enormous, black truck dieseling in the driveway. "You the Morgans?" he called out through the drivers-side window, eyeing Scooby-Doo cautiously.

"You've got the right place, but please—" I pointed at the dumb dog, "don't let him scare you. You'll just confuse him!"

Dave ambled out, shook John's hand and followed us to the backyard. "Let's see what you got going on around here."

As we rounded the corner of the house, his eyebrows shot up into his wide forehead. "Whew! Nice place, but you're right—definitely need some equipment around here." He walked toward the stumps.

John and I began to explain our ideas and outline the problems.

"There's a mound in the backyard. We'd like to know what that's all about. Level the yard out…" John gestured toward the yard and let it speak for itself.

"And the stumps have got to go!" I added, as though there was a question about the need for them to disappear.

Dave listened and nodded in all the right places. We liked him immediately, mostly because he saw no problem with our plans. We talked and joked, each of us mentally congratulating ourselves. John and I were pleased to have hired such a smart man. Dave thanked God he'd answered the phone that day. Our yard represented a goldmine for his business. We shook hands and set a time and a date for Saturday.

Michael jogged toward me, interrupting, which was totally out of character. "Mom, have you seen Scooby?" he asked, obviously concerned. I made a face at his rudeness, dipping my head toward Dave.

Michael got the hint, offered a quick apology, and got right back to the problem. "Have you? Seen Scooby, I mean?"

"He was here a little while ago, honey. I heard him barking— way out in the field."

Michael took off running, calling his beloved friend. I excused myself to go find Spencer. He hadn't been with Michael and surely that could not be a good thing. My mother's instincts were correct. I found him zipped inside a sleeping bag and sliding down the backstairs. "Look, Mommy, I'm sledding!" He'd at least thought to fill the bottom of the stairs with pillows and blankets.

Michael trooped in the back door, sad and obviously in need of mothering. "I can't find Scooby, Mom. I've looked everywhere!" he wailed, and his lower lip trembled once.

Hugging him close, I promised I'd help with the search as soon as I got Spencer squared away. Dave left, and Michael and I wandered acres, including neighboring land, calling and yelling for poor, sweet Scooby. I felt awful about all the mean names I'd called him, and my condescending attitude. Maybe he'd heard me, picked up on my negative vibes and run away to find a more compassionate owner. "Let's go get the car, Michael."

Car windows down, cold air whisking through the openings, we drove slowly down country roads. ""Ssssccooobbbyyyy," Michael called over and over, and my heart broke. Spencer echoed the plea from the back seat until they were both hoarse and crying. I imagined Scooby alone, shivering, and lost. I was consumed by guilt. I looked harder, squinting against the gathering gloom. I finally gave up and drove a silent car toward home.

"We'll keep looking," I promised unhappy boys, as we tucked them into bed.

John and Deanna took their turns too, driving, calling and looking. Days went by, and we finally admitted he was gone. Michael was inconsolable. He sat dejected, unwilling to go outside or play.

"Now what?" I asked John on Friday evening. I hated being so helpless.

"Maybe he'll still show up." John shrugged, taking the loss better than the rest of us.

"We've got Dave coming tomorrow!" He changed the topic, determined not to get too down about the situation.

"Hey, I've got the night off," Deanna chimed in. She'd been at the table, eating a late dinner and listening to our conversation. "I'll take the boys to a movie. Maybe that'll get their minds off it for a while."

I hugged her and John smiled as she went off to make things better.

Saturday arrived clear and bright. Fall was giving one last hurrah, swirling a kaleidoscope of color as far as the eye could see. I took time to enjoy the view. John spent the morning clock-watching and waiting for Dave. I trudged upstairs to find Michael and try another one of the hundreds of tactics I'd employed to cheer him. Nothing worked, and he sat in his room absently tossing Scooby's ball.

"Poor little thing," The Old Woman said, peeking in on Michael. "Ain't nothing worse than a boy losing a dog."

I heard Dave's big truck and scrambled toward the door, eager to see our yard transformed. "Come outside!" I yelled to the boys, "This should be fun!" Michael didn't look convinced. Spencer, however, was already glued to the window. The Old Woman looked over his shoulder and frowned at the machine she saw.

Dave stepped down from his truck, smiling and laughing. "Let me introduce you to my son Bob."

I looked in the truck, expecting to see a teenager. Dave followed my line of sight and grinned. "Nope, not in there. This here is Bob." He pointed toward his small bobcat, strapped to the back of the truck. "He's a big part of the family, so we named him."

Dave seemed to have a joke and a smile for everything, and we were enjoying ourselves. He wore an old baseball cap pulled down low on his forehead, and his tee shirt was stretched tight over his belly. He kept tugging at his jeans and shifting from foot to foot, like a child anxious to play with his toy.

He fired up Bob and noisily drove it off the back of the trailer and headed to the back. The boys flew out the back door, and I noted

Michael looked excited again. The Bobcat was the first piece of big machinery they'd ever seen up close. In their haste to get outside, they'd done half a job of dressing. Michael's shirt was on backward. Spencer had on mismatched shoes. Early signs of testosterone were popping as they cheered and ahhed, watching the machine crawl through the yard, chugging smoke and making noise.

The scoop lowered onto the mysterious mound of dirt, near the house. Huge chunks of it were torn loose. Dave's head popped in and out of the cab, checking the mound, his equipment. "There ain't nothing here. Just dirt," he yelled over the noise. "Maybe from where they dug out a septic or had a pool. Let me work Bob up near the house, and I'll start pushing this stuff toward your yard. Level it out like you want." He smiled again, obviously enjoying himself.

John and I grinned back happily.

"Stay back, boys, he can't see you!" John warned.

Spencer and Michael were a little disappointed, but I watched until they'd settled themselves by the back door. They still had great seats and watched the activity with big eyes.

As Dave got close to the house, the bobcat shifted and, like the home inspector months before, nearly fell into the old cistern. I'd filled it with rock, but Ol' Bob was heavy and cracked right through my feeble attempt at camouflage. The machine hung half in and half out of the hole, while Dave slammed gears and cussed.

We Morgans stood there, eyes wide, the boys half-hoping he would fall in, too young to understand the danger of such a thing actually happening. More astute, we parents wondered if we would be liable. *Does home insurance cover this?*

Dave backed up quickly, finding solid ground. He removed what was left of the cracked concrete lid, and, with Bob's help, carried it to the weeds. We looked into a deep hole despite all the stone I'd shoveled in there. The cistern had two compartments, something we'd not been aware of at all. My stone barely filled one side.

"Good damn thing you got this pile of dirt. I need it to fill this shit in. That's dangerous as hell!" Dave wasn't nearly as happy as he had been.

John and I thought it dangerous too but were disappointed to watch all our extra dirt land in a hole instead of across the yard. *So much for that idea.*

Dave climbed down, took off his cap and wiped dirty hands and sweat across his brow. *Why do men take off their hats to think? I had to wonder if it was related to the Y chromosome. I'd seen Gene do it, and now Dave.*

"You got a Coke or something?" Dave asked, plunking his hat back on his head. I ran to the house as fast as I could. I didn't want him to give up and go home.

"Anything else I need to know 'bout?" he asked, slogging down half the can. "A little warning goes a long way, ya know?"

John and I made eye contact and grimaced. "There's a well near the driveway—probably needs some work," John admitted and went over to show Dave the cover. The two of them pried off the lid and looked into a long, brick tunnel.

"See? Right there. That's the shit I'm talking about." Dave stood up abruptly and blew out a breath. "I need to know about stuff like this. Working on your yard is one thing, getting hurt is another." He raised his eyebrows, chastising us.

Taking the hint, I piped up, "There's an old septic out here too," I walked out to show him where I thought it was located. The price went up, but what could we do?

An hour later, the well, the old septic, and the cistern were filled, and a trickle of dirt had been spread across the backyard. Dave started on the stumps, revving the machine to full throttle. The boys brought out cookies and sat on the step, munching and watching the show.

I offered Dave another Coke, which he took gratefully. "Whew! Well, we got the worst of it done. Let's start on them stumps." He kicked absently at them, bent down to get a better look. He hauled himself back into the Bobcat, ready to get things fired up again. He lowered the scoop and plowed forward, thinking the momentum would help loosen the stumps. Bob hit the stumps and stalled. Dave hit levers and pushed harder, revving the engine to full throttle. Bob was bucking and shaking, with the rear end coming clear off the ground. The stumps, however, stayed stubbornly planted.

"Cool!" One boy said.

"Awesome," the other answered.

"What the hell you got going on out here?" Dave called, removing his hat again.

"We're just trying for a backyard."

"Well, it's killin' Bob! Wish I had his brother Bull today!" He backed up and made another run, slowly forcing the ancient stumps free and carrying them to the woods. He leveled the yard and the holes where stumps had been as best he could. He shook his head at the mess of a yard. "You got anywhere else we can get dirt from?"

"The pond!" John and I both shouted at once. We were anxiously trying to explain things.

"It's too shallow, and we want to dig it out."

"How 'bout widening the stream and taking dirt from there?"

Dave laughed at us as he walked toward the water. He squished around, assessing the situation. "I can't do much now, it's kinda wet, but we can shape it up a little, grab a little dirt."

He took the Bobcat to the mouth of the pond where the stream rolled in. The area there was always wet, but he was convinced that if he widened it, the pond could fill more completely.

"That's not a good idea. That mud is weird, Dave," we warned.

Dave didn't seem to think it an issue and maneuvered Bob into place. He took one full scoop of that thick mud and began to falter. John and I watched in fascination as Dave tried to dig himself free. Michael and Spencer crept closer.

Dave slammed the scoop through the muck, making a mess of the stream and effectively damming it closed. The machine spun left and right, whining with the effort and belching out plumes of smoke. The more he struggled to get free, the deeper the mud became. It was halfway up the tracks and showed no signs of giving in at all.

Dave leaned out the cab to see the mud. "I need my dump truck to pull Bob out."

"Naw, I can get you out with our truck," John suggested and sprinted toward the house for keys.

"I don't think so, man. Bob's heavy," Dave called to John's back. He looked at me for help.

I shrugged and smiled. "You never know. Look at the tree we pulled out." I pointed at the still drying swamp willow lying by the pond. Dave didn't look convinced.

John connected logging chains to Bob and my 'Gator, threw the truck in gear and started pulling. Without much effort, Bob and Dave were extracted from the mud, the stream, the pond. The boys and I cheered. Dave climbed down, laughing and smiling again. "Well, I'll be damned. Bet Lincoln would like to see a tape of that!"

I handed beers to adults and Sprites to boys. Dave ran the cold can across his brow, "Bob can't take this mud. Let's try this next summer when things dry out."

The Old Woman stood in the backyard frowning, her lips small and thin. "What a mess.

Grass ruined. Mud everywhere. Pond dammed shut." She shook her head the whole way back to the house. "Why can't you two just relax? The yard was fine. It's not a competition, ya know?"

She slammed the back door, muttering about our need to have everything perfect.

Little could we know that things would not dry out or get better for a long time.

Chapter 30

With a Cherry on the Bottom

Between the pond and the yard, we'd spent more than a month outside, and it looked worse than ever. We gave up, moving our energies back inside.

Fall had folded in on itself, allowing for another change of season and we moved steadily toward our first holiday season with The Old Woman. The changing of the guard was symbolic, allowing us the luxury of replacing our anxieties with anticipation.

Early on a Saturday morning, John snuck out of bed and began making an enormous country breakfast. Following the scent of bacon and fresh coffee, I found him puttering around the stove, babying his skillets and almost happy for a change. The children followed their noses as well, and a boisterous gathering resulted. I relaxed, and smiled at John, silently thanking him for his foresight and helping us to turn a corner.

Lazily, I watched mammoth snowflakes drift past the kitchen windows. They clung to branches and against window screens, sashaying toward the yard. They were beginning to layer themselves into, what looked to be, several inches of winter. It was a bit early for such weather, but the kitchen, so warm and cozy, made it magical. Cardinals gathered in the lilac bush near the kitchen window, and we watched quietly, enjoying their close proximity. Slowly, the kids and I crept forward until we were kneeling at the window, our breath leaving fog on the glass. They cardinals hopped from branch to branch in obvious irritation.

They were looking for food, and I understood; someone, along the way, had hung a feeder there. The cardinals, creatures of habit, were letting us know how things were supposed to be. I made a mental note.

"Since I did the cooking, you guys get clean-up," John announced, interrupting our voyeurism. He'd put on a coat, gloves, and boots. "I'm heading to the barn."

I looked questionably at him. Normally, I was invited along on such outdoor projects. He winked and headed out the door. In between washing dishes and removing grease from the stove, I peeked out the kitchen window, trying to locate him and figure out what he was doing.

I heard Gene's old '57 Ford tractor fire up from the equipment barn. He'd brought it to us on the pretense of storage, but we knew he intended us to use it on our little gentleman's farm. It chugged and bounced its way toward the field, gray smog rolling along behind it. The blade was on the back, hanging a foot or so above the ground. I couldn't imagine what John intended to do and scrubbed faster in my haste to get outside.

I slid on my own coat, laced up my boots and opened the back door just as John drove up. He was all smiles, and I stood mesmerized by the effect. It had been a while since I'd seen his face look young, excited.

"Good! You've got your coat. Get the kids. They need to get bundled up too," he gushed before I'd even walked through the door.

"Why? What's up?"

Taking a secretive peek around, he tugged me outside and gestured toward the back of the tractor. There, tied together tandem style, were four sleds. He'd roped them all together and attached them behind the blade. "We're going sledding!" He looked like a little boy with a secret.

"Sledding? How can we go sledding? We don't have any big hills."

"I know." He winked, checked the knots and climbed back on the tractor.

I ran back inside to find the kids. I didn't have to go far. Having heard the tractor, all three children were in the kitchen, looking out windows and hopping around the room excited.

"We're going sledding!" I yelled, as though they needed an explanation.

Spencer made a beeline for the door.

"Not yet, little man!" I laughed at his eagerness. "You've got to get bundled up first."

Gloves, scarves, coats, extra socks seemed to fly in a frenzy of excitement. Deanna pitched items to the boys, while I zipped, tied and fastened as fast as my hands would go. We spilled out the back door, eager for the new adventure.

Hours went by, as we laughed and sledded and crashed. John had used the blade to smooth an oval around the perimeter of the field—our own NASCAR lap. We each climbed on sleds, balancing and screaming as John rolled us faster around the circle. The sleds tied together, made a crazy line of drivers, sometimes ending up side-by-side, sometimes passing one another. Physics took control of the last person, and they would slingshot around curves at invigorating speeds. It was impossible to hang on, and we took turns flying through the air and landing in snow. Gloves and hats were askew, often coming loose and landing far away. Winter paraphernalia littered the field, a late-season yard sale.

The Old Woman wrapped a shawl around her shoulders and tried to follow our movements from the back door. Able to see only a small section of the field through the trees, she climbed the stairs to look out the unobstructed, landing window. "Well, isn't that clever? No one's ever tried that one before."

Clumping toward the house, ice was crusted in our hair, balls of snow clung to the tops of boots, and our cheeks were flushed with cold and happiness, we five were once again a family united. Snagging a few small logs from the brush pile, I carted them with me toward the kitchen.

Hot cocoa was hastily stirred, stale marshmallows rescued from the back of the pantry, and a toasty fire built in the fireplace. "Boy, do we owe Mr. C. another thank you. This is awesome!" I exclaimed as John watched me blow on some of the more hesitant sparks.

The fire crackled and threw out welcome heat. We gathered near, watching the small flames dance in the grate. Deana and the boys ran off to change clothes, throwing around ideas as to how to spend the rest of their day.

The Old Woman stood in the foyer, watching John and me, in the kitchen, and listening to the satisfied voices of children. There were no arguments, no yelling. "This is more like it." She smiled, feeling warmed and satisfied too.

John and I snuggled together on the little hearth rug, finishing our hot chocolate and leaning into one another. "I've got a ton of laundry thanks to the sledding, but I don't care. That was fun."

"Yeah, it was. Next time, I'll teach you to drive the tractor. I think I might like a turn on one of those sleds." He grinned, and I rolled my head against his chest, pleased to see him still smiling.

"What else do you have in mind today, Mr. Morgan?" I was half-asleep and lazy.

He woke me immediately, with the announcement we could start on the foyers.

"Really?" I pulled myself into a sitting position, looking at him, surprised.

"Don't see why not. Seems as good a day as any." He was smug, a king, hero for the day.

I couldn't believe it. *John* was suggesting a project? "Wow, let's go sledding every Saturday." I smiled at him, already peeling off wet clothes and moving toward the front door. No way was I going to let an opportunity like that slip away.

"Where do we start?" I circled the rooms, noting the floor, the stairs, everything that needed to be fixed. None of us went barefoot across the separated and aged planked foyers anymore having dug out one too many splinters. Things had also been dragged and dropped down the stairs for decades. They showed the abuse with missing chunks and drips of paint.

"Tell you what, I'm going to grab a shower, change and run to the store. You start on the stairs, and I'll bring home the plywood for the floors."

We'd decided eons ago that we couldn't save the floors but didn't want to tear them out either. We would add underlayment, get them level, and put a new floor over the aged planks.

Nodding, I slid into work clothes and located tools. In sanding the stairs, I knew them to be mahogany-stained. I loved that dark look and knew it to be perfect for The Old Woman. She needed the dramatic to give her the proper clothing for her era—mahogany and cherry. I saw it done. John saw it done quickly. There was a difference.

John ruffled my hair on the way down the stairs. "Didn't take you long to get going."

"I'm no fool. You know that!" I blinked dust from my eyes.

He took a minute to watch Deanna, Michael and Spencer carefully sanding between spindles and near the curved wall. I'd invited them to join me, and, surprisingly, they'd agreed. I could only assume the snow had some sort of hallucinogenic effect.

"I'll see if they have floor samples I can bring home too," John announced.

What a great guy. I watched him drop a kiss on each of his children as he descended. I assumed he knew my thoughts and preferences concerning flooring.

I took turns teaching each kid how to use the electric sander. We were moving along well and had finished five of the steps before he returned.

John's homecoming changed everything; the mood, the patience, and all the wonderful serenity went right out the window. He had no idea his arrival would have that effect. In fact, he was quite pleased with himself. Proudly hauling in a box, he opened it, pulled out several pieces of oak planking and declared, "I went ahead and bought the flooring!" He smiled and waited for the enthusiastic hugs he was sure he deserved.

"What the hell is that?" I stood on the stairs, sander hanging limply and stared. I could not believe his presumptive attitude. It was very nice flooring, pleasing to the eye and easy to install. I did not care one bit. "I'm not putting oak in this foyer!"

He frowned heavily.

Michael and Spencer, smart little fellows that they were, simultaneously laid down their sanding supplies and tiptoed out of the line of fire. Deanna beckoned them into the kitchen with the promise of a late lunch. She was smart too.

Standing in the foyer, surrounded by underlayment, sandpaper, and a box of half-wanted oak flooring, John and I glared, each of us convinced we were unequivocally right. We lit cigarettes and sat down, anticipating stress.

"Why are you so upset? I thought you'd be happy as hell—we could do the whole foyer this weekend," he began, in what, I'm sure, seemed a reasonable tone to him.

"I do want to finish the foyer—but it's got to be cherry. We looked at it together remember? Why would you bring this stuff home?" I pointed and frowned at the oak again.

He went on the defense immediately. "The floor you want has to be ordered. We can't have every project take two or three weeks. This house isn't a career goal, okay?"

"I don't care if it takes a month. We'll do it right."

"I want to be done, Hon." He hung his head and pointed at the floor. "I mean, really, look at this shit! It's wavy and buckled. Do you know what it will take to put in tongue and groove slats?" He dropped his chin to his chest and sighed deeply at the prospect.

I said nothing.

"We could be done this weekend and move on to something else. Maybe even decorate for Christmas." He was talking softly and using my love of the holidays as a way to sway my opinion. He was somehow convinced my silence equated to acquiescence.

"We'll level the floor—whatever—but *that* flooring has to go!" I pointed accusingly at the offensive box, flicking ashes haphazardly as I talked. *Who cared?*

"It's an old farmhouse— oak is fine." He had the gall to stand up, signaling the argument was over. He had never walked away from me like that before.

"Where do you think you're going? It's not an old farmhouse. It's a country Victorian, and it's going to have cherry." Hands on hips, I demanded his agreement. I stood up too, ready to chase him down and tackle if necessary. I'd never felt compelled to pursue him before and had to wonder at that. "Our grandfather clock that sits in this foyer is cherry. The stairs are mahogany. Do you know how stupid it will look to put in an oak floor?"

John glowered at me over the word "stupid." I stared him down some more.

For some reason, the word stupid was not allowed in our house. We could drink beer, smoke, and cuss, but weren't allowed to say that particular word.

Settling back down and sitting cross-legged on the planks, we each thought and plotted our next moves. John's cigarette had been practically chewed through. I picked at the gaping hole across my knee where jean material used to be. My own cigarette had been forgotten and burned down near my knuckle. We stared, eyes narrowed, daring the other one to speak.

Awakened from an afternoon nap, The Old Woman stumbled toward the foyer, confused by the loud voices and biting tone. "What's going on in here? It wasn't two hours ago that everything was fine."

Deanna snuck across the kitchen with a camera, walked to the doorway of the foyer and snapped a quick picture of us. She ran away, giggling. It was a completely different picture from the happy couple, standing arm-in-arm in the front yard, the spring before. Had it really been less than a year since the elderly ladies had asked to take our picture out there among the flowers?

We'd lost weight and been pulled taut. We were ogres snarling, snapping, unbending. Frustration had carved extra lines into our foreheads. Stress had added gray to our temples.

Startled by the flash, we paused momentarily. We heard the kids whispering in the kitchen but continued our argument anyway. That's what it was, an argument. We'd passed the point of discussion and were heating up pretty well.

"Not *one* piece of that flooring is going back, Katrina," John practically yelled through clenched teeth. His eyes glinted dangerously, but I was more concerned by his use of my given name.

Over the years, he had assigned dozens of pet names to me: Poopsie (which I hated), Honey, Cutie, Darlin', Babe, Boo, even Sugarbutt, which I'd only allowed the one time. Calling me Katrina meant he was seriously ticked. I checked his ears, and, as I suspected, they were red. He was definitely mad.

"There's a huge difference in just doing a job and doing a job right, *John*," I challenged right back, as I twisted my hair around fidgety fingers.

His head swiveled back toward me, alerting me that he'd heard correctly, and I'd used his proper name too. I had his attention and intended to pound my point home.

"What happened to our talking things through first?"

"You wanted a wood floor. You got one."

I leaned closer, stabbing his chest with my finger, "Don't you dare patronize me! I'd rather wait— keep this nasty floor until we can do it right."

"I'm telling you, it's not going back, and that's final. I bought ten boxes of the stuff. They're on the porch—ready to go."

"Ten boxes?" I opened the front door to verify that boxes were indeed piled there. "Have you lost your mind? You know what? *I'll take it back and do the right thing.*" I grabbed the few hateful pieces he'd brought inside and began shoving them back in the box. I taped it closed and began to drag it toward the front door. If I thought to goad John into taking it back or apologizing, I was wrong.

We were still shooting sparks at each other and not speaking.

I changed my clothes and stuffed my stubborn toes into tennis shoes, not even bothering to tie them. They flopped around as I hauled the ten heavy boxes back to my truck. I lost time because I kept stopping to glare at John, who was muttering to himself and beginning to nail down underlayment.

I drove subconsciously to the store. The car knew the way, and I was still replaying the discussion we'd just had. *Gonna try and rush the job, are you? Tell me we aren't taking the flooring back? I don't think so, buddy boy.*

I wheeled the big flat cart up to the counter and slapped the receipt down.

"Do you want a refund?" the perky little clerk asked

"No, I do not! Credit it toward the new purchase I'm about to make."

Not sure why I was angry, she nodded and processed paperwork, eyes downcast.

I headed to the flooring section, ordered cherry tongue and groove flooring, bought a dozen pieces they had in stock and used John's Visa to pay for the whole thing.

I calmed down on the way home, thinking through the day. We'd done a complete three-sixty; from sledding, and the first smiles I'd seen in months, to gladiators, squared off and spitting mad. He had been working hard. I couldn't blame him for wanting to be done. On the other hand, I knew we'd regret hurrying a process that required precision. I had rights too

Entering the house, I found him still hammering with gusto. Tapping him carefully on the shoulder, I smiled shyly. He rose, trying on a small smile of his own. I moved in for a hug.

"You didn't use to argue with me." I tilted my head toward him, wanting another hug, and wondered at the changes I saw in him; wrinkle lines, stubbornness.

"I know. You used to be more agreeable too." He tightened his hold, noticing my confident stance, something he hadn't seen in years.

"Nobody wants to be led around all the time."

"Damn straight. I don't like it either."

We grinned, looking at each other with new eyes. Holding hands, I took John outside to show him the few things I'd purchased.

The Old Woman peeked into the box, trying to determine what all the fuss was about. Looking at the dark, shiny pieces of cherry, she oohed and ahhed. "For me? This is beautiful."

A month later, we stood together in our new foyer, admiring the finished product. We'd just moved the grandfather clock to its place of honor, across from the front door. I squeezed John's hand, and he squeezed back, awed by the overall effect.

We were ready to celebrate an old-fashioned, country Christmas with the Old Woman. Excited by all the nooks, crannies and archways available, I'd draped garland and decorations everywhere, reveling in the gaudy freedom allowed once a year. She loved being dressed so thoroughly and hummed carols as she admired all the ornaments, sure things were on the upswing.

I happened to know that Santa would be delivering a new puppy to our house; an adorable yellow lab. I'd followed a 'Free to good home' Ad and knew the boys would fall in love with this dog, too. I wrapped up the toys, bones, and the trapping such a present required. It was time for new beginnings.

As I took in rooms, I was glad we'd reached for the exceptional and not settled for the available. We'd painted and wallpapered, and nailed chair rail into place, giving the rooms a complete makeover. The dark stained stairs and rich, gleaming floors set it off. They were the Coup de grace and restored The Old Woman to grandeur. Although it pained me to be silent, I knew I'd been right —clearly placing a *cherry* on the bottom had topped it all off.

Chapter 31

I'm Stuck

January brought colder, gloomier weather and post-Christmas blues. Well, the adults were feeling blue. The kids spent every available minute with their new friend Bear. Fat Cat Chance hadn't been particularly pleased by the puppy, and did his best to ignore him, or stop his antics with hisses, growls, and claws. The boys, bless their hearts, spent equal time with Chance so he wouldn't be so affronted. He had been with us far longer and needed to be assured of his place.

Meanwhile, John and I decided that we'd finish the rooms over the kitchen into a bedroom and sitting area. It would allow Michael to move to a larger, more private room. Spencer could then move to Michael's old room, giving him more space too.

The rooms, originally displaying red handprints, had seen very little activity. We'd replaced the broken windows, removed the saloon doors, and painted over the handprints, period. We'd walked past them for as long as we could, choosing other projects. It was a true, "out of sight, out of mind" phenomenon. To get everyone settled into new and permanent surrounding, the two areas had to be finished. The two rooms didn't seem like they'd be much work. How difficult could it be to do some more dry-walling and add some lights? John actually looked at them and said, "Piece of cake. We'll be done in a weekend."

The room had become our storage area, for tools, and "Stuff." And, like everyone else, over the years we'd accumulated stuff: totes full of various holiday decorations, accessories for the house that we weren't using, extra pieces of furniture, tanning bed, and weight lifting equipment. It was an impressive conglomeration of dusty boxes and piles. Relocating them meant we could march forward unfettered.

It became my job to clear out those two rooms during the week so we could start working on Saturday. It required a complete inventory of "What the hell is in here anyway?" and about twenty-five trips down the curved stairs, through the house to the shed, or to the dungeon, requiring still more stairs.

The Old Woman watched my comings and goings with interest.

The whole re-arrangement was complicated by a secret. Months prior, I had surreptitiously purchased a Victorian lady's chair. It was a great find: cherry, as was to be expected, tapestry-covered, nail-head-finished and gorgeous. I planned to display this piece of furniture in our bedroom but hadn't shared the news with John.

The problem with the chair was that it had been expensive. I'd been avoiding the confrontation I knew would ensue. Therefore, I hid it until the opportune moment came for the unveiling, a day when John was in a particularly gregarious mood. I would then admit to half the purchase price. "It was on sale," I could hear myself reassuring John.

Having laid out a phenomenal amount of money over the last year, I knew it was also a bit frivolous of me to have bought the thing but had somehow reasoned that all out. *A person needs to be rewarded from time to time or what's the point?* I'd given myself a prize for all the work in crawlspaces and attics. I would probably never let anyone sit in the thing, which was also going to be hard to explain. My Grumpa Ben would have called it "eyeball."

Secreting the chair had been easy because the rooms over the kitchen were so full of junk that no one had noticed one more box added to the mix. Now that work on those rooms was to begin, my day of reckoning had come. There was nothing to do but 'fess up and bring it all out in the open.

Did I make an announcement? A confession? Hell no. I waited for a time when everyone was gone for the unveiling—John was at work and both Deanna and Michael at school. Even Spencer, normally home in the afternoon, had a play date and was gone for the day. The other mom had even volunteered to drive him both ways. Hallelujah!

Thinking myself quite clever, I unboxed my new chair, carried it out of the storage room and placed it proudly, if not a bit defiantly, in our room. It looked great. At least it would, once I removed the existing wing-backed chair already located there. So it began.

Dragging the old green chair out of our room, I worked it down the five steps in the hallway and nearer to the sitting area by the front staircase. I was supposed to be emptying that room, but what the heck? *I may as well get things where I want them. I'll just move this chair around as we work.*

Still another chair, already in the sitting room, further exacerbated the process of all the chair-switching. That presented a problem. I couldn't move the wing-backed chair from our room to the sitting room until the big, pink, overstuffed chair that I no longer even liked was gone. It had to go, or the two chairs already moved around would have all been for naught. *Sigh.*

I found myself wishing Deanna would please hurry up and finish her degree, get a good job and buy a house. With all the extra pieces of furniture in the way, the logical solution was to give all the excess to her. Eventually, she'd be set, and I would buy more traditional pieces for the old house. Lucky girl. Lucky Mom. Poor John. Until such a move-out date though, I had to find a place to put that damn pink chair.

It should have been simple. Unpack new chair, insert into bedroom. Drag wing chair to sitting room. Transfer pink troublemaker to the den. It would mean taking the pink chair down the curved staircase and to the other end of the house, but that was okay. I could do it. *No problem.* Sounded a bit like John's "piece of cake."

Being Superwoman, I figured going down the curved stairs with a large chair wouldn't be so bad, given gravity and such. I would just bounce or drag the chair down each step, ease it around the curve, and then maneuver it through two more rooms and into the back den. What I didn't count on was the bulk of the chair and the degree of the turn. It got stuck. Really stuck.

I wasn't going to be able to move it on my own after all. I couldn't drag it back up; it was too heavy, and the gravity I'd been counting on would become an issue. I couldn't go down without losing control and strewing chaos along the way. Well, I could have, but not without tearing up the wallpaper, peeling the paint, chipping the molding, or smashing the spindles we'd already completed. The stupid chair was going to have to be lifted up and held over the railing in order to make that turn. Not good. A large pink chair lodged in the curved staircase left a lot to be desired. I was also beginning to panic. Things were not going quite as smoothly as I had hoped. All chairs should already be in position.

"What in the world are you doing?" The Old Woman questioned. "Why do you think you can do everything by yourself?"

She had a point. I was going to need some help and quickly checked Deanna's schedule. She had no classes that afternoon and would be home in plenty of time to assist with the chair situation. *Thank goodness.* She wouldn't mind lending a hand; she would be the eventual recipient of all that furniture anyway. Besides, she'd been in these messes with me before and always helped save the day. Together, we could remove the chair and fix the whole furniture mess before John got home. He would be none the wiser. Oh, what tangled webs we weave when we practice to deceive.

I couldn't call her yet, so I left the chair on the staircase and marched to the den to see what I could get done in there. The room presented another immediate problem. It wasn't overly large and was already compact with a faux leather couch, a loveseat, a TV, a stand, and a lamp. Before placing the stupid pink chair in there, I needed to carve out a large, square space.

"Fine. The loveseat has to go," I decided. "We'll put it in the barn." The one well beyond the house, across the yard, through the snow and as far away as could possibly be imagined. It could sit there, wrapped in plastic until Deanna moved.

I should have stopped right then and there. But, no, not me. *Must keep going.* I marched to the den area with the idea of getting the leather loveseat out of the way so we'd have room for the chair that was soon to be dislodged. The intent was to have as much moved around as possible before Deanna got home so that the balance of the operation could go quickly. If I had the loveseat out of the room, the pink chair could be rescued from the stairs and inserted in the den in less than ten minutes.

I shoved and pushed and piled furniture every which direction and could not figure out how we got the loveseat and couch into the den in the first place. Chair rail, doorframes, and doorknobs thwarted my every attempt to get the loveseat out of that room. The stupid thing, which also happened to be overstuffed, sported huge attached pillows along its spine. I could only assume that we'd finished the rooms around the furniture, with no forethought as to how to get it all back out again.

All I wanted to do was move the damn thing out of the den and into Deanna's room. Once there, I could slide it out onto the second front porch, using the larger front door that led outside. The rest would be easy. At the very least, Deanna and I could carry it to the barn. I had high hopes. But, if Deanna wasn't up to the task, surely John wouldn't mind moving it since it was already outside. He would hardly be inconvenienced. No big deal. Piece of cake even.

No matter how I maneuvered, rammed, cussed or removed cushions, the loveseat refused to go through the doorframe. I was sweating, bullets really, because I was getting in deeper and deeper. I considered removing all of the doors, but wisely determined I wouldn't be able to re-hang them in time. On to Plan B, C, or whatever it was at that point.

Unfaltering in my determination, I decided if I couldn't get the loveseat to the front porch, I could at least get the thing outside by using one of the other two doors in the den. Unfortunately, both doors had been sealed closed to keep out the drafts. I peeled off the caulk and threw it away. Desperate or loopy by then, I don't know which, I figured I could re-do the caulk. *"I can fix this,"* was my daily mantra.

There were no porches or patios outside those den doors yet. We'd removed the rotted bathroom and had dreams of adding a grand, back porch. It just hadn't happened yet. We'd been busy with other more important items. So, anyway, the door opening simply dropped off to the yard.

I shuddered one of the doors open to evaluate the situation in more detail. "Hmm. If I push it halfway through, I can go outside and pull it the rest of the way free." The loveseat could sit in the yard until help arrived. "It'll work."

I rearranged all the cushions and began to push. I was doing pretty well until the feet of the seat got stuck on the frame. (Sounded a bit like Dr. Seuss) Yes, I said stuck. Like the chair. The one still lodged in the curved staircase.

"Oh, Girl! You are too much! You know that, don't you?" The Old Woman was leaning on a doorframe, taking in the haphazard den. She was laughing though, knowing I had gotten myself into another mess.

The loveseat was approximately twenty-five percent through the door and wouldn't go one way or the other without absolutely destroying either the couch or, again, new molding. At least the weather was good, or I would have really been in deep poo.

I checked the clock and frowned deeply. A loveseat wedged half in, half out of the house had not been in the day's plan, and the afternoon was half done. The phone shrilled sharply in the background. I climbed over the furniture and sprinted to the kitchen.

"Hey, Mom!" Deanna sounded happy and in a good mood, and I was pleased.

"Hey yourself! I was just getting ready to call you. I'm in a hell of a mess and could really use you here. The sooner the better." I outlined the various challenges.

"Oh no." She drew out the words in a tone that could only spell disaster. "Mom, I'm not going to be home 'til this evening. That's why I was calling. I've got a group project due tomorrow, and we're all meeting this afternoon."

"Uh-huh." I didn't know what else to say.

"Maybe Michael can help? I'm really sorry." She hung up the phone, and I hung my head. *Man, I'm in trouble now.*

I couldn't do a thing to remedy the problems until somebody came home. *I just hope it's not John.* What else to do but clean the house thoroughly? Using the back staircase for access, I got everything spiffy then made a lovely dinner, hoping to soften the blow by presenting a fine meal and a sparkling house. It was a good thing we had two staircases, or I would have been climbing Mt. Pink Chair.

I was optimistic that Michael would be able to help me when he got home. He was getting taller, and stronger, He might be able to add some muscle to the situation. Alas, my skinny boy was not up to the task. He might have been but was too busy laughing at me and making all kinds of disparaging remarks about what was going to happen when Dad got home. *I thought the parents were supposed to use that line.* I had destroyed all leverage for future discipline.

Spencer came home from his friend's house and was enthralled with both pieces of problem furniture. He was either trying to sit on the stair chair or climb out the house seat. The dog, who, unbeknownst to me, had been untied, was trying to enter the den via the self-same loveseat.

I had one kid trying to get out and one dog trying to get in. Ever the opportunist, Bear saw the open door and bolted eagerly toward the house. I think Spencer may have been encouraging such behavior, but I lost track since I was trying to get out of the house and tie up the damn dog before he got to my loveseat. I might be giving it away to Deanna, but that didn't mean it could be ripped to pieces by the dog. A dog who had, by the way, taken a quick dip in the partially frozen pond.

Bear thought the whole thing was a game and kept dancing away at the last minute. He shook water off himself and all over the couch and me. The boys hung through the open door frame, laughing their little pointed heads off and offering no assistance whatsoever. I lobbed threats their way, but they were unconcerned. I was outside, and they were in, and they knew it would take some maneuvering for me to get to them quickly. The dog, tongue lolling and tail wagging, did not agree with me on the merits of being tied again and continued to prance away.

I was screeching at this point. I know that I was. I'm sure my neighbors heard. My life passed before my eyes. The clock was ticking, and Dad was coming home. What would it be? Straight to bed without supper? A week with no TV? A time out? More cooking was required. Maybe I could whip up a batch of brownies? Everything would be better with chocolate.

Needless to say, John was less than thrilled when he arrived on the scene. The boys told on me as soon as he walked in the door, the little narcs. I didn't get the benefit of serving the nice dinner first or offering up the rare dessert. He didn't immediately catch the drift of the situation because my darling children were talking loudly, laughing and tripping over each other's sentences, wanting the privilege of telling first.

He finally got the chair and the stair part and went to look. I had already bolted up the back staircase to meet him on the curved staircase.

I was standing behind the embedded chair, eager to help. John hadn't seen the couch yet.

Vanna White would have been proud of the gracious way in which I displayed the chair, arms wide, smile bright. *Will it be chair number one on the stairs, chair number two in the sitting room or chair number three in the bedroom?*

His head flopped back on his neck, and he closed his eyes tightly, dealing with the instant migraine. We rescued chair number one. I was right about it having to lift it high over the railings. We carried it toward the den, and I braced myself for the reaction. He took in the open door and the couch. "Damn! Can't you ever do one thing at a time? Or how about simply? Can you do anything simply? Couldn't this have waited until we were ready?"

"You said you wanted me to clear the room." I was trying for some sort of defense, but not very hard. I knew I'd messed things up.

He was pretty mad, so I apologized and looked extremely sorry. He managed to tug the couch back into the room and firmly closed the door. I didn't think it wise to point out that the couch was supposed to go out, not in.

The room, which had already been crowded, was back to how it had been with the addition of an extra pink chair. We sat down to a cold dinner. Things got worse when he went upstairs to change his clothes and discovered yet another chair.

"At least it doesn't have to be moved." I tried on a guilt-free smile.

He was not the least bit impressed with my facial expressions or explanation. Nor did he buy, for one second, the idea that I had saved him money in the process. The "On Sale" technique had lost its charm with all the hauling he'd had to do.

"What makes you do this stuff?" John asked as we readied ourselves for bed. "I mean—who are you trying to prove things to? Me?" He sounded genuinely perplexed.

I didn't have an immediate answer and lay in bed wondering about it myself. Minutes ticked by and I heard what sounded suspiciously like a snicker. John rolled sideways.

"Are you laughing at me?"

I felt him shake with holding things in. He turned over and grinned at me, then laughed right in my face. "Only you could manage to get two pieces of furniture stuck in the same day. You should've seen your face!" He laughed again.

I playfully punched him in the arm, "Be quiet!"

A wrestling match began, both of us rolling across the bed, tangled in covers, laughing. It wasn't long before all thoughts of chairs and couches disappeared.

Chapter 32

Good Things Come to Those That Wait

She was late, and I was a bit disgusted. The news station had said she'd be arriving earlier than expected. Unfortunately, she'd been delayed somewhere over Minnesota, fighting one last cold spell sent down from the Canadians. She finally dragged herself through our yard, almost exhausted with the effort. I was pleased and happy to see her despite her tardiness. Spring had finally arrived.

Like a door too long unopened, the earth creaked out a hesitant welcome, unsure if the warm weather was to be trusted. After two days of suspicious waiting, Flora and Fauna decided it was the real thing, and grasses and flowers burst forth like children at recess.

February, although technically the shortest calendar month, had drug by, grey and dreary. So, no matter how March came in, lion or lamb, its advent was welcome. I stood just inside the back door, taking in the sights and sounds, listening to the ice, cracking and thawing the pond. Standing perfectly still, I could almost hear the reedy orchestra of grass pushing through the winter coverlet. The birds were singing, and I watched a robin, more confident than the rest of us, fly by. I just had to get out there. "Come on, boys. Let's go play!"

Bear was leaping in his excitement to go out too. Finally, he would have outdoor playmates. He tripped over his large feet and sprinted free. Loping back toward the door, his entire body wagging, he presented me with a soggy tennis ball recently thawed from the yard. He tilted his head and begged with big brown eyes. I never could resist such looks.

I threw the ball far and true. It, unfortunately, took a bad bounce and landed in the recently freed end of the pond. Not to be deterred, Bear dove in after the yellow ball, triumphantly running back to shake the water and the ball at me.

His lower half was black not yellow, and I assumed it spring mud until he got closer and I smelled the Sulphur and cloying smell of petroleum. "What the hell?"

Michael and Spencer turned at my shout. I tried to snag Bear, who happily sidestepped my attempts, convinced this was another game. "Grab that dog! Something's wrong!" They obeyed and tried to coax him their way. Bear, thrilled with all the attention, darted first left and then right, imitating a lithe boxer. He would draw near and then just as one of us reached for him, he'd turn and leap away in excitement.

I dropped to the ground, feeling the shock of wet and cold penetrate my jeans. "Come on, Bear," I called softly and gently. "Here, boy," persuading him I didn't want to play, and I wanted to pet him instead. That sounded good to him, and he flopped on the ground, presenting his belly for rubbing. I secured his collar and bent closer for inspection. "Look! He's covered in oil!"

The smell was awful, and the oil was globbed behind his knees. I handed off the collar to the boys and ran to the pond.

The thawed edges were yellow and foamy, and rainbow circles were formed everywhere the sun touched. Hoping we were the proud owners of some new underground oil source, I eagerly explored. Maybe we would be rich beyond our dreams and could finally finish our old house. I had no problem being labeled The Ohio Hillbillies.

I followed the stream and was confronted by one dead frog after another, upside down and bloated. The surface of the stream shimmered with oil, and the bodies of white, listless worms were drifting by. It was not pleasant to step past dead animals, and I gave up the oilrig idea quickly.

"The pond is full of oil," I whined, unsure what to do.

"Where's it coming from?" Michael asked, trying to contain an unhappy Bear.

"I don't know. We're going to need to see what's going on. I'll take care of the dog, and we'll check it out." I carried a reluctant fifty-five-pound dog into the house.

Not knowing what else to do, I got into the small downstairs shower with Bear. He was trying to get free and yapping at the water coming down on our heads. I shampooed him in the confined area, creating a mess that was truly awesome in its volume. In a hurry to get back outside, I decided to use the blow dryer on him, which did not go over well. He jumped and barked and twisted—anything to get out of the room. More or less dry, we exited and started our journey. I tied Bear to the old chicken house and started up the stream with the boys following behind.

"I saw a dead fish in the pond," Michael informed me.

I shook my head. "Man, this is bad. Hurry, let's see where it's coming from."

We traipsed through water and mud, following the stream a quarter mile or so and eventually found the source. Red, oily something was dripping from a pipe into the stream. We followed the pipe to a house. We banged on the door, but they weren't home.

I knew I was looking at home oil or transmission fluid or something deadly and toxic. Hurrying back home, I anxiously made phone calls to Water and Soil Conservation, the health department, the fire department and finally an emergency number at the EPA.

The pond was taking more and more oil as the ice along the stream melted and began to flow. The pond was only half-thawed, with the remaining ice acting as a break wall and stopping the oil. That was good, because the ice kept the toxins from moving toward the wildlife preserve area down the road.

Still making frantic phone calls, I finally convinced the EPA they should come to take a look. They showed up that afternoon, walking toward the pond casually as though there was no big deal, and I was some sort of alarmist.

Ten feet away they began to smell oil and picked up the pace. Kneeling and letting the water run across their hands, they held it to the light, to their noses and then made faces. Cell phones appeared out of pockets, and the three men were talking hurriedly to three other people at the other end of their lines.

They started picking at fish. One man carefully held up a dead bird he'd found by the side of the pond. The frog buffet had evidently been too much to resist. I explained where our water came from and where it went. "I found the source. It's further up the stream," I explained, pointing in the general direction. They took in the ice, still holding the oil, and ran.

Men in white suits showed up. I laughed, remembering how my friend Karen had predicted such a thing early into our project. "The men in white suits are coming to take you away ha-ha, they're coming to take you away," she'd chanted at a bonfire, almost a year prior. They were different men in different suits, but I still couldn't wait to tell her.

A small plane circled overhead, taking pictures and mapping out the flow of water. Suited men waded into the cold, cold pond, shoveling sand and dirt into the mouth of our run-off stream to make sure all the contaminated water went to the pond. They flung huge pieces of fiber-coated plastic across the water. "This will soak up the oil," they explained to us. We'd been hovering close by, watching the activity in fascination.

The EPA spent two weeks collecting dead fish, frogs, and oil-laden plastic. Everything was cataloged and placed into fifty-five-gallon drums. A large truck backed into the yard and the evidence was loaded and carted away.

They'd determined our environmental catastrophe had been the result of an accidental spill of household heating oil. The huge container had rusted at the bottom, leaking one hundred gallons of oil across the basement and down a drain. I hoped the EPA would dig out the pond. They would want to remove all the oil, and I would get my deeper pond. I was trying to take advantage of a bad situation.

"You can't dig here for at least a year," they informed me in serious tones.

"Why? Shouldn't you remove the mud-soaked oil?"

"No, digging will only disrupt it all again. Let nature do her job. Microbes will come and eat what's left, but you absolutely must not disturb this area."

I nodded dejectedly. There went another year for the pond. We looked around for something else to occupy our spring.

A few days later and the wind blasted past me, blowing west to east. I looked skyward at the heavy clouds piled one on top of another. I headed to the back door and noticed flower blossoms soaring across the yard. That got my attention. I hadn't planted any flowers yet and wondered where the petals had come from. I squinted through the rain. It appeared they were coming from the west side of the house. It was horribly overgrown there, but curiosity got the best of me. I waited for the rain to stop, pulled on my trusty boots and headed out to investigate.

Through the wall of vines and thorns, I could see color and plowed into the underbrush to find out what was blooming. Delicate, pink cherry blossoms covered the ground. I leaned back and saw that the stunted cherry kept company with the largest pear tree I'd ever seen. "I had no idea they grew so big." The four-foot base had been struck by lightning and was more than three quarters hollowed out, and still, the branches flowered. Tiny pink blooms showed on yet another tree. "Apple! This whole area is an orchard!"

There was a faint pathway leading from the upper clearing, near the road, to a lower area that was hard to discern. I followed the line, snagging most body parts on thorns. It was another clearing, and I stood in the center and marveled at my discovery.

From that vantage point, I could see nothing of the house or the road, meaning no one could see me either. Honeysuckle tumbled over a fallen tree, soon to release its' wonderful scent. Wild roses, having been unattended for so long, were pushing forward toward the center of the circle. A few jonquils laughed as they chased each other down another faded pathway which led toward the backyard. I knew I had stumbled into my own Secret Garden when I tripped, literally, over the bricks lining the perimeter.

It was a secluded and dreamy place. I knew someone, sometime, had spent many hours there. I stood in the middle of that small circle with my eyes closed and tasted sweetness on the wind. It was a place where souls and God could commune. I stood looking, listening, and realized it was the most at peace I'd felt in a long while. I knew I would put a bench there and let the area remain semi-wild. Like the women before me, I dreamed of wildflowers and quiet afternoons.

Standing at the back of the house, I suddenly knew just what to do. I looked at the space which used to house the rotted old bathroom. We'd yanked the room off the house, tentatively sketching ideas for a back porch. I knew the porch was now a certainty. I'd have to convince John to move it up the list but knew it would be worth it. We could work a little harder, because the view, the serenity that came would be worth it.

Walking around the corner to the area that faced the tangled, but blooming vegetation, I made another decision: "This should be a patio." I saw it completed and knew exactly how it should look. I wanted flat old stones, simplicity.

Eager to share my newfound garden and plans with someone, I grabbed my keys and hurried off to pick up Spencer from pre-school. We had a quick lunch and headed to the store. Although the patio was only a figment of my imagination, I couldn't wait to buy a little table and two chairs to place there.

Back home, Spencer and I raked, cleared, and had the area ready in no time. I marked and shaped my patio idea by drawing lines in the dirt with my feet. "Half a circle—moon-shaped. And stone, it definitely needs to be stone." I nodded at the picture, accepting my analysis. Spencer, always happy to use any type of tool, helped me assemble the bistro table. There were no stones yet, but who cared? We both tried out the chairs, pleased with ourselves. He was soon bored and went inside to play.

I stayed where I was, taking in the beauty and serenity. It was an intimate and private place where two people could talk or watch a reluctant sun sink behind the trees. I sat there thinking about my mom, some of my friends, people I would want to sit with.

Drifting in my afternoon daydream, I was brought back to reality when Spencer rapped on the window to get my attention, "Mommy! There's water coming out of the toilet."

Great. I ran to investigate and, sure as hell, lovely septic water had regurgitated all over the bathroom floor. I plunged and cussed until the brown smelly mess, swirling to the very top of the commode, slowly sank down the drain. Scrubbing vinyl floors and porcelain tanks, I tried to breathe through my mouth and not my nose. "I swear it's something all the damn time! An hour ago, I was feeling peaceful, and now I'm cleaning up shit. Are we not supposed to relax?"

John was less than pleased to hear about the toilet. It wasn't a very pleasant way to be greeted when coming home from work. He walked to the backyard and stood over the septic tanks. "Man, this system is old. It's damn near shot." He bounced on the ground and felt the soft ground give and sink. "Let's hope it'll hold a little longer."

It was not to be. Over the next few days, all the toilets backed up and refused to flush easily. The plungers were worn out with trying to stuff water and excess back through drains. We had no choice and stopped to deal with the latest crisis. The old tank needed to be caved in, the excess fluid sucked out and a completely new system sunk into the backyard. Machinery chugged in back, digging and literally sucking up crap. There were more piles of dirt added to the mayhem.

Bear, however, was ecstatic. He used the dirt piles as lookouts, running up first one then another, barking and ensuring his territory was accounted for and safe. The laundry doubled because Michael and Spencer couldn't resist playing "King of the Mountain" with Bear.

"Let 'em play. No use everyone being miserable," I told myself, trying not to stress as I threw another car and headed for the Laundromat.

With the septic system half-inserted, I felt no guilt in, once again, heading to the far side of our yard. I was on a mission and fired up our semi-retired, neighborhood-sized, riding lawn mower. We'd bought a huge new mower to help control the acreage but couldn't bring ourselves to throw the old one away. *If it breaks down, so what?* I convinced myself it was all right, despite the fact I knew John would not be pleased if I did further damage to the thing.

I plowed through the undergrowth between the upper clearing and the secret garden, ducking and bowing as I went, trying to save my face from limbs and burrs. It took a while as the mower quit twice. I yelled in frustration, "Go you stupid thing! It's downhill, for God's sake. Move!"

Reaching the clearing, I hopped off the mower and followed the path I'd just cut. I was not at all surprised to find stepping-stones buried along the entire length. They were supposed to be there, and I had done well to follow my instinct. Once upon a time, someone else had evidently felt and seen what I did.

As I cleared away the rotted logs and thorns, flowers long buried opened shy eyes and blinked at the unfamiliar light and me. They were sickly and translucent, having been denied the sun, but refusing to give up. I hummed unaware The Old Woman had joined me there. She stood quietly taking in the scene and swaying to music playing in her head. "You're finally gettin' it, girl. Sometimes you don't have to add or change a thing. Just enjoy."

"I can't wait to get this cleared!" I lugged more branches, thorns, and logs to the edge of the circle. The sooner it was tidied up, the sooner I could put a bench there. I hadn't shared my secret garden with the family yet, wanting to keep it to myself for just a little while. I wanted them to walk there and be amazed.

Saturday was declared, "Clean up The Yard Day." The mess was making John crazy. He couldn't do anything about the piles of dirt, but he could pick up everything else. A spring storm had dropped branches all over the place. Thorn bushes were trying to grow back along the property line, and things, in general, looked sloppy. "Go get the golf cart so we can load up branches."

With all that acreage we wanted the boys to enjoy, we'd purchased a golf cart for fun. It didn't go very fast and had a windshield and roof—a much better alternative to four-wheelers or dirt bikes. It was more a workhorse than a plaything and even had a hydraulic dump on the back. It was great for hauling leaves, dirt, kids, and had proven to be indispensable. I ran to get the cart with Michael, Spencer and even Bear at my heels. "I get the middle!" Michael called. Spencer ran faster, and Bear wagged his tail, eager for a ride around the property. They were disappointed to find, we were working, not riding.

John started another of our famous bonfires and began to burn the limbs and branches nearest to the fire. The boys picked things up and dragged them toward Dad. Seeing an opportunity, I slipped over the hill to the secret garden and piled a full load of debris into the golf cart. Driving toward John and the fire, I dumped my load and headed back. I made several trips before anyone got wise.

Good Things Come to Those That Wait

"Where are you getting all of this?" John wanted to know. "The backyard still looks horrible! It doesn't look like you've picked up one damn thing from back here."

The boys stopped to listen, interested because Mom was in trouble.

I managed to look a little sheepish and confessed, "I've got something to show you guys. Come with me."

They followed me, curious. I went to the upper clearing and showed them the path I'd cleared. "Wait 'til you see where this goes!" I headed off, assuming they'd be right behind me. John had stopped halfway down the stone pathway. He looked around and frowned. He leaned down to look at a few small trees I'd plowed through. "How'd you get this path cut? You used the mower, didn't you?"

I nodded, crinkled my eyes and pointing out the attributes of what I'd done. I redirected John's attention to the daffodils that shouted by the hundreds. "Oh—and look at this pear tree, guys, you won't believe it!" Spencer stood inside the base and laughed. John continued to try to catch my eye, not done discussing the mower. I skipped happily away and called to them from the garden circle. The hillside was purple with creeping myrtle, the roses, and honeysuckle buds, near to bursting. I held my arms wide and turned a slow circle. "Isn't this incredible?"

Spencer ran off to explore the pathways. John stopped in his tracks again, taking in the flowers, the seclusion. He looked at me, shook his head and smiled. I hoped that meant the mower wasn't such a big deal after all. Michael, who had grown taller and worldlier, stood nearby watching my animated face. "You know what, Mom? I think this is your house. Maybe you lived here once before."

I raised eyebrows at his statement. "Maybe. I do feel like I'm finally home."

"It does seem like it was made for you. I know how you love flowers." John took my hand. "I guess I know where you've been getting all those branches from."

I dreamed of planting flowers and creating more landscaped areas. I remembered myself as a little girl, putting in flowers for the first time, digging in the dirt with my mom. I couldn't wait to get started again.

I was glad to have shared my "Secret" with the boys and was looking forward to sharing it with Deanna as well. Joy, after all, should never be singular.

Chapter 33

I am So Blessed

I presented John with a card before he left for work.
    He looked at it puzzled. "What's the occasion?"
    "Just open it, Silly!"
He tore open the envelope and pulled out an Anniversary card. "I don't get it," he said. "Our anniversary isn't until September. It's only March."

"It's been a year since we started on this house," I announced happily. "Look how far we've come!" I pulled him into a happy dance,

He rolled his eyes at my antics but smiled. "Been a hell of a year."

The Old Woman walked through the house slowly, memorizing each room. She saw them as they had been, sad, neglected and filthy. She looked at them now, completed; beautiful woodwork, wallpaper, color, the rooms draped with small but homey accessories. "My but how things have changed in a year."

Her hand trailed gracefully down the curved railing on the staircase, and she remembered the weeks it had taken to refinish the stairs and install the gleaming floor. She stood in the kitchen, shaking her head at the transformation.

She looked out the door to the back porch, hardly believing it had been a caved- in and decrepit bathroom once upon a time. Landscaping was starting to take shape and flowers bloomed in abundance. A tree fort stood near the pond in early construction, and she smiled, at the boys and their Daddy as they hammered away at yet another dream. Everything was neat, tidy, and more spacious than it had been.

Back inside, she admired the new fireplace in the living room, the books stacked on shelves, and thought back on the holidays and birthdays that had been celebrated inside that room. "So much laughter here."

She stood under pretty ceiling fans, grateful for their ability to push cool air through her rooms. She looked through new, shiny windows and saw a lawn carefully cut, bushes recently trimmed. New plantings and flowers crowded against each other, eager to be noticed and admired by their caretaker.

The sun glazed off every surface and still was not satisfied. It relentlessly blasted the leaves until they curled in surrender, allowing the heat through to the soft green grass beneath. They'd had a burst of rain the night before, but not enough to soak. Instead, there was a heaviness in the air, and she knew, without having to go outside, it would be humid. She watched the road lazily and could see the shimmer of heat rising up from the asphalt.

The similar weather was triggering memories of the day her current, beloved family had moved inside her rooms. What a happy time that had been, chaotic and crazy, but happy, nonetheless. After months of working, building, fixing and adding, they'd slogged through heat and humidity to move their things inside, determined to meet the deadline.

Before they'd arrived on the scene, she'd been so close to folding, to simply closing her eyes and sleeping forever. They'd awakened her just in time, and she'd dared to take a chance on them. They'd seemed so happy and full of plans. She'd decided she could endure one more set of changes and that she would dance once more.

It had taken them awhile before joining her in the waltz, and she laughed at the ridiculous obstacles that had gotten in the way: bats, squirrels, strange spirits, gaping cisterns, and mysterious bones in the basement. The family had slogged through contractors, tempers, mud, oil, and injuries and yet they'd made it through. She was awed by how they had spoiled her, revamping her wardrobe with wonderful colors and shiny new jewelry.

She remembered meeting their children and how they'd run through her rooms in eager anticipation. They'd chased after first one dog, then another, and even lightly argued over who got to sleep with the cat. They'd grown and changed in the last year. The oldest was off to college and falling in love. Would there be a wedding? Oh, she hoped so. The boys were becoming young men, and she was pleased with who they were turning out to be.

The couple, though, they were the ones who'd stolen her heart. It had taken some time to get used to him. He'd been rather quiet and stressed initially. She'd watched him, though, and learned his one true desire had been to make the family home a place that shone with pride and happiness. He loved his wife to a fault, and The Old Woman could not argue with such devotion.

The lady had changed the most though. Gone were the days of her needing approval and validation. She'd grown strong in the knowledge of who she was and where her life was going. Oh, she could be manipulative at times but softened it with laughter. That girl could land in mud, literally, and still find something funny about the experience. Her love of the house, her family and the land surrounded her like warm light, radiating out to those around her.

The Old Woman watched the lady working in the front yard, wiping sweat away, as she tried to replant the flowers. She tilted her head back to feel the sun, and stayed that way for several minutes, just soaking in the day. That the lady appreciated the joy the flowers gave, that she stopped to feel the sun, brought a smile to The Old Woman's face.

I remembered an old Bible verse I'd learned as a little girl, "To everything there is a season and a time for every purpose. A time to be born, a time to die, a time to plant and a time to pluck up that which is planted." I ambled toward the house, eager to do more planting.

I sat in the warm sun and dug fifty small holes. Each hole was given a new crocus bulb. Although I sat among the spring crocus, there had been fewer that spring. I worried. We'd been unkind to the yard in the last year, driving vehicles, and machinery every which direction in our attempt to fix, correct, build. I wanted to ensure the crocus' burst forth every spring, flinging hope from the porches to the road. Hence, the new bulbs going in the ground.

Completing the last hole, I brushed my hands across my jeans, rolled my neck to get out the kinks and smiled—tired but so very satisfied. I made my way to the porch where a book and cold glass of water were waiting. It had been ages since I'd allowed myself the luxury of reading, and I looked forward to the moment with great anticipation.

No matter how I tried, I couldn't make my eyes stay on the page. I felt so full of awe, so full of wonder at all I had learned and experienced. I sat cross-legged in the wicker chair, just taking in my surroundings and loving it all, loving life, happy to be there. The words from a popular country song kept popping in and out of my head.

I ran inside, found my Martina McBride CD, put it on the stereo, and fast-forwarded to the selection I wanted—*I Have Been Blessed*. The song captured how I felt, and I wanted to hear the words completely. I opened the windows wide and went outside. The music drifted past the porch and out into the yard. Several phrases held my attention, and I ran back inside to replay the song, turning the volume up louder.

The chorus pulsed out the windows, and I sang along, meaning every word. With the last words of the song hanging in the air, I closed my eyes. They encapsulated everything I was feeling, deep down into the far reaches of my soul.

The Old Woman watched the lady curled up in the chair, eyes closed and singing. It was finally time to dance, and The Old Woman knew it would be her last. There was no sorrow in that. It was time to go. She knew her legacy would live on in the lady who lived there now. She would watch over the rooms and guard those who lived there for many years to come. She would love the house and tend the land and find her own dance. For now, though, it was time for them to join their spirits into one, the past, the present, and the future.

I sat on my porch content, finally. I'd come to understand that we don't have to earn the right to dance, to rejoice, to celebrate. It's not necessary to have everything in our lives orderly and perfect before enjoying a day, a moment. We have only to listen to the sweet voices around us—the older voices echoing softly in our hearts and the newer ones swirling around us every moment. Echoes of yesterdays turn into the sweet music we enjoy in the present.

Back of House Before

During

Back of the house After

Rotted foundation. This is where we went under the house to add supports and jack it back into place.

These were our original bathroom choices

Some of the handprints from the 'Manson Room.

Same room After

The Falling apart garage before

Crooked Back Stairs

Kitchen Before (Yes, we really bought it like this!)

Kitchen After

Foyer Before

Foyer After

Front of the house following all remodels, including the breezeway and garage

www.ingramcontent.com/pod-product-compliance
Lightning Source LLC
Chambersburg PA
CBHW030107100526
44591CB00009B/308